The Final Prophecy

A Jewish Perspective on
End Times & Eternal Life

By H. Jay Schein

"And it shall be in the last days" God says,
"That I will pour forth My Spirit upon all mankind;
　And your sons and your daughters shall prophesy,
And your young men shall see visions,
And your old men shall dream dreams;
Even upon my bondslaves, both men and women,
I will in those days pour forth My Spirit
And they shall prophesy."

The Final Prophecy
© Copyright 2004
by Jay Schein
All Rights Reserved

Published by Master Press
8905 Kingston Pike Suite 12-316, Knoxville, TN 37923
Master Press website: www.master-press.com
1-800-325-9136

Distributed by Master Press

ISBN 0-975904914
All Rights Reserved.

Any form of reproduction in print or through any type of transmittal or duplicating device of any kind whatsoever is prohibited without the expressed written consent of the Author, with the exception of direct and accurate quotes with quotation marks and references to this Book appropriately displayed.

Scripture References:
Tanakh, the Holy Scriptures, a new translation of the Holy Scriptures according to the traditional Hebrew Text, 1985, Library of Congress Cataloging in Publication Data Bible, O.T. English 1985 and Scripture taken from *New King James Version*—Copyright 1979, 1980, 1982 by Thomas Nelson, Inc. Used by Permission. All rights reserved.

Printed in the United States of America.

Cover Design by Aaron Spring

Lenora Walker,
May God's Word guide you, strengthen you and enlighten you in following His plan for your life. Be blessed in every kindness you show, every smile you give and every word of encouragement to others you impart.

This book is dedicated with thanks to our Messianic Jewish brothers and sisters whose welcomed presence in the Body of Christ is bringing restoration to the ruined and desolate cities.

God bless you
Jay Schwem

Dedicated to All
Seekers of Truth

Contents

Acknowledgements:	13
Preface:	15
Introduction:	19
Chapter One: Wisdom	29
Chapter Two: What's It All About?	37
Chapter Three: God and Choices	45
Chapter Four: Godly Wisdom	51
Chapter Five: The Word of God	61
Chapter Six: Introduction to Prophecy	81
Chapter Seven: Prophets of Israel	95
Chapter Eight: The Promises of God	117
Chapter Nine: Facing Truth	129
Chapter Ten: Glorifying God	137
Chapter Eleven: Daniel	151
Chapter Twelve: The Final Prophecy	177

Chapter Thirteen: Who is Messiah	187
Chapter Fourteen: Messiah in Prophecy	217
Chapter Fifteen: Sin and Salvation	239
Chapter Sixteen: The Final Prophecy	247
Chapter Seventeen: The Great Tribulation	277
Yeshua in the Bible	304

Acknowledgements

To Diane - My Wife and Best Friend - You believed in me, encouraged me and you are all of Proverbs 31 -Thank you--Eternally

To Natalie, Brandon, Brittany and Jennifer - My Children -you are my joy in this earthly life and so special in our Father's heart...

To Bob Coy - You led me to God's truths and then taught me all the Biblical precepts of those truths. Your love and devotion to teaching the Word of God has touched thousands of lives who now possess the hope of eternal life. May the Lord richly bless you and your family.

To George Verwer - A continued source of inspiration and a friend. Your life is a testimony of unyielding service in answering the call to bring God's Word to the entire world. May the Lord richly bless you and Drena for all you do.

To Krista Werner Velarde - Contributing Editor -Thank you so much for your faithfulness and professional devotion to this project. I could not have produced such a work without your God-given skills that you unselfishly devoted in helping to bring this book to God's chosen people and all seekers.

To Every Servant of God who has received the call, answered the call and has been faithful in fulfilling that call. As were the prophets of old, we are but seeds of God's love for His children. May you continue to plant, to sow and to reap and in the end of days, may we gather one and all in Jerusalem to worship and serve the King.

Preface

This book is about life, a renewal of what is now and a promise of what is yet to come. God has promised His beloved Israel that she will one day have peace. God has also promised His children of Israel that they will share in that peace. God's promises are never broken and His final prophetic fulfillment that is known as the Final Prophecy is the key to all that has been foretold since ancient times. This final prophecy will be carried out starting with the day that God permits it to begin a countdown of a period of seven years. Eternally sharing in that new life is a matter of individual choice, a decision that I pray is correctly made once you have internalized the truths of this writing that will assist you in eternalizing a life when this one has ended.

I have rarely known anyone who did not have a thought as to what is on the other side of this life when it ends. I think it somewhat strange how we never seem to reflect on our birth but all of us have considered life's end. I would attribute that to our growing further away from the first event and nearer to the second! I have known people who have actually feared the thought of death, considering it morbid to even discuss the subject at all. Man should never fear the end of his days but embrace them as the culmination of a life well lived in the proving grounds to greater things.

Alfred L. Tennyson once stated, "Death is the bright side of life." The former United Nations leader Doug Hammarskjold said, "In the last analysis it is our conception of death which decides our answers to all the questions that life puts to us." Charles Kingsley stated, "What better can the Lord do for a man than take him home when he has done his work." Helen Keller stated, "Death...is no more than passing from one room to another. But there's a difference for me, you know, because in that other room I shall be able to see." Victor Hugo, "The tomb is not a blind alley; it is a thoroughfare. It closes on the twilight, it opens on the dawn" and Henry Beecher stated, "Death? Translated into the heavenly tongue, that word means life."

Talk about any subject you want to, dream any dream you dare to and set any goal your heart desires but the end of life as we know it is inevitable. If however, you should possess an eternal hope, a belief that there is truly a spiritual life beyond this physical life (a transition from flesh to spirit and from earth to heaven) there would not be the slightest regret or fear when you faced that inevitable day. The question is, why do so few of us believe in eternal or everlasting life? Could it be that somewhere along the line of our upbringing we were misled or not properly instructed about the most critical day of our lives-the day that we leave it? Man cannot fear death when he knows where he is going-especially if it is right into the arms of God. In that very thought exists our main topic, a subject that has received a great deal of attention in the past several years- the subject of our not having a choice concerning those final days for they could be cut short by the end of days,[1] the prophetic ending of this world as we know it. The prophets of ancient Israel have warned us of these end times for thousands of years. We should also know of the Biblical event within these times known as the Day of the Lord, the judgment day for the world when God pours out His wrath in judgment of our sins. Most of the religious leaders of the world now agree on one thing concerning this prophetic declaration-our time is running out and the fulfillment of that final prophecy is closer to becoming a reality than ever before in the history of mankind

If someone presented this book to you as a gift, I would not feel presumptuous in stating that the giver possesses a heartfelt concern for your eternal destiny. The end of days—rooted in Messianic prophecy in the Old Testament and addressed in part by the Left Behind series of recent years [2] has many Jews believing that these books and the movie series were solely a Christian belief and one that has no significance for the

Jewish community. This is simply not true, for it is our own prophets of Israel that have foretold of these events from Isaiah to Micah. It has everything to do with our people and their involvement in these times as it all comes to pass. This book is not about changing or converting any of our beliefs except to open the doors to the understanding and the knowledge of truth.

Notes

1 You will see references to end times and end of days throughout this book. It is the Biblical phrase to identify that period of time in which life on this earth as we know it now, will cease to exist and will be replaced by the reign of God on earth, referred to as the New Heaven and the New Earth.

2 Used as a reference only. Left Behind, Books and Motion Pictures are not affiliated or connected with this work in any way and are Copyright by the Authors and professionally related parties.

Introduction

You are about to take a literary journey down a path of discovering historic, Biblical truth. The presentation is simplified in the interest of complete understanding, but the content is fact and not opinion—unless indicated as such in the footnotes. This is not just about *end times* or the final prophecy in itself but rather about providing factual and documented information about the prophetic history of our people, Israel and the world, entirely foretold since the ancient days of the Jewish prophets. Surely you have heard the terms end times, the end of days or perhaps The Day of the Lord. These are terms that are specifically linked to our own Biblical prophecies, signifying the end of this world as we know it now. When I say the end of the world it is not some scare tactic or a quotation from a science fiction novel. These are prophetic words from God that have been revealed to us by His prophets of the Old Testament. The topic of end times has never before been so widely talked about and regarded as a major issue for religious leaders and theologians throughout the world— regardless of their individual religious beliefs.[1] They all continue to express their learned views that the world has never been closer to the fulfillment of these prophecies as it is right now. Despite this reality, the questions I hear posed are, "Of what concern is this prophetic declaration to our (Jewish) people?" "How will these prophecies affect us and how will they affect the nation Israel?" "How, why, when and where will these final prophecies take place?" These are honest, heartfelt questions that any reasonable person should not only be concerned with but

The Final Prophecy

should also be seeking the answers to. That is why I stated that this is a journey of truth— to find the truth. You cannot find truth in rumor or in man's teachings but only in God's Word—the Bible. The prophets have long ago told us where and how these prophecies will take place but not when. The timing is totally up to God as they are His prophecies and the Final Prophecy to be fulfilled is a seven year period that can only begin when God allows it to begin.

In this explicit writing of the truths of these prophetic declarations, I pray that it will guide you in learning and understanding the prophetic secrets of the Bible. I present these truths to you from a reasonable and Biblical Jewish perspective. The average person should find this book extremely helpful rather than confusing—especially if you have had little or no formal Biblical or Theological education. I have purposed this writing to open your eyes and your heart to prophetic insight in a progressive teaching and an easy to understand dialogue. If you have followed and stayed with me so far, you will have no problem throughout this book. It is a matter of reasoning instead of lecturing and my prayer is that this book will assist you in unlocking the truths of Scriptures so that you may know beyond any of your doubts what those truths hold in store— for you individually, for the Jewish people of the world and for Israel. God promised that this would occur and His Word never changes.

> "For I am the Lord, I do not change; therefore you are not consumed O sons of Jacob. Yet from the days of your fathers you have gone away from My ordinances and have not kept them. Return to Me and I will return to you." [2]

When the prophecy of end times is completed, Israel will be the focal point for worshipping God—for the entire world. Messiah will take the throne of David and the whole world will instantly know Him as the prophesied King of Israel. That is why the prophecies of the end of days are not just about us. They are about every man, woman and child on planet earth. God did not simply allow a chosen few to be informed about His judgments or to be excluded from worshipping Him when He rules from Zion. He provided all of mankind with the words of the ancient prophets so that all might learn from them and prepare for those days. Preparation is made by acquiring the knowledge and the enlightenment of Scripture. It is there that you will find the key to what is either waiting for you or not waiting for you when life as we know it ends. Under the right circumstances, God has promised us that we may live in His presence forever—yet getting to heaven is not an open door policy! We live in a worldly testing place where we all make certain choices that affect not only our natural lives but our eternal destination as well. The good news is that while we are still here it is never too late to reverse previously made bad choices. We serve a God who will forgive our sins and blot them from His remembrance as far as the East is from the West—providing that we ask Him for that forgiveness with a pure heart of repentance.

> "As far as the east is from the west, So far has He removed our transgressions from us. As a father pities his children, So the Lord pities those who fear Him." [3]

That is why I ask that you put away fantasy, dismiss the claims of soothsayers and turn away from self-professed psychics— those who would be foolish enough to state that their knowledge of eternal matters surpasses God's specific Word on the subject. All that I have written is from His Word— the very words God spoke to His prophets for the world to see.

What did we know?

Most Jewish men have shared the tradition of graduating [4] from boyhood to manhood in the Synagogue—our Bar Mitzvah. If your experience was anything like mine, we were taught our portion of the Torah, the prayers for the opening and closing of the portions of the reading and of course our speech after the reading was concluded. We were not taught the prophets or the prophecies and we did not study Proverbs to gain a portion of Solomon's wisdom! Since the prophets were not of the first Five Books of Moses, why confuse us! After our Bar Mitzvah most of us never went back to Hebrew School or continued in Biblical studies. We simply wanted to learn what we were required to learn for our big day—unless one aspired to become a Rabbi. The point is, how did we know then that the prophets were the keys to unlocking the knowledge and the understanding of the prophecies of end times or eternal life? We didn't.

On that thought of studying the prophets, don't you think it's somewhat ironic that so many Christian have read, studied and quote the Old Testament while we turn our noses up at the *New* Testament, referring to it as the Christian Bible? I believe that for the most part, this is attributed to a lifetime of established prejudices and the lack of knowledge as to what the New Testament contains. It was not until I read and studied the New Testament that I realized it was actually the *Old* Testament fulfilled! It was then that I realized so many truths that opened the eyes of my heart to the prophecies of end times. God spoke to us through the prophets, desiring that we all know His Word, especially in these volatile times of world conflict. We must face the facts that if these prophecies are not fulfilled in our lifetime then it could come upon our children's or grandchildren's lifetime. The signs have never been clearer and the prophecies ever appearing closer to their foretold Biblical fulfillment.

Then there is the hope of eternal life. Surely the reality of God's wrath being poured out on the entire world should stir your thoughts! Unfortunately, most of our people never read through the entire Bible thoroughly, thus remaining either uninformed or misinformed about eternal life. If the prophecy of the end of days is upon us and having never been closer to that prophetic time in man's history, one should wisely explore all the possibilities and where those possibilities lead. It is about the knowledge of Scripture and the ageless record of prophetic predictions that we Jews have not realistically come to terms with— intellectually and spiritual, but we must, for it is our destiny—simply because

INTRODUCTION

God said so!

Author's Note to the Reader

Central to every known religion is the perceived idea of faith. Man seeks a spiritual reality that is perhaps not instantly detectable by his endowed natural senses. That is simply because those senses have not been spiritually tuned— for man is caught up within the reality of the world he is in and does not look beyond it. Religion is ultimately about God and drawing near enough to Him in love and awe-inspiring respect while making Him the focal point of our everyday life. That would require putting off any and all perspectives of our own importance, the "me first" thinking. It's about seeking a personal relationship with God and pursuing that relationship as it was intended to be when God declared, "You shall be My people and I will be your God."[5] Love should be the foremost attraction and the only motive that one should have in seeking to know God— the quest to establish a spiritual connection with Him. The reward that transcends the joy of His love is the promise of eternal life. Then you know that you will receive that love forever. Until you discover how to have that personal relationship with the Lord you will never come to know the depth of the meaning of love—in the way that God intended it to be.

> "And you will seek Me and find Me, when you search for me with all your heart." [6]

If all you personally derive from reading this book is a topical insight into prophecy then you will have missed the intended purpose as well as the understanding of what to expect should God's timing place the fulfillment of Final Prophecy in the path of your own lifetime. That is not a nightmarish thought to those who understand and believe that God intended more than just this earthly life for us. However, if you are convinced that death is final and that's all there is, obtaining some insight into prophecy may provide you with a more hope-filled perspective on end times. It takes a thinking person and a spiritually-filled person to possess a realistic outlook on the subject of heaven and eternal life—an outlook that is grounded in the belief that there is a spiritual life after physical death. For those that believe there is nothing beyond the grave you are naturally lacking any eternal hope and a life without that hope greatly diminishes one's quality of life (in a spiritual sense) because of an underlying fear of death. I for one have never believed that God simply created us one day after the earth was totally formed, allowed us to live out our pre-destined seasons of life and then we simply cease to exist— returning to the dust of the earth from which Adam was first made. What I do believe is that we have a place, a spiritual home that God has prepared for us at His designated time. I also believe that the Day of the Lord is not just a Biblical story but a reality that will inevitably come to pass, just as every single prophecy already has— with one final prophecy still ahead of us.

Heaven or Hell

On the subject of heaven, there are many who believe there is actually no such thing as heaven and hell, which is named "Sheol" in the Old Testament. If that is possibly your belief I submit to you that if God's Word tells us that Elijah and Enoch were "taken up and never tasted death." [7] I ask you where did these godly men go to? God surely did not take these righteous men of the Bible to nothingness and nowhere! God brought them unto Himself— to spend eternity with Him. If you have questioned this place we refer to as heaven than I submit to you that heaven is not an exclusive club for Biblical greats such as Moses, Abraham, King David, Solomon and those who came after them. It is for all who belong to God—who are His children. That is why the word "faith" has so much meaning, intellectually gathering enough information so that you are filled with Biblical wisdom and then the heart is opened to eternal understanding. That which is in the mind must travel

INTRODUCTION

downward, a distance of eighteen-inches to the heart where absolute faith becomes a result rather than just a thought. I have met so many people who possessed a solid understanding of the Scriptures and of prophecy but all of that understanding in their heads never reached their hearts! God allows us to take a peek into the heavenly realm through the prophets of Israel who have recorded every word of the visions they received from God. We can review the prophecies and the lessons of the past, delve into the historical truths of our ancestors which allows us to gain a great deal of insight into the times to come— before the Kingdom of God is established on this earth and the old earth passes away.

> "The test of our faith is our willingness to suffer for it...the supreme test of faith comes in our belief in a life hereafter." Alice H. Rice

> "No ray of sunlight is ever lost, but the green which it wakes into existence needs time to sprout, and it is not always granted to the sower to live to see the harvest. All work that is worth anything is done in faith."
> Albert Schweitzer

Perhaps you are one who believes the "Doomsday Theory" somewhat popular among some of the radical ecological groups. They believe that someday the water supply will be totally polluted, the ozone layer completely destroyed, the Arctic melted, and food supplies diminished to the point that we cannot feed the world's population any longer and starvation begins to plague the nations. Then what would occur? They theorize that war would break out in every Nation and every Country as we all fought for the remaining supply of food, water and medicines. Considering the number of nations that possess nuclear devices, they ask, "Could it all simply come to an end in that way?" I believe they call this

THE FINAL PROPHECY

the "Who pushes the button first theory." How could any person who believes in Creation as opposed to believing that we grew from a single cell over billions of years even consider that God had these intentions when He created us? I believe that when God created the universe in its perfect balance, the earth itself and then human life, it was so that we could be a part of His blessedness and His holiness— dependent upon Him for the essence of these very virtues. We are here to worship Him and abide in Him as His children with eternal love, affection and revering Him as our God. He placed us here for a season according to His will and according to the predestined purpose we were to achieve in the balance of His plan for all of mankind. Then, when our time here is completed and by our free choice we chose God over evil, He will take us home [8] to forever be with Him. That is precisely what God's Word promises us and what a person of faith believes.

> "It gives me a deep comforting sense that things seen are temporal and things unseen are eternal."
>
> Helen Keller

It is my personal plan, prayer and purpose to offer you a dialogue of simple understanding as we go through the truths within this book. I know the questions and the doubts that people have including their individual fears of death and dying. The traditional answers and those "pat" remarks will and should never satisfy a genuine seeker of truth.

Before understanding the truths of the Bible, there was a great deal of personal challenge of the beliefs I am now addressing. As I began to delve into the concepts of heaven, hell, *The Day of the Lord* and several other significant subjects of the Bible, it seemed that the more I learned, the more I realized how unknowledgeable I was and how much there was to learn. It's not something you simply decide to do one morning and by bedtime you have accomplished it! Biblical truths require years of study because there is a nugget of learning on every single page. You see, God does not allow a middle of the road, lukewarm heart to inherit wisdom and understanding. God is looking for on-fire seekers of His truths. Faith is something that can be achieved when the mind understands the basis for those truths. When God's Word tells us, "the truth shall set you free," it implies a release from doubt, from not knowing what is beyond this human form of life. Truth alone completes us— in knowledge, in wisdom and in our faith. Know that when the light of revelation loosens the truths from the darkened state of confusion, the results are bringing the mind and soul into the illumination of spiritual truth. This is an inner joy that you will surely proclaim for your heart will be overflowing with God's love. I pray that this will be a journey of revealing all that the Bible discloses to those who seek God's wisdom. May this be an educational and spiritual filling that will change your perspectives on life—forever!

> "I will ransom them from the power of the grave; I will redeem them from death. O Death, I will be your plagues! O Grave, I will be your destruction." [9].

Notes

1 Jewish and Christian Bible scholars alike.

2 Malachi 3:6-7

3 Psalm 103:12-14a

4 This is the traditional passing of a boy into manhood and considered a man able to sit among the other men of the Congregation.

5 Jeremiah 30:22

The Final Prophecy

6 Jeremiah 29:12-13

7 Elijah and Enoch never experienced death. God "took them up" which is to say that one moment you are talking to someone or simply enjoying a scenic view and the next moment you are in heaven with the Lord. You never knew what it was to experience death itself.

8 Heaven

[9] Hosea 13:14

Chapter One

Wisdom

Opening new doors of wisdom and enlightenment requires one's willingness to reason through all the facts that are presented to them. I also encourage you to suppress emotionally-based reasoning, prejudices and opinions— applying only God-given enlightenment and wisdom to the process. One of my favorite sayings is, "There is no replacement or substitute for wisdom." Wisdom is the supporting strength of the individual process of decision-making. Wisdom is ultimately the backbone of all decisions in our life that are appropriately made. I believe that wisdom is the forerunner of understanding— especially in supporting the various seasons of life that we go through. We historically have acknowledged the wisdom of noteworthy people in every era of history that in one way or another made our lives easier or better. They are the innovators, the men and women of vision and unyielding faith who individually and collectively forged the very pillars of progress that allowed this Country to become the most powerful and wealthiest nation in the world. We immortalized them by the written word or perhaps their portrait hanging in public institutions or in monuments that are admired for generations—until the tribute fades or crumbles or is forgotten. You see, it is the only accomplishments that are immortalized, those that have been made to society and what those contributions meant to us individually and collectively. Contributions such as medical and industrial discoveries that have improved the quality of our lives.

The Final Prophecy

Would you agree that most of us try not to leave this earth without some sort of legacy— as simple or as large as it may be—legacies that will benefit our children and their children and so on? In speaking of and planning these legacies, I ask you to consider the time required to properly plan and build one's legacy—from the moment you perceive it to the moment it is fulfilled. It seems as though noted people of fame always had a vision that was rooted within them, never giving up or giving in until that vision was fulfilled. They did not just live for the day at hand but were constantly looking towards the future. They were not simply content in what was but rather dreamed of what could be. To bring this all into a semblance of simple understanding, just about every great human being I have ever read about and respected had a strong connection to God or developed an inseparable connection through their human trials. Even those who lived most of their lives in unbelief—attempting to prove that there was no God, found Him and never let go of all He had in His Word to grow them and prosper them

> "To find God is but the beginning of wisdom, because then for all our lives we have to learn His purpose with us and to live our lives with Him…" H.G. Wells

Those who searched and found the Biblical truths of God's advice for life were people of determination and conscience. Many were ordinary men and women, some without even so much as a formal education-- simple every-day people who sensed there was more to life than what we could see. We study scientists and inventors of machines in the classrooms of education, but are forbidden to discuss the man who led an entire nation out of bondage. (Moses) We consider a psychic's predictions of the end of the world with awe and even buy the tabloids of sensationalism that headline their predictions. Have you ever considered that God's

CHAPTER 1

Word informed us of the predictions of the future long before any psychic known today was even born? Are we saying that we trust their predictions more than the Word of God? I don't think so but most of us have not read the Word of God and have only heard these human predictions. The psychic's of the tabloids sought fame and fortune. God's prophets came from various walks of life, but were universally condemned and persecuted for their prophesies.

Unless you are retired or have an inordinate amount of idle time on your hands, very few of us spend all of our waking moments attempting to acquire future visions. We are usually far too busy with the reality of today which includes our occupations or jobs, our families and our involvement in social and religious organizations. Most of us give very little thought to the ultimate future which is conclusively the end of our lives— especially if you are very young. We do however seem to talk about and consider our time— needing more of it or making more of it. As a society, we have created all types of inventions and services to save as much time as possible. Most live a fast-paced life and we always seem to need more time. That is probably due to the fact that we know our individual time allotment is running out. What is surprising to me is that so many people tend to negate any thoughts of eternity or eternal life and yet we talk about having enough time to accomplish all that we have aspired to! Perhaps that is why we need an occasional reality check to aid us in remembering that we are not in control of our destinies – God is. We talk about time and yet time does not really belong to us—it belongs to God. He gave it and He can take it away. We have become a society that is preoccupied with living life amidst a volatile climate in a sin-infested world of religious and political unrest. Some learn to live with it all by approaching each season of life with simplistic philosophies but whom do we look to for emotional and spiritual support during the times it all seems to be falling apart? May I suggest looking upwards and seeking the answers from God? Only He can provide the wisdom of the ages and the wisdom to survive the end of the age as well.

Considering that our topic in this Chapter is wisdom, I personally look to Solomon, son of David, out of all the Biblical men of wisdom in the Scriptures. Whether it is the teachings and words of Proverbs, the reality

The Final Prophecy

—of Solomon's views on life in Ecclesiastes or the greatest love affair I have ever read in Song of Songs, Solomon's words of wisdom and understanding all lead to God. In the words of other great men who looked to God for wisdom, Ralph Waldo Emerson said, "We learn that God is, that He is in me, and that all things are shadows of Him." The famed Author C.S. Lewis who upon relinquishing atheism stated, I gave in and admitted that God was God." Henri Bergson stated, "Why should God need us, unless it was to give us His love?" Doug Hammarskjold said, "The day I first really believed in God, for the first time, life made sense to me and the world had meaning." William Penn whose statue rises from the top of City Hall in Philadelphia once said, "Those people who are not governed by God will be ruled by tyrants." Henry Wadsworth Longfellow stated, "To do God's will is the only science that gives us rest." And speaking of knowledge and wisdom, Albert Schweitzer declared; "The highest knowledge which man can attain is the longing for peace, that our will becomes one with the infinite Will" (God's will) and on the subject of gaining our knowledge and wisdom from the Bible which this entire book is based upon, James W. Alexander stated, "The study of God's Word for the purpose of discovering God's will, is a secret discipline which has formed the greatest characters." Meister Eckhart said, "It is the will of God that we surrender our wills---yield completely to God and then be satisfied." Finally, though I am far from exhausting the list of quotes from great men, I felt this quote was significant for understanding that life in this form as you have seen it, lived through it, experienced it, felt it and suffered through it is not all there is. We tend to grow negative and distrusting as we suffer the trials of this life, even to the point of turning away from our religion and our God. But do you recall that I stated emphatically that God has a plan for every life? Horace Bushnell said it for me. "God understands His own plan and He knows what you want a great deal better than you do. What you call hindrances, obstacles, discouragements, are probably God's opportunities."

In short, life apart from a relationship with God, our attachment to Him, abiding in Him right down to daily praise, prayer and discourse with Him is no life at all but a vapor— a pursuit of "grasping for the wind."[1]

CHAPTER 1

> "What profit has the worker from that in which he labors? I have seen the God-given task with which the sons of men are to be occupied. He has made everything beautiful in its time. Also He has put eternity in our hearts, except that no one can find out the work that God does from beginning to end. I know whatever God does, It shall be forever. Nothing can be added to it, And nothing taken away from it. God does it that men should fear before Him. That which is has already been; And God requires an account of what is past. Moreover I saw under the sun; In the place of judgment, Wickedness was there; And in the place of righteousness, Iniquity was there. I said in my heart, God shall judge the righteous and the wicked, For there is a time there for every purpose and for every work." [2]

God told Solomon that he could ask for anything he desired and God would give it to him. Solomon asked God for wisdom and from that wisdom Solomon became the wealthiest and wisest man known in that time. It is the impetus of this journey into the knowledge of Scripture that cries out to be heard and absorbed— and for you to sense,

> "To everything there is a season, a time for every purpose under heaven." [3]

As we look to and learn of the various times in Biblical history, we also look to the history of Israel. We should know of and understand the prophets who were called by God to deliver His Word for living as well as His warnings about the way we were living in sin. It was most unfortunate that our ancestors did not heed these warnings and admonitions of the prophets, despite the fact that every word of warning was from the Lord. They were our people and they suffered greatly in trials and punishment for their disobedience, their iniquities and their sins against

The Final Prophecy

God. Through it all, God continued to forgive and forget but not without great consequences. Have you considered that we are a people with a very realistic perspective on life, one that has earned us a renowned reputation as survivors? We have realistically embraced our heritage with sound understanding, and yet we have historically overlooked specific words from Solomon that related to our destinies when Solomon declared, "He also put eternity in their hearts." [4] For all the years of wandering in the desert, for our suffering and persecution in the ghetto's of Warsaw to the showers of Auschwitz, the Six Day War and the terrorist bombings of today— we survived. Have we considered and taught our children Solomon's admonition of "eternity in their hearts?" If we take these words and couple them with the very first verse of Solomon's overview of the "seasons of life" from Ecclesiastes, Solomon also declared that there was "A time to be born and a time for dying."[5] Coupled with the first words of the concluding verses of those thoughts before Solomon speaks of judgment, "I realized too, that whatever God does, it shall be forever."[6] In those verses you have the intent, the motivation and the purpose behind allowing yourself to remain open minded while reasoning through this book. It's about tracing God's own Word—methodically and intelligently leading to a point of consideration and conclusion as to what God tells us is on the other side— our eternal destinies when Solomon exhorted us to place the thoughts of eternity within our hearts. The realities of Solomon's wisdom is that all he has declared realistically points to time and timing, for this could be your time to plant those seeds of wisdom from God's Word. These are seeds of learning that can unlock the doors of knowledge and provide perspectives that are purposeful and eternal. Once you have understood these timely truths of the Scriptures, you could very well find the faith and subsequent strength of inner peace that leads to an eternal hope. Once a person possesses that eternal hope and it is firmly planted in faith, it can never be taken away from you and faith occurs when one acquires the wisdom of why one should have faith in the first place.

You have to know about what you believe in before true faith can be instilled within you. True hope that was built on strong faith is rooted deeply and forever— a hope that I pray you one day possess. I submit to

CHAPTER 1

you that the time to understand all that is under heaven is second to finding the path to all that awaits us in heaven. The former is so temporary!

> "It gives me a deep comforting sense that things seen are temporal and things unseen are eternal."
> Helen Keller

> "I do not feel badly about those who have no sight as much as I feel badly about those who have no vision."
> Helen Keller

Notes

1 Ecclesiastes 4:4

2 Ecclesiastes 3:9

3 Ecclesiastes 3:1

4 Ecclesiastes 3:11 Tanakh, Pg. 1444

5 Ecclesiastes 3:2

6 Ecclesiastes 3:14 Tanakh, same page

THE FINAL PROPHECY

Chapter Two

What's It All About

Perhaps you have heard of a song, "What's it all about Alfie?" It is the theme song from an older movie by the same name. I find it appropriate for exploring the implications of the question, "what's it all about— this thing called life?" The words of this song provide a purpose, a point and a place in time for you to ponder the three part question that the song asks as we delve deeper into the subject of eternal life. It wasn't that long ago that this song echoed the very thoughts of so many searching Jewish hearts who asked, "Where did I come from, why am I here and where am I going?"[1] There have been seasons in the history of our Country when the lyrics of songs such as this one appeared to capture our thinking at just the right time. It's when people pause in the routine of everyday life and come face to face with the significance of these questions that concern life itself— the substance of our own existence and wanting to know if death is absolutely final. There was the assassination of John F. Kennedy, the Viet Nam War and more recently the horrors of 9-11 that is certainly more prevalent in the minds of today's youth. Our kids witnessed 9-11 as it occurred, on giant television screens. Unfortunately many shared the loss of a life—a mother, a dad, a grandfather, a relative or a friend. This tragedy was not in some foreign land but was right here on the soil of our own country. The verses of "What's it all about Alfie" provoke a question that should be highly significant for in the very next verse the songwriter goes on to ask, "Is it just for the moment we live?"[2] For the many who never gave much thought to eternal destinations, that "moment" is often translated as, "live it up now for you never know what tomorrow brings."[3] Living just for the moment sounds exciting, tempting, daring, adventurous, self-indulging, passionate— but think about this; the *"moment"* in terms of any lasting quality or significance in relation to one's total lifespan is exactly what the term denotes - a moment. It means nothing more and nothing beyond that particular point in time. That is a most serious consideration to keep in mind when there are eternal alternatives.

Most people do not go around thinking about the subject of death and for the most part choose to ignore the fact that their biological clock will ultimately run down and cease to tick someday. It's not the kind of thoughts anyone likes to entertain on a regular basis but the thought of the process of aging occurs to even the young and the young at heart. The reality of death and dying most often occurs when you lose a friend or a family member and there is a tug at your heart during the funeral when the Rabbi declares, *"I know he (she) is in heaven and has found eternal rest."* I found myself questioning, *"Are they really in heaven? How do we know?"* I believe that it's a fair question and one I posed to my Rabbi in the naivety of my youth. His answer to my question was, *"Faith son, have faith."* My mind could not fathom what having faith had to do with the subject of everlasting life. That encounter led me to think about Abraham, Moses, Enoch, who I previously spoke of and what about Elijah—all the great patriarchs of the Bible! Surely these great men must be in heaven! When serious thoughts along these lines begin to emerge, one might think, "I know God loves me but what about getting to where He is? Do I automatically appear there? Do I simply stand before God while He opens the Book of Life and He looks for my name? What if I did not get to Synagogue on Yom Kippur and I die or I'm killed? What if my name isn't in the book and it has been a hoax all along to give us something to believe in?" Many of our people have an absolute conviction of the heart that if we follow Torah and are a "good person", God will take us to heaven when we die—after all, don't all of God's chosen people go to heaven? But as a young man and as it is with most young men, I was

CHAPTER 2

convinced that I was going to live forever. I reasoned that I had plenty of time to dwell on the subject and hopefully find the truth someday. That is akin to thinking, "If I simply ignore whatever it is, it will go away!"

SEEKING LIFE'S ANSWERS?

Did you actually know that the answers to these questions can be found in the Books of the prophets of the Old Testament? The problem with most is, who has time to study all that there is about every major and minor prophet and what they predicted? Orthodox Jews and even several Rabbis tell me that the prophets are "good and interesting but their main purpose was to serve God and carry His messages to the people of Israel." They went on to say that, "Most of what they (the prophets) said were merely admonitions or rebuke of the people's sins because our people did not uphold the Law. The first five Books, Torah, that's what you need to know!" That is what my own Rabbi told me and went on to say, "It's the Law, our traditions and how we live our life that is important." I am not attempting to portray that all Rabbis have these traditional pat answers to timely questions however I did at one time ask a simple and rather fair question after I had actually began studying the prophets. "What about the prophecies of Daniel, known as "the Seventy Weeks? What was to come out of Daniel's prophecy for the Nation Israel?" The answers I received were nowhere sufficient enough to quench the thirst of my seeking nature. It was in the late sixties that I began to read my way through Zechariah, Isaiah and began to superficially understand some of the prophecies and saw some type of correlation between Messiah and of whom Isaiah was speaking. At that time, I didn't give a second thought to The Day of the Lord. My first thoughts concerning Messiah, was that they must be referring to Elijah. Again I returned to questioning my Rabbi, asking, "Who was Isaiah speaking of — was it the Messiah?" "Didn't God promise David that a king from his own seed would sit on the throne of Israel forever?" They were questions that I continued to ask and not just of our Rabbi but of others in our Synagogue, elderly men whom I considered to be Old Testament scholars. The more people attempted to confuse me with less than appropriate answers the more determined I became to find the truth.

Since I was about eleven years old, I believed that whatever was written in the Bible had significance and meaning or it would not be there. I did not intend to stop until I understood what God was saying to us through His prophets. Have you ever experienced the frustration of not knowing the very things that bring us Divine understanding instead of trusting in tabloids or the evening news! Like so many of us at any time in our lives, young or old—I was seeking answers to life's questions. Sadly enough however, I came to a place in my life that I gave up this quest until many years had passed and the time for my individual re-awakening occurred according to what God had planned. The question still remains for any of us who at one time or another were seeking these answers, "Did God purposely hide these truths from us for some unknown reason? Were the truths of the prophecies of Isaiah and Daniel veiled from us because of the limitations of our finite understandings or was it our blasé attitude towards the study and understanding of the Bible?" Think about it, why should the future be made known to a person unless that person is truly seeking truth? Were the Israelites ready to receive the Ten Commandments at Mt. Sinai or did they lose both patience and faith and act as though Moses never went up to the top in the first place? Obviously the latter occurred and they made a golden calf and took part in lewd and sinful acts as though God did not even exist. There is no difference in modern times where our sins separate us further and further from God and all that He wants to reveal to us. We are too busy living life against His precepts and cannot see the glory of His presence as He fades from our eyes. That is because the sin we are indulged in all too often becomes a matter of habit until we do not even realize that we are pushing ourselves further away from God.

God had messages for us and the prophets carried those messages to our people. God was angry with our people and the prophets let us know. God wanted us to do something and the prophets guided us in understanding God's will—not just for our people but for all of mankind. How incredibly blessed our people were in those ancient times to actually be the recipients of a direct line of communication from God through His prophets— speaking to us and providing us with supernatural wisdom from above. That's how one might reason over the prophets today, however back then the prophets were an annoyance and not a blessing to most. They were a constant reminder to our people of their sinfulness in worshipping idols and marrying women from conquered lands who were not of our faith. Adultery and lewdness was also rampant and we turned out to be a poor representation of the God of Israel, sinning alongside the heathens and conducting our lives as sinfully as they did. God had a plan for us and it included our actions and our deeds as a people and not willingly joining the ranks of sin.

> "I will also make you a light for the Gentiles, that you may bring My salvation to the ends of the earth."[4]

FINDING ANSWERS WHEN GOD IS SILENT

Then came the time in our history when neither God nor His prophets spoke to the people of Israel and there were surely no contenders for the vacant prophet jobs. The prophet Malachi had said the last of what was to be said [5] and the final events in Israel to be recorded were those of Nehemiah.[6] God spoke to no one—for about four hundred years. All that was left were the recorded prophecies, waiting to be fulfilled. This silence was as though God closed the door of interaction and gave us four hundred years to figure out all that He previously said. It was a time for us to witness the fulfillment of many prophecies that had not been taken seriously. It was time to make some drastic changes in our overall understanding, belief and acceptance of Biblical prophecy. This period is known as the *Silent Years* and there are several factors regarding this period that many of us have neglected to teach our children—the fulfillment of all that the prophets predicted. I can well understand the Rabbis

THE FINAL PROPHECY

wanting to avoid studies such as the declarations of the prophet Daniel. His prophecies were exacting and history validates their accuracy. These were precise prophecies both in the time of their occurrence and the details, such as Alexander the Great defeating the Persians who had ruled over our people for about two hundred years. Daniel prophesied that the land of Israel would pass from the hands of the Medo-Persian Empire to the Greeks and then to the Romans. Again, history dictates that this was all the historic future based on the king of Babylon's dream that God allowed Daniel to interpret.[7] Then there is the matter of Daniel Chapters Nine and Twelve, with special emphasis on Daniel 9:24 and Daniel 12:1-13. The verse Daniel 12:11 declares the event that begins the countdown of the last three and one-half years to the fulfillment of the Final Prophecy.

In keeping with my opening challenge of allowing reason to prevail and not emotions or prejudice as we explore Biblical prophecy, I have listed seven reasons that should bring you to an inquisitive state of mind— wanting to know more, study more and understand more about prophecy and end times. Can you be objective and relate to any of them?

1. You have not come to a point of total peace, an inner hope and a complete understanding of what will happen to you after you die.

2. You have read some of the prophets and attempted to figure it all out but you could not arrive at complete or satisfactory answers.

3. You thought you knew about eternal destiny but are now becoming anxious or confused, wondering if you were truly correct in your assumptions.

4. You have experienced a kind of empty feeling inside (likened to having a small hunger pain that you simply cannot satisfy) and you thought it was the "Is that all there is" syndrome!

5. You do not have a clear understanding of Torah or The Bible and you don't trust the reliability of The Bible or the study of Prophecy, the Prophets themselves and why they prophesied what they did.

CHAPTER 2

You do not know Ancient Jewish History and how it ties to the present as well as the future. You do not have a clear understanding of "what it's all about." More importantly you need a better understanding of God and your own place in His plan for your destiny.

6. You have become exasperated reading books that used terms or phrases that you did not understand and because of the tone of the book, were led to feel a sense of guilt for not knowing your own history! You did not like the book preaching at you instead of providing supportive, documented information that brought everything to a point where you could draw your own conclusions.

7. You now desire to take a step in the right direction— heading towards God and not away from God.

Seven is the number of completion in the Scriptures and as the seven statements above provide visually what some might have not been aware of internally, I ask only that you seek the truths for yourself. Solomon with all that he possessed maintained that *a* life outside of a personal and close relationship with God is no life at all. We are not complete and can not find the answers we seek without a total spiritual attachment to our Creator. Our spirit must be connected— plugged in so to speak and His power should be lighting us up from within and not the world's power darkening the process of our thinking and keeping all truth from us. If you follow the world and all that the world offers you will walk in that darkness all the days of your life—only thinking you are complete. In contrast to the joy you could have, you will remain unfulfilled and incomplete. The seriousness in all of this is that far too many people do not understand the need for that attachment to God— until it is often too late. As time is not on our side, now is a good time to make the effort to pursue God's Word. Regardless of what your personal issues are or how religious you are or are not—even how you feel about anything I have said thus far, let us just reason about it all, one step at a time. All that will be spiritually discerned has to come from God. I can only present you with Biblical truths and God has to do the rest. Remember that nothing of eternal consequence can come from man— especially any manner of fulfillment in the highest spiritual sense. That is why we must explore, reason and understand the connection between God and mankind for He has called you by name and knew you before the foundations of the earth. When you were born God's Word declares that it was not a random birth but rather a predestined birth and God had a plan for your life. Perhaps not of greatness, wealth or power but then again where do all of those things leave you when your time here has expired? These are God's realities and man's lessons to learn. Truths that have been declared in the Scriptures for mankind to discover and to embrace—if mankind desires to do so—remembering that God gave us the free will to make these choices.

In the next Chapter, I ask that you give some serious consideration to your present connection to the Lord and ask yourself how it lines up with any of the Scriptural truths we have discussed and are declared within God's Word.

Notes

1 A question I would often be asked in counseling someone who was weakened in their faith upon experiencing a tragic event in their life. Having worked with Hospice, I heard this question many times.

2 Original song taken from the movie "Alfie"

3 Italics mine

4 Isaiah 49:6b

5 Malachi 1:4-6

6 Nehemiah 13:4-30

7 The king of Babylon whom Daniel interpreted the dream of which led to the Biblical prophecies of Daniel

Chapter Three

God and Choices

I have often heard people say, "In this world it's nice to have the right connections." I wholeheartedly agree to the right connections part but not in this world. Why seek a finite or earthly connection when you can have an infinite one—obviously referring to God. When you get right down to truth instead of ego and worldly desires, what can your earthly connection do for you of any lasting value when you draw your final breath— besides attend your funeral? The connection to God is likened to a spiritual lifeline that has existed within us from the moment that God breathed life into man at his creation. In that breath was the source of our soul— our spiritual lives. You see, when the breath of God entered the body of man, it became the spirit of man but when the spirit reacted with the body that God had created, the soul of the man was formed. As Job said, "The breath of the Almighty gives me life." [1] Every man has that spiritual connection but may not know or understand how to use it to tap into God's power. That would be the power and ability to have a close, intimate, personal relationship with God. The majority of us thought that only the Rabbi could have such an intimate connection to God and the Rabbi spoke for all things that were related to God— just as Moses spoke for the people of Israel. That connection was a sort of lifeline to the Creator who gave that spirit exclusively to mankind. The animals of the world do not have it and God created them as well. It is man alone that God-breathed life into. You see God treated the soul of man as something very unique. The angels were created as spirits and man was created predominantly as a living soul. Man not only had a physical body after he received the breath of life but became a living soul as well. Your soul is the organ of a man's free will where spirit and body are completely and totally merged. If the man's soul wills to obey God then it will allow the spirit to rule over the man as he is guided by God. The soul can also suppress the spirit and choose some worldly delight apart from God to rule over the man instead of man's total obedience to God. Why do I pursue this line of understanding after talking about wisdom and reasoning? Because developing this connection between you and God is the method by which spiritual awareness is awakened, eventually leading one to wisdom and understanding.

How is this possible and how are we connected? A simple explanation of this would be to compare all that I have said to a light bulb, somewhat far-fetched from a man but bear with me and follow this analogy for simplified, illustration purposes only. Let us say that the light bulb represents the total man. Within this light bulb there is electricity, light and wire or three things in one light bulb. The spirit is like the electricity, the soul is the light and the body is the wire. Electricity is the cause of the light within the light bulb while that light is the effect of the electricity. Wire *(body)* is the substance to carry the electricity and for displaying the light. Do you see the significance of the three working together in harmony? However, turn off the electricity and you still have a light bulb with the same wire but the light bulb will be void of any light. The Spirit feeds the soul and the soul feeds man. The soul being created by the breath of God alone is basically God's source for that interpersonal relationship that is capable within every one of us. We can call upon that relationship when the moment for us comes –which is different for every human being as to when it comes. You see it is basically our choice to exercise and not God's to impose. The calling to Him must come from within us and in no other way, such as emotional reactions to outside stimuli. [2] We express that desire in sincerity, in truth, and by our own will— when we call upon the name of the Lord. We have the power to turn on the electricity and produce light or unplug from the source and just exist as a light bulb without light. Relating that to the condition of the heart, what a dull and cold life that would be!

CHAPTER 3

As long as we reason together and understand that the soul of a man represents all the elements of seeking spiritual insight and wisdom, you can't get that kind of power without plugging into its Source. God provided His creation the opportunity to receive that power and the free will to make the choice of connecting *to* Him and abiding in Him forever. Would this not provide us with a spirit to continue when by natural process the flesh ages and dies? Our bodies are of flesh and can only come into contact with and be a part of this world in its present form. The spirit of a man can only be given by God. Where the body provides us with world-consciousness the soul makes up the intellect which is the individual personality of a man. It is that individuality that gives us self-consciousness. The spirit within us provides us with spiritual-consciousness so that we are able to worship and commune with God.

Exercising our free will is our individual choice to connect. It is the search for truth that can only be encouraged within the soul of man as the flesh of man is basically sinful, corrupt, selfish and weak, especially when it comes to temptation. We have yet to learn this simple truth. Isn't it amazing that we who were created in the image of God are the only ones who have the capacity to rebel against Him! Animals are ruled by instinct alone so naturally they do not have a connection to God. They (the animals) are not aware that there *is* a God so they can't possibly rebel against Him! The Rabbis point out that both the lower animals and the higher angels have the same Hebrew name which is "chayot." Does this mean that man is somewhere between angels and beasts? One would agree that within us is a sinful nature that appropriately provoked could lower us to be as hostile as the beasts of the animal kingdom. You see, mankind has choices and every day we make a conscious choice in most everything that we do and in all actions that we take. There is no middle ground so one must choose sides—either evil ways or God's ways. Man can choose to do the things that will lead him to the place where he rises like the angels or he can make the choices that lowers him to the level of the common beasts of the field. According to the ancient Rabbis, "Everything is in the power of Heaven [3] except the reverence of Heaven".[4] "Man's freedom to resist or to obey the will of God is a restriction of the Deity's power that is totally unknown in the physical universe." [5]

The Final Prophecy

In His love for man, God has set aside an area of freedom in which man can elect to live right or do it all wrong. God always provided the guidelines but man is free to provide the response. The choice must be good over evil— either following God or being separated from God. According to God's Word, there are no "good people" so you are either on one side or the other. [6] God leaves no room for the middle road. One cannot dabble in sinful things and then claim that they are not too bad of a person. What I have personally heard said to me was, "I'm a good person. I did not murder anyone and I go to Synagogue." So therefore the usual belief is that they are righteous—in their own eyes perhaps, but not in the eyes of God.

When Moses came down from Mt. Sinai, God gave our people ten rules to live by.[7] Man had choices where he could simply elect to live by those rules or take his chances in dealing with the consequences of breaking those rules. Sin has a way of being passed from generation to generation, in lifestyle, in upbringing, in parents influencing their children with the very same basic choices that they had in their own experiences in life. Misinterpreting the Bible and the plan of God that has been shown to us through His prophets can also be passed down from generation to generation. Why do you think there is so much misunderstanding about end times and eternal life among our people? If you grew up with the understanding that this is the only life we have, you will tell your children, "Make it the best possible—you only have one life to live"—the result of what you yourself were told! That belief having been instilled within you since childhood would usually be passed along to your own children— unless you discovered that there was so much more beyond what you were led to believe. It is not that your own parents thought differently or tried to hide anything from you. It is simply that their own parents, your grandparents told them the very same thing they are probably telling you. If you did not seek the truths and simply passed along an old belief, what would you say when your grandchildren came to you and asked, "Grandpa (grandma) what happens to us when we die? Do we go to heaven? What's heaven?" Surely one can see evidence of cause and effect resulting from the lack of Biblical wisdom. Case in point is God's admonition to the Israelites,

CHAPTER 3

> "May they always be of such mind, to revere Me, and follow all my commandments, that it may go well with them and with their children forever."[8]

Again, Scripture declares;

> "But if your heart turns away and you give no heed, and are lured into the worship and service of other gods, I declare to you, this day, that you shall certainly perish; you shall not long endure on the soil that you are crossing the Jordan to enter and possess." [9]

Choices are given to man either to accept or to ignore God's Word. If man ignores the Word of God, he is taking his chances with the *wrath* of God rather than the blessings of God. History has shown us in great detail that God's wrath does not come upon us immediately. He is patient and waits for repentance, rather than immediately pouring out His wrath upon us for our disobedience to His commandments. God waits for man to return to Him and turn away from his sins. Making those choices and the consequences of having made those choices is further declared by God when He stated,

> "See, I set before you this day, life and prosperity, death and adversity." [10]

Personally I do not believe that the choice between life and prosperity or death and adversity is a difficult choice to make! It is quite simple and made perfectly clear within that same Chapter of The Book of Deuteronomy what God wanted from the Israelites who were about to cross the Jordan river into the Promised Land after forty years in the wilderness.

The Final Prophecy

> "For I command you this day, to love the Lord your God, to walk in His ways, and to keep His commandments, His laws and His rules, that you may thrive and increase, and that the Lord your God may bless you in the land that you are about to enter and possess."

History dictates in all that transpired during the period of the silent years that man made the wrong choices. He did not follow God's commandments, he did not obey the laws and the rules set forth by the Lord, thus leaving Israel far from being blessed. They had choices they could have made, however they chose to make the wrong ones to satisfy themselves and their own wants and desires.

Notes

1 Job 33:4

2 Referencing emotion-stirring preaching or teaching where the emotion of the moment makes us think that we have accepted and recognize what the Spirit alone can provide within.

3 Heaven is capitalized as it refers to the dwelling place of God in Talmud.

4 Talmud Bavli, *Berachot 33b*.

5 Shumuley Boteach-- 'Judaism for Everyone'

6 Man is born in sin and his nature is sinful according to God's Word, he is either saved or unsaved.

7 The Ten Commandments which were commandments for all mankind to live by

8 Deuteronomy 5:29

9 Deuteronomy 30:17

10 Deuteronomy 30:15

Chapter Four

Godly Wisdom

You can sit for years in the lecture halls of the most respected Universities and listen to every word of the most respected scholars. You can read every great literary classic that has ever been written. You can spend years in studying the great philosophers and the teachings of the proclaimed geniuses of our time. You can make every effort to seek wisdom and greater understanding of mankind and his destiny but none of these resources can provide you with the wisdom of God's Word—only studying the Word of God itself can accomplish that. I am not speaking of learning occupational or professional knowledge such as Medicine, Law, Engineering or Public Accounting. I am not referring to the courses at MIT or Harvard or Yale. I am speaking of the Biblical wisdom that calls aloud to be heard. The wisdom one should seek as though they were seeking after silver or gold. I am referring to the wisdom of the Bible and in this scenario, the incredible and timeless insight found in the Book of Proverbs. God's Word and the wisdom of Proverbs (as well as other Books in the Bible) provide you with the education for living life itself.

Most scholars agree that the Book of Proverbs was written by Solomon, son of David. The title in our Hebrew Bible is "The Proverbs of Solomon" and wisdom is the opening subject. "The proverbs of Solomon son of David, king of Israel. For learning wisdom and discipline; for understanding the words of discernment"[1] In his time, Solomon penned approximately 3,000 proverbs of wisdom[2] with the intent of encouraging people to contemplate, somewhat along the lines of my encouraging you

THE FINAL PROPHECY

to contemplate or reason through the thoughts and the facts within these pages. I do not have anywhere near the wisdom that Solomon possessed, however I have God's own Words of infinite wisdom from which all of us can draw from. How did Solomon become so wise? He sought God for all of his acquired wisdom.

> "And Solomon said to God: "You have shown great mercy to David my father, and have made me king in his place. Now, O LORD God, let Your promise to David my father be established, for You have made me king over a people like the dust of the earth in multitude. Now give me wisdom and knowledge, that I may go out and come in before this people; for who can judge this great people of Yours?" [3]

Once we know God we understand the source of all wisdom and look only to that source for direction in our lives. The next natural step in that process is the application of acquired wisdom and how we use it. "For the Lord gives wisdom; From His mouth comes knowledge and understanding; He stores up sound wisdom for the upright; He is a shield to those who walk uprightly; He guards the paths of justice, And preserves the way of His saints."[4] Having wisdom without applying it to our everyday lives is wasting God's gift of Divine enlightenment. If you seek wisdom with only half a heart you will never find all that a determined and believing seeker acquires. "Yes, if you cry out for discernment, And lift up your voice for understanding— Then you will understand the fear of the LORD, And find the knowledge of God."[5] Each day we notice various world events, hear different opinions and points of view. How does one discern that which is truth and that which is the "spin" on the truth? How does one truly discern the lies of men who seek only to prosper at your expense and whose concerns in life are centered solely on themselves and their own needs? God's wisdom allows the truth to be known and the deceivers exposed— a most important factor in the times of The Final Prophecy. That is why possessing God's wisdom is imperative for there

CHAPTER 4

will be deceivers, false prophets, falsely claimed miracles and only those who know the Word of God will know the difference. Knowing truth from deception is the key to discerning spiritual warfare in every- day life and in end times.

Can you even imagine a soldier going off to fight in a war without first going through basic training? He would be at the highest level of risk in surviving the ordeal. Understanding the Word of God is your personal basic training. It prepares you for not only the events of the end of days but also for every circumstance of life that may come your way in this volatile, fallen world we presently live in. The countdown to Armageddon could begin with tomorrow's sunrise and those who do not know God's instructions for surviving will likely perish— just as uncontrolled sinfulness can lead to perishing in that sin instead of inheriting eternal life. Why do I tend to emphasize the understanding of God's Biblical wisdom? Because it is imperative for us to understand the Biblical account of the prophecies of ancient Israel so that we fully understand past history and the predictions of our future history. How can one know where we are going if you do not understand where we have been? How can we trust certain predictions if we do not have a general idea of how and why these prophecies came to pass and how they are all tied to the final one that is yet to come? Have you ever questioned, "How did such a thing happen?" History may appear to be a series of unrelated events to unstudied eyes however I submit to you that there is a master plan for it all that is God's alone. This "plan" was from the beginning of time and links all the historic events of history to what appears as a hidden and supernatural mystery between the pages of the Bible— just waiting for you to discover and spiritually understand. If I first show you the foundations of all that has occurred in Biblical history, perhaps you might catch the vision of all that God has in mind for His people Israel and for His future world.

It is as though a story was unfolding about things that we are not spiritually attuned to. Stories such as those foretold in the Bible that we have never read. If our minds and our hearts were not opened and prepared to receive such wisdom from God, it would be like seeds being planted in a garden at the very surface of the soil. Those not planted deep enough would be eaten by birds before they even had a chance to take root. That would be likened to your turning a deaf ear to instruction because you had no belief in what was being said. Before real knowledge had a chance to root itself, you dismissed it as though the seeds of that information were never there. You have surely heard the expression, "The truth fell on deaf ears." You would then be missing the depth or the main points of the story and surely missing the picture as a whole. The truths did not take root and soon they become a passing thought rather than an internal understanding. Men and the world would be able to convince you that their way was a better way. You had no roots of truth to ward off the lies. Those that heard, listened and learned by believing in God's Word are as the seeds of truth that are planted deeply— fed by the waters of God's Spirit. These are the seeds that take hold and grow into the fruits that sustain life. So you see it is important that we allow these seeds of knowledge to go deeply and become rooted within us. It is following God's commandments that make the difference, not just possessing the knowledge by itself. God wants the changed man who knows Him, loves Him and respects Him by living a life worthy of that relationship. Putting feet to your faith is demonstrated by the fruits of what one does and not what one says. "Trust in the Lord with all your heart, And lean not on your own understanding.[6]

If we gathered the greatest combination of minds in the entire world, we could never hope to possess the intelligence necessary to actually figure out and totally understand all the mysteries of life. We need the expressed guidance of God and His teaching, His Word, His Spirit which is the source of all knowledge and understanding. We must never close our ears to the hearing of wise men for even the Talmud declares, "Who is a wise man? He who learns from all men."

Of all the wisdom that has come down from man through the ages, even those who were agnostics readily admitted that when they read the Bible they derived both learning and guidance—receiving inspirations that led them to other thoughts and discoveries. There was a pattern of continued discovery in addressing the secrets of life. This is the deep, spiritual understanding that only God can provide. One never ceases to learn, for one who is finite cannot possibly understand all the mysteries

CHAPTER 4

of the universe— simply because those things are infinite and are of God. Man is not big enough to understand all that there is to know, for if he did, God would not be God and man would not need Him!

When it comes to knowledge of the Scriptures, we all have varied levels of understanding—which could range from no knowledge whatsoever to studied, Biblical understanding. Not all of us have the same desire to read or study the Bible or the prophets and the prophecies they declared. Some of us may have been misled, perhaps by a Rabbi or parents who thought they were explaining Scripture to us or possibly wanted to avoid some truths that they thought would lead us to exploring other than traditional understandings. When I refer to truth I am talking about appropriate interpretation of the Bible. Not our guesses but what the writers were actually saying as God gave them the visions to write. An example would be Moses, for surely God Himself had to have given Moses the words when he wrote the accounts of Creation—the Book of Genesis. The intent and the meaning of Biblical truth can only be what God intended it to be, for He alone was and is the Author of all truth.

How do all of these things work together for the greater good and the greater understanding? When one is faced with making important life-changing decisions, there is only one place we should go for advice— God's Word. Understanding prophecy and the fulfillment of those prophetic events are also matters that go beyond the concept of simply reading Torah. We as Jews need to expand our desire for Biblical knowledge and go further into God's Word, including knowing the prophets and understanding their prophecies because God is not finished teaching His chosen people.

With the Old Testament containing the historical accounts of ancient Israel, the Creation, the prophets and their prophecies, you will discover the most fascinating, historical, non-fiction work of not only our past but also what is yet to come. Then, if an open mind permits, you will find the fulfillment of those prophecies in the New Testament.

The question one may ask at this point is, "Why do we need the New Testament to tell us what our prophets have already told us? What application does the New Testament have for the Jewish people?" The answer is that both the Old and the New Testaments are given to us by God and

The Final Prophecy

contain both halves of the "big picture," the past and the future. In the Old Testament, Daniel predicts and the New Testament clearly shows the prophetic fulfillment. Isaiah predicts and the New Testament demonstrates the fulfillment once again. Zechariah and Joel predict and the New Testament explains and points to their prophetic statements, those that were fulfilled and those yet to come. If the New Testament supports and validates all that the Old Testament has shown, why would you call the New Testament anything other than the completion of God's Word? The Bible in its entirety was given to all of humanity by God however the Old Testament is the unique, historical account of His chosen people. Remember that we are but a part of humanity and not humanity itself because we were chosen by God. If a person or a group of people is selected to perform specific tasks and fails to do so, God will simply select another group to fulfill His will. We were God's chosen people to be the light of the world, but time and again we forgot Him, persecuted His prophets and walked in the ways of sin. Finally God made a new covenant and turned the task over to another group whom we call Christians to complete the task that we Jews were supposed to do.

As for the two Testaments, allow me to clarify this issue with a simple illustration. A chain comprised of individual links needs to be assembled in order for you to tie-up a boat to a dock. You have the links and all you have to do is attach them to each other to achieve the appropriate length of chain you need. You measure the distance from the deck where the chain will be attached (the cleat) to the piling where you will secure the chain. Having all the information you are sure of what you need and you attach the links, produce the length of chain and go back to the dock to secure the boat. However, there is now a problem. From the time you left the dock, certain you were correct in your assumptions, God kind of changed the tide and now your boat is much farther from the dock. You cannot reach it and the tides change daily—no way of knowing what tomorrow will bring in the fate of your vessel! Perhaps you should have read the new tide charts! Symbolically, you may or may not have read the Bible and acquired all the information necessary to have the proper discernment on the tides of the times. Then, the tides changed between the Old and the New Testaments (about 400 years worth between the close of the Old and the opening of the New) and you are now further behind in spiritual knowledge and understanding because you have not measured the affect on your life from the Old to the New and are acting under assumptions that are no longer valid. Are you waiting for the tides to slam into your life or is it not wiser to simply read the New Testament and get all the information first hand? The chain length one needs to connect all the understanding of the tides of life are precisely sixty-six links! The New Testament represents the missing links.

If we combine the Old Testament with the New Testament, the Bible is broken down into sixty-six smaller Books as I illustrated with the number of links. You will find that the sixty-six Books are all connected— threaded together as would the strands of wool on a large loom. If you are standing on the weaver's side of the loom you will see various strands of colors— a series of knots and a pattern of weaving, that makes no sense to you at all— until you walk around to the front of the loom. It is there that you will see a beautiful multi-colored picture or design as it was meant to be seen—the total picture. How did it become clear? You simply viewed the front and the back, the entirety of the work and not just one part of it. As we study and look deeper into each of the Testaments, the picture of God's Word will become clearer, more defined, more understandable as well as the connection—the threads that are woven to complete the Master Weaver's work, revealing all that God (the Master of the entire work) wants you to discover. That is the connection of obtaining wisdom—by going to the place that God provides us with that wisdom for every human being to simply read and understand.

Each one of the individual Books beginning with the Old Testament renders a portion of the whole, a snapshot of a larger picture. God must certainly be grieved at the lack of faith and the lack of spiritual discernment in many of us for not reading and embracing that (the Bible) which opens the rusted locks of apathy and the door to eternal understanding. You should put aside religious prejudices, old fashioned thinking and years of misguided understandings and allow the truth of God's Word to remove the veil and open your spiritual eyes. As sad as it may be many of our own people have expressed at one time or another that much of the Bible is a fabrication. Many believe that some of it is true however

The Final Prophecy

most of the stories are not.[7] Some believe that the Bible is used to control society which in itself is an interesting statement and here is why. How could society possibly be controlled by something that they do not believe in? As for the Laws, many non-Orthodox Jews believe that no one is able to keep the over 600 laws and the stories of denial and rejection of the Bible go on and on. We are a divided people and should be unified in the Spirit of God. As trials prevail, many of our people, especially in Israel, allow their hearts to be hardened towards anyone who is not Jewish. This type of thinking is old fashioned but in the past was literally one of the common threads that held our people together— being unified and possessing the will to survive. Let us not forget that back in 1881 there were no more than about 25,000 Jews and dry desert land in the area where the independent State of Israel is today. As the years passed, realizing that which was and is now behind us, we continue to forge our own concepts of religion in the practice of our traditions. What many of us have not realized is that we are missing the very essence of our faith which is learning and understanding the Word of God. I submit to you that the rejection of God's Word is likened to rejecting God. To even entertain the thought that one word of God's Word is fabrication, denies all the wisdom that God has placed before our people for thousands of years. Did we not learn from the example of forty years in the wilderness for the lack of our faith and patience at Mount Sinai? Did we not reject the God-given wisdom of the prophets when they told us that an enemy was coming against the chosen people of Israel and we would suffer exile in Babylon for seventy years? I often feel as though God is watching and listening to these comments of rejection and is sadly shaking His head and knowing that in all these centuries we have not learned our lesson well. I have actually had a Rabbi tell, "I should not believe everything I read in the Bible—outside of the first five books." So if God's Words comprise the Bible in its entirety, whom do you trust? God is the source of all truth and it is God that I choose to believe and not man. The Bible contains God's messages, His declarations of all that He wants to make known to mortal man, from warnings to prophecies and from judgments to covenants. All of God's Word is divine revelation and every nugget of that wisdom is waiting for your discovery.

CHAPTER 4

H. G. Wells once stated, "To find God is but the beginning of wisdom, because then for all our lives we have to learn His purpose with us and to live our lives with Him."

That is what man said, however God said,

> And God said, For thus says the Lord, Who created the heavens, Who is God, Who formed the earth and made it, Who has established it, Who did not create it in vain, Who formed it to be inhabited: I am the Lord and there is no other. I have not spoken in secret, In a dark place of the earth: I did not say to the seed of Jacob, 'Seek Me in vain' I, the Lord speak righteousness, I declare things that are right. [8]

The Psalmist also said; [9]

> "The law of the Lord is perfect, converting the soul, The testimony of the Lord is sure, Making wise the simple, The statutes of the Lord are right, *Rejoicing the heart:*

God's testimony of Himself is sure, for without His testimony would you begin to understand Him? Could you fathom the mind of God? Could you explain all His mysteries and His ways? That is why He is the source of all truth and the source of all wisdom. Reliability of Scripture is based upon study and familiarization of Scripture and a strong inner belief in God and faith in His Word. You simply can't believe in one without the other. To know God is to know His Word.

Notes

1 Proverbs 1 – Page 1285 Tanakh, Revised Edition

2 Reference 1 Kings 4:32

3 2 Chronicles 1:8-12

4 Proverbs 2:6-8

5 Proverbs 2: 3 & 5 (verse 4 deals with seeking (her) wisdom as one seeks silver or hidden treasure)

6 Proverbs 3:5

7 Isaiah 45:18-19

8 Psalm 19:7-8

Chapter Five

The Word of God

One obstacle that man faces in his quest to acquire Divine knowledge and wisdom is that God has not directly spoken to mankind in over two-thousand years. There has not been a new prophet declaring prophecies in Israel or a voice for God's Word outside of the Pulpits of the Synagogues and Churches of the world. It would appear that God gave us a very long time[1] to figure out the event that broke the first four hundred years of silence. Unlike the days of our ancestors we do not have to look very far to find what God has to say as well as what He historically has said in the past. It applies to all of our lives, specifically the message He has given us for every human being who believes in Him and calls upon the name of the Lord for their salvation. It's all in writing, every vision that God allowed the prophets and the Patriarchs to see and to write about. It's in that one Book of sixty-six smaller Books, printed in black and white and all we need to do is to read it! Excuses such as, "It's too difficult" no longer applies as most Bible's today provide you with reference pages of insightful information on interpreting God's Word and even precise word meanings from the original Hebrew and Greek text. You will also find references to similar verses in the Bible as cross-references, allowing you to compare the unity of God's Word. God's Word is available to every human being yet how many of our people actually seek the knowledge and wisdom it has to offer? Chances are you have not really studied or read every Book, chapter and verse prayerfully seeking truth and understanding. Personally, I could never make it through Leviticus as a

The Final Prophecy

young man. However, I understood why I needed to do so when I began delving deeper into the amazing account of all there was, beginning in Genesis and all that will be in the Book of Revelation. If you recall the illustration I presented earlier about the weaver and his loom where God was creating a picture that appeared to be a bunch of threads and knots when looking at it from the weaver's side. Excluding any single chapter of the Bible from our study would be the same as the weaver eliminating a huge part of the picture he was creating. This would leave an empty, unwoven space that would literally disconnect or confuse the vision of the rest of the picture. How can we even consider delving into a Book that reflects our past and our future without knowing something about the Book itself? Would a novice who was attempting to work at a loom be able to create a woven masterpiece the first time he sat down to use it? Let's delve into some understanding of this Book and reason it through together. Personally, I usually want to know a little bit about the Author and the book itself before I invest precious time in reading it. Here it's a no-brainer. The Author is God and the Book is about life—past, present and future and well worth our reading time!

The Bible is also a truly unique Book, standing alone and above all the books that were ever penned anywhere in the entire world or at any time in the history of mankind. No book, religious or otherwise has withstood the test of time and persecution as much as the Bible. Men have tried to ban it, change it, deny it, disprove it, reject it, outlaw it, burn it and when they could not succeed, they finally began to study it in an attempt to understand it so that they could ridicule it. The Bible however, remains the most read book in the world and most of those (as I stated in the previous Chapter) who ridiculed the Bible eventually became strong believers. You see, anyone who has the desire to disprove something will search it that much more closely. When they could only find God's truths and not what they first perceived they would find, it changed not only their way of thinking about the Bible but blessed their lives in many other ways as well. These were not simply casual readers or uneducated people. Many were scholars, highly respected in their professional fields and did not simply glance through the sixty-six Books. They studied every verse and in the original languages. All these men eventually arrived at

CHAPTER 5

their individual moment of truth, fully believing in God's infallible Word. Abraham Lincoln had this to say. "To believe in the things you see and touch is no belief at all; but to believe in the unseen is a triumph and a blessing." The Bible is also the largest selling, longest survived book of all books and has been translated into most languages of the world's major populations and even some remote populations. Several organizations serve in translating the Bible into some of the most difficult ancient tribal languages. How does it strike you to know that as you are reading this book, some remote villagers in Tibet are reading about Abraham, Isaac and Jacob in their own language!

To truly understand the uniqueness of the Bible, let us consider that the Bible has been written over the span of 1,500 years, over the course of forty generations and by over forty authors. The authors consisted of men from almost every walk of life including kings, peasants, poets, scholars, fishermen, statesmen, and others. Some of its Authors were Moses, educated and trained in Egypt, Peter who was a fisherman, Amos who was a herdsman, Joshua a military man in the battles for the promised land, Nehemiah who was a cupbearer, Luke who was a physician, Solomon, king of Israel and son of David, Matthew, a Jewish tax collector, Saul who became Paul who was a Rabbi and of course Daniel who became a Prime Minister in captivity in Babylon. The Bible was written in many locations from the wilderness during a span of forty years by Moses to a dungeon where the prophet Jeremiah was incarcerated. The Bible was written under varied circumstances and at different times. David wrote in times of war, contrasted to his son Solomon who wrote in times of peace. Consider the fact that the Bible was written in three different languages, beginning with Hebrew, which constitutes major parts of the Old Testament and in 2 Kings 18:26-28 it was referred to as Judean. Then in the Book of Isaiah, it is referred to as *the* language of Canaan in Chapter 19, verse 18. Then there was Aramaic which was the common language of the Near East up until the time of Alexander the Great. Major portions of the Book of Daniel 2-7 were in Aramaic, followed by the Greek language which was an international language at the time that the New Testament was written. The Bible was also written on three continents, namely Asia, Africa and Europe. One of the most amazing facts that I yet marvel over

The Final Prophecy

is the harmony of the entire Bible, meaning how every one of the Books of the Bible are knitted or fit together. With all that diversity within the group of the Bible's Authors, the times in which each lived, the circumstances surrounding their lives and their varied levels of or their lack of formal education, every Author agrees with one another— a unity from the Book of Genesis to the Book of Revelation. I compare that to being as incredibly unique as attempting to gather up a dozen Authors from different times, different circumstances, different ages and different places. Give them all a subject and then find that they agree on all aspects of explaining that subject! It just doesn't happen—except in the Bible. The Authors of the sixty-six Books of the Bible do not question or ridicule each other in their individual writings and admonitions. They agree on what they have written over different times and in different places. Have you ever said; "I don't read the Bible because it does not make sense to me." This is not an excuse or a reason not to read the Bible or reject the Bible. It is a reason to study, explore and learn the historical and spiritual wealth of knowledge that exists between its covers. Why? It's your life, your future and mankind's future that we are exploring. You are linked to the long chain of our people and you are one who will ride the waves of destiny whether you want to or not. God is not going to stop the prophetically scheduled events of mankind because you didn't know about them! Additionally, interpretation itself should not be the primary goal of any student of the Bible, but rather the application of God's Word in your everyday life, how it applies to you and the life you are living. How else can you really know the essence of what this finite life is really about?

Speaking of reliability, any student of the Bible knows and trusts the omniscience of God. (God is all-knowing and sees the past, the present and the future at one time) To explain this in relatable circumstances, everyone at one time or another has been to and has seen a parade. You are watching the parade's participants go by you and you are even catching a glimpse of those who are following. You may also see the backs of those who just passed you by however God sees and knows the people who are in that parade before the parade ever started. He sees the beginning of that parade, those who are passing you by and the end of the parade—all at the same time. A simple enough explanation of omni-

CHAPTER 5

science and explaining God's Word is just as simple. I always turn to the best reference on the Bible—the Bible itself. If I want to clarify, support or check on someone quoting the Bible, I simply go to the Bible itself. The Bible provides us with more than one Biblical figure and more than one prophet and they are all saying the very same thing. No conflict, no disagreements and no contradictions. We literally have thousands of years of statements that provide us with the historical facts to compare each and every one of those statements or predictions and see their accuracy first-hand. If all that we read of God's Word demonstrates to us that it all came to pass, how could one doubt when the results are right in front of you? His Word is pure, historically shown to be truth and without any deception. God cannot lie. The Book of Proverbs declares, "Every Word of God is pure; He is a shield to those who put their trust in Him. Do not add to His words, Lest He rebuke you and you be found a liar." [2]

King David stated, "The words of the Lord are pure words, Like silver tried in a furnace of earth, Purified seven times." [3]

It is impossible and beyond any understanding to imply that one single word in the Bible could be false, especially when we consider that every word in the Bible was inspired by God. The heart that does not believe God's word would surely doubt many things God has said, those things that He has done and prophecies that our eternal destinies rely upon. If a man does not believe the Word of God he has no belief in his eternal future let alone a belief in anything— except himself. He is his own god and will perish in that belief as surely as he lives it. You see truth is the very core of God's character, for He is holy, loving and just. God *is* holy and God cannot look upon sin. To lie is to sin.

The Book of Psalms has also declared, "Who made heaven and earth, The sea and all that is in them, Who keeps truth forever." [4] David cried out to God in praise and thanksgiving and declared, "And now, O Lord God, You are God, and Your words are true, and you have promised this goodness to Your servant." [5]

This was at the time that David learned that his seed, his own son Solomon would build the Temple in Jerusalem. But God had given David more than a man could ask and David gave thanks to God, knowing the promise to his son would be kept and that his seed would rule over Israel

The Final Prophecy

forever. Solomon became David's successor to the throne of Israel and built the Temple that God promised his Father he would build.

I have heard many statements over the years about the Bible. Men who thought they were wise, until they were confronted with the wisdom of God. One man, who confronted God with his questions and his condition of life, received very direct answers. His name was Job.

> "Where were you when I laid the foundations of the earth? Tell Me, if you have understanding. Who determined its measurements? Surely you know. Or who stretched the line upon it? To what were its foundations fastened? Or who laid its cornerstone, When the morning stars sang together, And all the sons of God shouted for joy? "Can you lift up your voice to the clouds, That an abundance of water may cover you? Can you send out lightning that they may go, And say to you 'Here we are'? Who has put wisdom in the mind? Or who had given understanding to the heart? Who can number the clouds by wisdom? Or who can pour out the bottles of heaven?" [6]

Have you answered any of these questions or challenges yet? These are some of the challenges that God put to Job who questioned all that God was doing which can theoretically be compared to a man who doubts God's Word. (I would encourage you to read the Book of Job in its entirety, especially Chapters 38 to 41) We are just human and finite and we surely have not known the ends of the universe. We are men and women limited to our own world and often not even aware of what is going on in it because we are so caught up with our own problems of everyday life. We have not seen the furthest point of the galaxies that scientists (who are also mere men) continue to find are infinite. We have seen only a tiny corner of this universe and what we individually [7] know and understand about its infinite vastness would not fill a thimble. What's more, our very nature is plagued by a perverseness that often looks to and accepts vagueness instead of truth— electing to be gullible and believe in something other than admit to what we cannot understand or fathom.

CHAPTER 5

I submit to you that an unwavering, total belief and faith in God's Word is the most important thing for you to have before we even begin to talk about prophets or their prophecies that will lead us to the discussion of The Final Prophecy. To fully understand the complexity of the Bible's prophesies, especially The Day of the Lord, one must have some basic understanding of Scripture and at the very least (regardless of how much of Scripture is understood) you must believe in it! Man should gratefully receive the teachings of Scripture and allow the Spirit of God to minister those truths to his heart and to his soul.

> "The teaching of the Lord is perfect, renewing life; the decrees of the Lord are enduring, making the simple wise; The precepts of the Lord are just, Rejoicing the heart; The instruction of the Lord is lucid, Making the eyes light up; The fear of the Lord is pure, Abiding forever; The judgments of the Lord are true. Righteous altogether." [8]

To possess a more educated concept and vision of the future it stands to reason that we should learn all that we are able to about our past. That is where we begin to see direction— a type of order to things and even a pattern to that order. Once we see direction, we have a greater understanding of the journey and where it might be headed. If need be, history also provides us with the opportunity of not repeating or making the same mistakes of the past—provided that we learn from those mistakes. I am referring to not only we as individuals, but also as we the Jewish people— as one people and the Nation Israel. That is why I have spent so much time on the Word of God and explaining your personal connection to that Word. Simply stated, the Bible is God speaking to us, advising us, warning us and encouraging us to take heed of His Word. Do we really need a thunderous voice amidst a towering pillar of fire or a burning bush to convince us that every word within the Bible is from our Creator? All you have to do is consider the fact that no man can predict what is going to happen in a few hundred years or so and be precisely accurate in every way when it finally occurs! Obviously you can not go to whoever made that prediction and challenge them—neither of you would be here! In contrast, the predictions of the Bible that were made not hundreds but thousands of years ago need not be challenged because they have historically been fulfilled. We need only to go back to the original prediction and measure the accuracy and the precise details of the published events to see that these predictions were from God and not from man. God did not leave us hanging or wondering about how we should live our lives or what has happened to those who chose other than His way and His will. He told His prophets and they told us. They simply passed along the visions of things to come that God gave to them. When every prophecy, save the final one is shown to have already been fulfilled, one should not have any doubt that the last one will be fulfilled as well.

The original copies of the Old Testament were actually written on pressed leather or papyrus from the time of Moses, which would have been about 1450 B.C. up until the time of the prophet Malachi which was around 400 B.C. Copies of the manuscripts of the Old Testament were extremely scarce and it was not until around 895 A.D. or so that authenticated copies were discovered— simply because they were buried! You see, our ancestors of that time period were superstitious about the original text copies and when they became old they buried them! This act of course declined the number of available copies with each burial. It was between 600 and 950 A.D. that the Masoretes [9] standardized the Hebrew text by adding vowel points and accents to it, thereby increasing its readability. They also safeguarded against anyone making copies of these texts by implementing a numbered system that was very complicated. It dealt with words, pages and sections that were carefully counted from the middle of some pages to provide a sort of secret formula in which to identify the originals that were established from the old texts. This was actually helpful in giving us a safeguard for the accuracy of the older texts. Whenever anyone wanted to emphasize or support the accuracy of a passage of Scripture, they would simply refer to the Masoretes or the most accurate text.

CHAPTER 5

CHECKS AND BALANCES

Then in 1947, the critics of Scripture were pushed further back then they had ever been when by Divine fate, God stepped in to provide[10] the skeptics or unbelievers with irrefutable evidence concerning the accuracy of the Bible. A boy playing among a series of caves tossed a rock into one of them and heard the sound of a clay jar breaking as the rock struck it. Curious and excited, thinking perhaps that he had discovered a treasure, the boy climbed into the cave and discovered what would later become known as the Dead Sea Scrolls. These Scrolls provided us with the original Hebrew texts from the second to the first century B.C. and covered all of the Books except one, Esther, with the rest of the Books all in tact. This was extremely important to the reliability factor as these original manuscripts eventually proved the accuracy of the other texts that were in our possession at later times. Once all were painstakingly compared by the foremost authorities in the world, the Masoretic text officially became the reference point for checking the accuracy of Scripture until this very day. Other forms of early scrutiny that were conducted on the Hebrew texts included the Septuagint translations which were from the middle of the third century B.C., the Aramaic Targums which were fundamentally the paraphrases and quotes of the Old Testament and the Latin translation of Jerome from A.D. 400 which was actually made from the Hebrew text that was available in his time. If you place all of these checks and balances into a single statement, we had and still have an accurate text of the Old Testament.

Regardless of your beliefs concerning the New Testament, I would be negligent if I did not provide you with some of the facts in the New Testament to illustrate how the Old and New Testaments are threaded together. The Old Testament is the origin of the prophecies and the New Testament is the fulfillment of Biblical prophecies. This all relates to the reliability and authenticity of all sixty-six Book of the Bible. Let us reason through some Biblical facts for your own process of deliberation. A great deal of the New Testament writings point to Moses and Abraham and many, if not most of the Old Testament prophets. Equally important at this juncture in our reasoning is that we approach this from a thinking

The Final Prophecy

person's frame of mind. The more we look at truth instead of educated guesses our conclusions will not be clouded or blocked by speculation or prejudices. They will be supported by truth. That permits us to explore these revelations openly and not be hindered by preconceived notions or past teachings that were handed down from prior generations.

The Facts Supported

The more manuscripts that exist of a work, the more accountability, reliability and authenticity the work has. You just can't slip in a counterfeit text when there are so many originals available to compare it with. The philosophers, also known as the Greek thinkers, are fortunate if there are 25 complete manuscripts to check on their philosophy.[11] And yet, everyone I have ever heard who quotes Plato or Socrates, believe that they are quoting fact! They don't have a question in their mind about the authenticity. There are over 5,000 ancient manuscripts of the New Testament that exist today, making this text the most authenticated ever. Of the copies that are in existence there are about seventy-five fragments of Scripture (pieces of Books) that are written on the original papyri that dates back to the eighth century. When I say fragments, they cover parts of twenty-five out of twenty-seven Books [12] and the parts themselves render about forty percent of the text. Don't you wish you could have forty-percent of next week's newspaper! I believe that after the events of that week unfolded, having forty percent of those events in writing from before they occurred would render the information accurate. You would also know if its content covered enough insight of the other sixty percent so as to leave you with no doubt whatsoever of the genuineness of the content— and its reliability. If that is not enough, there exists today over 2,000 lectionaries that were early religious service books that contained many of the Scripture portions and 86,000 quotations of the New Testament. I believe you would agree that there is more than sufficient resource here to insure that we have an accurate text of the New Testament from which to discern its historic reliability.

CHAPTER 5

FROM THE OLD TESTAMENT TO THE NEW

The Old Testament is the guide that opens the history of our people and takes us from Genesis to the 400 years of God's silence. The Scriptures to Orthodox Jews are the first five Books of Moses which are known to us as Torah. It appears from the reading in the Synagogue that the Torah has all five Books joined together in one continuous scroll which originally it was. At what point it was divided into five separate Books remains unsure, however the English translation of the first five Books is believed to have originated or made available in its original language and form sometime around the third century B.C. This is the name by which the first five Books of the Old Testament are designated, known as the Law or The Book of the Law and placed as the first five Books of the Bible. That is because they (the Books) rendered detailed accounts of both Creation and the origin of the law as well as providing us with all the civil and institutional laws that went with it. The first five Books of Moses were placed in all translated Bibles (Jewish and Christian alike) because they fit chronologically and gave us an indispensable introduction to the remaining Books. *Without the first five Books at the forefront (Torah) the remainder of the Bible would be unintelligible.* Why? The rest of the Books of the Old Testament as well as the Books of the New Testament make reference to events in the first five Books both in Doctrine and in rituals. My emphasis on this fact is to support the importance placed on Torah by all if not most Rabbis, however the Rabbis and our people should never diminish the importance of the other 61 Books of the Bible that support Torah, refer to Torah and fulfill Torah.

THE CHALLENGES

As in any great work that challenges the human intellect and imagination, there were challenges from critics who stated that Moses was not schooled enough to have written these Books because the Hebrews could hardly read or write. There are critics for everything formed or made so

The Final Prophecy

let us not forget the obvious. Moses was not raised by his birth family. They (his mother and sister) protected him and gave him the chance to live (by God's will and providence) by setting him afloat among the reeds of the Nile which even non-Bible readers are familiar with for who of us have never seen the movie "The Ten Commandments." It was from that fateful day that Moses was taken from the Nile and raised by the daughter of Pharaoh. As such, Moses had all the educational privileges that went along with his destiny. Moses had the best of all available education by the Court Tutors through his entire childhood. One need not speculate any further on the literacy capabilities of Moses any more than one would speculate on his spiritual capabilities. Additionally, if God wanted an uneducated man to write the historical accounts that God wanted on paper, do you really think that his education would matter if it were God doing the dictation? Did Elijah or Joshua go to College? There are critics for everything, with the problem being that the more critical a person is or becomes, the less they understand. To further support this point or any other, I always turn to God's Word.

> "So Moses came and told the people all the words of the Lord and all the judgments. And all the people answered and said, 'all the words of the Lord we will do." And Moses wrote all the words of the Lord." 13

Then again in the journeys of our people, the Biblical Book of Numbers declares in the Thirty-Third Chapter;

> "Now Moses wrote-down the starting points of their journeys at the command of the Lord. And these are the journeys according to their starting points."

As we look more closely we see that Joshua reinforces the actual writings of Moses—God commanded Moses to write and Moses wrote.

CHAPTER 5

Joshua declares,

> "There was not a word of all that Moses had commanded which Joshua did not read before all the assembly of Israel, with the women, the little ones and the strangers living among them." [14]

Sometime around the seventeenth century there were further challenges when some scholars began questioning how Moses could have possibly known such details about the creation and the early days of human history, obviously having taken place long before Moses' birth. Just a short ways back I related their first questioning his education. What source for example did Moses use to write the Genesis account in such detail? Scholars began to study different possible sources of the Pentateuch [15] comparing and studying some of the ancient Egyptian and Babylonian texts. Not a single theory could conclude that Moses was not the author of the Pentateuch. This was supported in truth some years later when numerous archeological discoveries were uncovered in the Middle East. These discoveries affirmed the historical accounts of the Bible-especially the writings of Moses. One of my favorite undertakings is actually reading about great scholars that refuted facts set forth in the Bible and set out on a personal quest to disprove them. After intense investigation and studying archeological reports from the discoveries in Israel and the Dead Sea Scrolls, these critics soon become the most ardent believers. They learned first hand that God is Sovereign and His Word is true and accurate. You see Scripture is pure, without adulteration, falsehoods or pretenses that would lead man astray. The Bible declares this of itself, throughout Scripture, saying exactly what it is.

> "The law of the Lord is perfect, converting the soul: the testimony of the Lord is sure, making wise the simple. The statutes of the Lord are right, rejoicing the heart: the commandment of

The Final Prophecy

the Lord is pure, enlightening the eyes." [16]

And

"Every word of God is pure: He is a shield unto them that put their trust in Him. Do not add to His words, less you be reproved and found a liar." [17]

And,

"Forever, O Lord, Your word is settled in heaven." [18]

There must be a personal *belief* in Scripture in order for anyone to discern the prophecies of God. One cannot look at one verse and believe, then look at another verse or Chapter and discount it as untrue. It is or it's not. Scripture is simply God's advice for today— and His awareness for tomorrow. It is God's way of communicating with us and providing us with His wisdom to lean on instead of our own understanding. (Paraphrased from Proverbs) Solomon makes this very clear in Proverbs, saying;

"The Proverbs of Solomon the son of David, king of Israel: To know wisdom and instruction, To perceive the words of understanding" [19]

Solomon then confirms,

"Trust in the Lord with all your heart, And lean not on your own understanding." [20]

CHAPTER 5

I have yet to meet a person who did not derive blessings and opportunity from following Scripture in their lives. If you haven't been receiving such blessings, isn't it time that you began to? I have previously stated that the key to perceiving an eternal future lies within our understanding the declarations of the kings of Israel and the prophets of old. Only God's Word will enlighten you to these truths. I can point you to books that can provide you with historical overviews, commentaries on the Books of the Bible and even some insight into God's Word. However the Bible itself cannot be replaced by any other source from which to learn absolute truth. That is why I encourage you to look up the footnote references and read the verses for yourself. This provides for God's Word to speak to you spiritually as you read them in the context of the whole passage— reassuring you that the verses I have rendered serve as an integral part of your understanding.

God did not give mankind His Word, His Scripture, His Bible for us to remain unaware of the truths of life as God meant them to be. We as Jews were supposed to teach God's Word to all nations so that all the people of the world would come to know the God of Abraham, Isaac and Jacob. In the times of our forefathers, Gentiles regarded the God of the Jews as a conquering God who would smite an entire population for their wrongdoing. When our people sinned at Mt. Sinai, Moses pleaded with God not to destroy our people. In my own paraphrasing, Moses' plea to God, (I wish he was my Attorney if I ever needed one!) was how it would look to the non-believers of the world for God to have lead His people out of bondage from Egypt and then destroy them! Moses had a valid point and God accepted it. It was all about sin—the repeated warnings about sin and the consequences of sin. The Gentiles of that era did not understand what righteousness under a Holy God meant for they were mostly heathens and could not relate to that kind of a relationship. We Jews were to be the ambassadors, the emissaries and the light of the goodness of God to the sinful populations of the world in ancient times. Instead of doing so we fell right into the traps and the lures of evil and wound up involved in the very same sinfulness as the people to whom we were sent to bring to our God. We began to act and believe as the rest of the world did and surely that was not being a witness for a God who only wanted mankind

The Final Prophecy

to love Him as He loved mankind. A God who encouraged our worship, our friendship, our love and thankfulness for all the blessings that He had waiting for us— had we faithfully and fearlessly fulfilled what we were challenged to do. Since we did not fulfill God's expectations, He had to make other plans when it became apparent time after time again that we would not carry out His mission.

An interesting point I must make is that I have found that Christians study, learn and interpret our Old Testament more than our own people do! They believe that it is but one Bible in sixty-six Books—and not two separate Bibles. They turn to the Old Testament for the richness of God's Word and the teachings of Creation, the history of mankind and the Old Testament prophets. They then look to the New Testament as the fulfillment of all they read in the Old Testament. The complete Bible is our guide to the history of our lessons on morality, raising children, conducting our family life, our business life and social lives in the world around us—and not just among each other, but rather one to another. We have sadly allowed the knowledge and understanding of our Bible to be replaced with devotion to our traditions which we confuse as our religion. The Bible, the Word of God is our heritage and the traditions should be keeping that heritage alive. That has been our focus, our way of life and yet, God meant them to function side by side, learning from the Bible, understanding the Bible and celebrating our rich heritage. How can one say that "I know God" when they do not know His Word? If you truly love God and want a sincere relationship with Him and you desire to possess the power of His love within you to guide and protect you, one must first have a relationship with Him. If you sincerely want this for your life, then you will get to know Him through His own Word.

By the time you have reached this point in the book you will surely have a topical understanding of how I as the Author feel about several issues concerning the Bible, our religion and a relationship with God. You only know these things because you took the time to read and understand my book—thereby knowing me and how I view these subjects and how much I want you, the reader to learn them for yourself. It is no different with any other Author. To understand how and what God feels about the issues of life you simply have to read His Book. Just about all of the

CHAPTER 5

men who have written books on godly issues first read God's Book long before they wrote their own books. In the Bible, God has expressed and made known His promises, His unconditional love, His wrath over sin as well as his forgiveness for genuine repentance. More importantly, God has made perfectly clear His commandments on living life itself— right up to the end of days. A finite man can only observe and write about what he saw in the past and what he sees now. God has written about all that has been in the past and all that will take place in the future. For me to write about, understand and advise you of the future there is but one source from which I obtained that information—from God's Book. You either accept Scripture on the basis of it being God's truths or you do not. You cannot pick and choose, debate what is believable and what is not, for once a person declares that a source of information is tainted or untrue that colors the entire work as tainted or untrue. You cannot say that you believe some of the things that Moses said and not all of what he said. That would mean he lied about some things and if he did than the content of the entire work is debatable.

The question of the worth of human existence is a question that the majority of human beings ask at least once in their lifetime. If a person does not ask that question they have ceased to think, to question, to discover or it is possible that you are one of the very few who have been blessed in finding exactly what God had planned for your life and you are living it. Even so, referencing this life and all of your contentment in it, how does that affect you at the end of this life? Does it guarantee you another life?

Are you one of the millions who have ceased to think higher thoughts and to dream higher visions, living day-to-day questioning your own mission in this life? If you are, than that is usually the result of a non-purposed life. You could be highly successful, even rich, but remember that all you have will eventually rust and grow old and fade away. You know the saying as well as I do—you can't take it with you. I have been to numerous funerals in my life and I have yet to see one single casket filled with cash, cars, jewelry, houses, boats and you get the idea! The luxuries or material wealth of this life are temporary. Only God's kingdom is forever. So in summary of all this admonition and encouragement, here is

The Final Prophecy

the bottom line. You really need to discover it all for yourself in the Book that God has written and has had your name on for years— waiting for you to pick it up and discover the very essence of the word hope, inner peace and life eternal. Don't be put off by your prior attempts to read it or what you don't understand. Remember that God Himself will strengthen and guide every attempt that we make to connect with Him.

Notes

1 A thousands years is likened to one day for God.

2 Proverbs 30:5-6

3 Psalm 12:6

4 Psalm 146:6

5 2 Samuel 7:28

6 Job 38

7 The reference is to most of us who are not trained Scientists in this field, and even they do not have most of the answers.

8 A Psalm of David 19:8-10 Tanakh, The Holy Scriptures, 1985 Revised Edition

9 Jewish traditionalists who refused to part from their exacting ways in preserving the Word of God.

10 A personal belief from the study of the Commentaries on the Dead Sea Scrolls

11 Known historic records

12 Number of Books in the New Testament

CHAPTER 5

13 Exodus 24:3-4

14 Joshua 8:35

15 The Pentateuch is the five-fold volume of the first five Books of the Old Testament that was originally on a roll and then divided into five individual books. *(when is not known)*

16 Psalm 19:7-8

17 Proverbs 30:5-6

18 Psalm 119:89

19 Proverbs 1:1-3

20 Proverbs 3:5

THE FINAL PROPHECY

Chapter Six

Introduction to Prophecy

The prophecies of end times have been associated with controversial issues that we as Jews consider to be outside of our Judaic sphere of concern and have therefore dismissed as irrelevant. Most of us who have never studied or understood the prophecies from the Old Testament, do not fathom how these predictions could include Israel and her people, thinking it's just another Christian tool to subvert Judaism. We could never be more misled. These prophecies apply to every human being on the face of this earth. The prophets who foretold the events of end times and The Day of the Lord were faithful men of Jewish belief and heritage. Men whom God called into His service in a way that is no different than when God called Moses or any other man throughout Biblical history to serve Him. God will often use the most unlikely people to accomplish His will, for as Solomon well stated, the foolish shall confound the wise. None of the prophets had formal training, nor were they skilled in the tasks that God called each of them to perform. All of the prophets had no prior job experience and were not highly educated in prophecy. God does not always call the equipped—God simply equips those whom He calls. I picture God chuckling when mortal man and his finite wisdom tries to second-guess Him! Man often refuses to admit that he does not have all the answers. The prophets of ancient Israel had only the answers to the question of what God intended for His people to know. They also provided rebukes or admonishment for sin and foretold of those

The Final Prophecy

things that were yet to come, such as the judgments in the days that God would cleanse the earth of its sin. Their words were visions of what God instructed them to do and nothing more or less. In those tumultuous times it was not an easy task or profession to be in! God inspired the words and they spoke them when and to whom God instructed them to do so.

Prophecy, in its simplest terms is a prediction or the foretelling of events and circumstances that will take place sometime in the future from the time that the prediction(s) is (are) made. If one wants to understand the nature and the completeness of God's Word then one must have some basic knowledge of prophecy. I have previously stated that in order to know what the world is coming to we must first look to our past. It is in that past that God has told us what would occur in the future!

If we topically separate the entire Bible we would find that one-fourth of the Bible is related to predictive prophecy. These predictions were made by the prophets who were given predictive capabilities by God. Prophecy is a powerful word for students of the Bible for they are the promises of God and not simply the idle words of man. That means that when God spoke to the prophets and predictions were made, they come to fruition within the time-frame predicted. There were also covenants that were made by God Himself when He was still speaking to His chosen leaders— the Patriarchs and the kings of Israel. A time-frame of over 5,000 years provides a great deal of history to turn to and verify the accuracy of the prophetic record. To not consider prophecy is likened to not considering the future. To reject prophecy is turning away from all the possibilities of life –not being aware and not having an understanding of the power, the providence and the plan that God has predestined for all of His people, those who have purposed their hearts to follow Him. Each prophecy in the Bible is with definitive purpose— another piece of the big puzzle of mans ultimate destiny.

The Biblical Books of 1 and 2 Kings were originally one Book, titled "Kings." This was taken from the first word of the first verse. When the Septuagint [1] was written dividing the one book into two, and was specifically done for the purpose of making the scrolls for this lengthy Book manageable and not for any changes or other interpretations then those already written by the ancient Scribes. The two Books were written by eyewitnesses to the events of these times which covered a span from the death of David (971 B.C.) to the destruction of the Temple by the Babylonians. (586 B.C.) The first Book begins in the time of the reign of Solomon, son of David. Kings depicts the people's outcry to be ruled by kings rather than priests. The Books also provide us with the first major mention of prophets in the Bible who were active throughout the split kingdoms of Judah and Israel. However, it is not the first mention nor is it the first prophecy in the Bible. The Book of Numbers, Chapters 22-24 tell us of the pagan prophet Balaam, (not to be confused with God's anointed prophets) who lived among an entire cult of professed prophets who were practicing magic and divination rather than being in the service of God. When Balak the king of the Moabites (the descendants of Lot, Abraham's nephew) saw the multitude of Israelites on the plains of Moab, he began to seriously worry. He should have worried for it was from that very location that the Israelites would invade Canaan under God's protection. Knowing that he had to do something outside of going to battle with an army he could not defeat, Balak sent for Balaam and hired him to curse Israel. That did not work very well for instead of cursing the Israelites he offered up blessings for them! You might enjoy reading this section of the Bible, especially noting how God even uses a donkey to achieve His purposes! 2

There are those who were also regarded as prophets although they were not called by God to specifically be prophets—familiar names in Biblical history. For one, there was Samuel who was the great leader in the last days of the Judges. (The Book of Judges in the Old Testament) Even King David had two prophets in his court, namely Nathan and Gad. Both of these prophets provided Divine guidance as well as Divine rebuke for David in specific matters of ruling Israel. Jewish tradition refers to the prophets of Joshua in the Book of Judges and 1 and 2 Samuel. 1 and 2 Kings mentions the Former Prophets as opposed to the group who are referred to prophets such as Isaiah, Hosea and Jeremiah (and others) who are referred to as "Latter Prophets," such as Isaiah, Hosea and Jeremiah. The first of the Latter Prophets was Amos who provided a turning point in the perception and knowledge of prophecy. You see, up until the time

The Final Prophecy

of Amos (the middle of the eighth century B.C.) all of our knowledge concerning prophecy depended on stories about the prophets. Beginning with Amos we had (and still have) the opportunity of studying the prophets own words and the actual contributions that each made with regard to the fate of Israel.

Prophecy is regarded as a unique and divine characteristic of Israel, considering that it was not prevalent anywhere else in the ancient world. There were both prophets and seers and it was said of the seers that they would receive divine revelation in a trance-like state, possessing what was referred to as the eye of vision.

> "The oracle of Balam, son of Beor, the oracle of the one whose eye is opened, The oracle of the one who hears God's words and sees a vision of the almighty, swooning but with his eye uncovered. [3]

This would be representative of a seer whose prophetic insights and revelations came through a type of third eye as the seer refers to as being opened and then uncovered. If you recall from the Bible, the prophet Samuel was able to recover lost objects as well as see distant events. Here is a Biblical example.

THE SETTING

Saul was searching for several donkeys [4] belonging to his father whose name was Kish. The donkeys had gone astray and Saul was sent out to find them, accompanied by a servant from their household. When they could not find the donkeys after traveling a great distance and

CHAPTER 6

had reached the district of Zuph in the hill country of Ephraim, it was then that the servant suggested that they seek out a seer by the name of Samuel. This was a man of God and well known in this particular territory at that time. Saul, who was frustrated by that point, wanted to return home but took the advice of the servant. They came upon Samuel who had just heard instructions from the Lord to seek out a king for Israel. It seemed that the people were crying out for a king to be sent to them.[5] What Saul did not know was that as he (Saul) was on his way to find Samuel, it was Samuel who had come to bless the sacrifice of the town. God had already instructed Samuel on who would be the king that the people were praying for and had delivered up a sacrifice for him. As Saul found Samuel and approached him, the Lord spoke to Samuel and declared that this was the man to anoint as king. [6] Was this prophetic? Yes, for it was a short term prophecy that was made under divine instruction from the Lord to his elect prophet or seer and the prophecy came to pass when Saul became king. The evidence of the anointing was short term and made known. In fact, Samuel told Saul every detail of what would occur, including the location, the band of prophets that would approach him and the Spirit of the Lord gripping him and changing his heart. [7]

> "As [Saul] turned around to leave Samuel, God gave him another heart and all those signs were fulfilled that same day. And when they came there to the Hill, he saw a band of prophets coming toward him. Thereupon the spirit [8] of God gripped him".

The prediction by Samuel that was relayed to Saul came to pass the moment that Saul reached the Hill and was approached by the group or band of prophets. This was a short term prophecy but assuredly not a case of coincidence.

My question is what would be the difference if the Lord, appearing to

The Final Prophecy

a prophet in Saul's time, in David's time or at any point in our history and provided that prophet or seer with divine revelation (as it was just illustrated with Samuel) of what He (God) is going to do about the sin of His people if they do not repent and stop worshipping false gods? Suppose God said that the chosen prophet must warn them for His (God's) patience is drawing to a close. The prophet then tells the people, informs the elders and has done what God has told him to do. Suppose the consequence was a year into the future and God gave them that time to comply with His admonitions but they did not listen? What is sad is that the Israelites either disbelieved the prophecies or simply chose to ignore the warnings. Then a year later, when Israel was attacked, would anyone then doubt the word of the prophet who in essence was speaking for God?

At this very time in our history, God's Word is warning His people and the entire world, crying out from the pages of the Bible that there shall indeed be judgment upon the sin of this world. The terrible Day of the Lord shall surely come to pass and all the prophetic warnings of end times shall be fulfilled. In the prophecy of the Babylonian captivity, God gave His people a single year. In the case of this prophetic pronouncement concerning the entire world, God has given us thousands of years to prepare. Let's not forget that thousands of years seem like a very long time— however the Bible tells us, "With the Lord, one day is like a thousand years." [9] Acknowledgement in the case of the Israelites came with the sorrow and realization of how right the prophets were and how wrong the people had been.

The first major lesson to our people was when they were brought out from Egypt. Idolatry, quarreling, complaining were the sins that cost them a lesson of forty years in the wilderness. The Babylon lesson would cost them seventy years in captivity. The greater lesson of eternal life could cost those who do not heed God's warning just that— their eternal lives. When will we ever learn? This is what we see throughout the Bible, prophecies of different proportions and of varied magnitudes as they relate to the life of the people and to the life of Israel. You see, the significance of Israel's prophets lies not only in what they predict but also the circumstances surrounding the prophecy. We need to fully understand who they were, what happened to them and when and why God called them. Was it for a specific purpose? Was it to serve Him as a prophet all the days of their lives or for a specified period of time to accomplish a specific purpose? Isolating human revelation will cause one to lose sight of prophetic origin— such as who declared it and why. You really should know more about the prophet first— before you ponder over his prophecy. If you focus on the revelation you may lose sight of the response by the prophet and by the people as to that specific prophecy. Why didn't they heed the warning? Did they not know the prophet or were the prophecies he made in the past not yet fulfilled? That would account for the people being hesitant to act on the prophet's word or were simply being skeptics instead of the grateful recipients of that prophecy! How would you feel if you were the prophet, confronting facts that concern the future of the world and the lives of your own people? Surely the revelations of what was to come would have perplexed the strongest believer and the holiest of men. Here is an excellent example of the prophets and what I often refer to as the perils of prophecy. This is where God tells a prophet to announce harsh words of rebuke or deliver news of some impending tragedy and even death. One example would be the prophet Jeremiah who cried out in great despondency after he announced the forthcoming capture of Judah by the Babylonians to Passhur, the son of Immer the priest. (See verses below) If that wasn't bad enough, Passhur was also chief governor in the house of the Lord! It was just the day prior that Passhur struck Jeremiah and placed him in the stocks. He did so because he heard of Jeremiah's predictions of things he obviously did not want to hear. After all, no one wants to hear bad news. On the next day when he brought Jeremiah out, Jeremiah declared,

> "For thus says the Lord: Behold, I will make you a terror to yourself and to all your friends; and they shall fall by the sword of their enemies, and your eyes shall see it. I will give all Judah into the hand of the king of Babylon, and he shall carry them captive to Babylon and slay them with the sword. Moreover, I will deliver all the wealth of this city, all its produce, and all its precious things; all the treasures of the kings of Judah I will give into the hand of their enemies, who will plunder them, seize them and carry them to Babylon. [1]

The Final Prophecy

Would you have wanted to be the one to make that announcement to a head priest of the Temple who had the power to place you in stocks and throw you in prison for the rest of your life? As if all of this was not bad enough, in the next breath Jeremiah told Pashhur that he and his family would be taken to Babylon and would die there. It seemed that Jeremiah had absolutely nothing to say that was encouraging to this man! Why all this bad news? Pashhur had given false testimony and false prophesy as a man of God. You simply do not go around announcing, "Thus say's the Lord" if the Lord did not truly say it! Jeremiah was not popular and he felt the isolation and the rejection. How would you hold up if you went to work tomorrow and told everyone; "You who are Jewish and have not been to Synagogue this year for Yom Kippur and who have not repented of their sins will all go to hell and burn there for the rest of eternity." How popular would you be with your co-workers? I believe this point is made so that you can readily see that being a prophet was surely not a popular profession. For what gain does a man have to tell you of something that he knows very well will bring him ridicule and rejection and the possible loss of his life? The prophets knew it was God alone who called on them so who was going to argue? They answered God's call. I believe it would be fair to say that no prophet did it for the glory. They lived lonely and often ostracized lives. Would you want to be known as the "gloom and doom" person in your neighborhood?

Types of Prophecies

It is important for you to know that there are actually three types of prophecies so that you will be able to differentiate between them.

- *Unconditional fulfillment*
- *Conditional fulfillment*
- *Sequentially fulfilled*

CHAPTER 6

Unconditional fulfillment mostly deals with the salvation of mankind and the covenants that do not require the fulfillment of any type of demands— from individual man or from mankind in order to maintain or fulfill their mortal side of what God promised. If God states that He will do something and the fulfillment is unconditional, He will do so as promised. There is no dependence upon the actions of man. An example would be God's covenant of the seasons, in Genesis 8 where God declares,

> "And the Lord smelled a soothing aroma. Then the Lord said in his heart, 'I will <u>never</u> again curse the ground for man's sake, although the imagination of man's heart is evil from his youth; <u>nor</u> will I destroy every living thing as I have done. "While the earth remains, seedtime and harvest, Cold and heat, Winter and Summer, And day and night, Shall not cease. [2]

In the very next Chapter of Genesis [3] God makes another covenant— this one with Noah, although it surely affects all of mankind. Verse 8 declares:

> "Then God spoke to Noah and to his sons with him, saying: "And as for Me, behold I establish my covenant with you and with your descendants after you" Verse 11: "Thus I establish my covenant: *Never again* shall all flesh be cut off by the waters of the flood; Never again shall there be a flood to destroy the earth."

In essence, God promises that He shall never again destroy the earth with the waters of a flood and God sealed this covenant or promise with His rainbow in the clouds. It is known as the Rainbow Covenant.

The Final Prophecy

If you look at both covenants, the prior covenant with the seasons and the promise with Noah never to destroy every living creature upon the face of the earth again by God's covenant with Noah, we see that God has declared a promise, a prophesy *never* to do something such as that act of vengeance for sinfulness again. Man has no role in this covenant that God made. There is nothing he must do or not do to prevent a worldwide flood. God promised it without conditions, requiring nothing of man to uphold this covenant. It is unconditional therefore never to occur again regardless of mans sinfulness, disobedience or falling away from God. God said it and mankind has no part in its fulfillment. However, don't think that if God promised not to destroy the earth, then why do we have all this concern over end times? Simply because God said that He would not destroy us by water. God did not say that He would not judge mankind by other methods. Did you not know that the opposite of water is fire? God specifically speaks of this in His warning in the Final Prophecy. It is also important to note that the unconditional prophesies or promises are not numerous in number with respect to all other prophecies. They are however central to the overall prophetic picture of God's plan.

Then there is God's covenant with Abraham in Genesis Chapters 12 and 15 that go something like this. Imagine coming home one day and telling your wife that you have some life-changing news for her. You tell her that there is both good news and bad news. The good news is that you are moving from Ur, a prosperous city in Mesopotamia, the town you live and worked in for many years. Then you tell her the bad news. You don't have a clue where you're going! Then you tell her that God said "If we 'get out of Ur, He will bless us and make us a great nation. He will make our name great. He will bless those who bless us! He will also curse those who curse us." Then the most awesome part of the news is related. God said, "Within me, all the families of the earth would be blessed!"[4] At first your wife is shocked, however since God said He would bless your household and she knew her husband as a man of God, that was good enough – let's go! And Sarai, (later to be re-named as Sarah) packed all their belongings and went!

Is this a conditional covenant? No, although some may say that Abraham still had to get out of Ur to receive the blessings of this cov-

CHAPTER 6

enant, God knew Abraham's heart and knew his answer—before he said yes. The covenant itself was unconditional because God promised him and despite Abraham's own mistakes and sins along the way, God was faithful in His promise. This covenant however is a covenant that is stated, confirmed and reaffirmed. In Chapter 12 of Genesis we see what will become known as the Abrahamic Covenant. For your own study and affirmation, the covenant is confirmed in Genesis 15:18-21, then reaffirmed in Genesis 17:1-21, renewed with Isaac in Genesis 26:2-5, and then Jacob in Genesis 28:10-17 and is portrayed throughout Scripture as a lasting covenant. It is unconditional in the sense that the ultimate fulfillment of this covenant is the fulfillment of a kingdom and the ultimate salvation of Israel. The fact that this covenant is everlasting and thereby unconditional does not make it an immediate covenant. That would be a condition or the part that is conditional. Israel is already here— it is a kingdom that exists. Abraham was blessed, his family was blessed and the seed of Abraham, promised to be passed down to generations that have spawned generations that outnumber the stars visible to man. There is a final fulfillment yet to come and we shall approach that when we talk about God's everlasting plan for Israel. God's covenants or promises are still interpreted as prophetic, especially when they are to be fulfilled in the future at some point in time— or fulfilled forever as a lasting covenant.

The prophet Jeremiah was promised a new covenant between God and His people and it was fulfilled.[5] This covenant declared by God, stated, "He would be their God and they would be His people." God said this and there was no condition placed on the covenant. God did not say "if" they do this and He did not say "unless" they sin against Me— it was a final and everlasting statement. Note that God did not say He would not punish sin. He said that He would "be their God." I believe you now see the nature of the *unconditional* covenants although the majority of prophecies are of the conditional kind that uses the word "unless" or the words "If you keep My commandments" which in itself declares the condition. In Jeremiah 18:7-10, we see a link to what I previously explained about unfulfilled prophecies. Take the situation of Ahab and the murder of Naboth in the Biblical Book of 1 Kings. God said in essence that although

The Final Prophecy

He pronounced judgment upon a nation for its sins, "if" the nation turned from its evil ways and repented, God would reverse the judgment. This is conditional and provides a chance to change sinful ways which is a sign of God's grace. This is also an example of how God's covenants pass to individuals and not just nations as a whole.

Referencing the simplified chart that was depicted earlier concerning God's promises, I stated that there were basically two distinct types of prophecies that come from God. One type being "conditional" in that there is something that man must do in order for God to fulfill that covenant or prophecy. The second is "unconditional" which means that God will fulfill a covenant or prophecy and man must do nothing in order for God to do so—all in His timing, of course.

Prophecy is essentially a man being chosen as a prophet by God to relay both God's promises and admonitions, thereby immortalizing God's Word. Prophecies that are to be fulfilled in the distant future represent another piece of the puzzle in God's master plan and will naturally not make a whole lot of sense to the prophet. God however, always provides a vision of that which is to come and the prophet sets that vision to words. As an example, if you were to receive a divine revelation, a picture in your mind of heaven and you knew it was not a dream, how would you react? There you were standing in the midst of your eternal destiny and taking in all you could see! You framed this picture in your mind and within minutes after your eyes had been filled with that picture of glory you immediately wrote it all down while it was a vivid image in your mind. Streets of gold, a throne with twenty-four Elders around the throne who fell to their knees, praising God, singing; "Holy, Holy, Holy is the Lord of Hosts, the whole earth is *filled with His glory."* God did not have to tell how to write those words and God would not be looking over your shoulder to make sure that you wrote it all down properly! You would have written precisely what He wanted you to write because that is what He allowed you see! The words that describe the vision may have been written by your own hand but it was God's vision that you wrote about. It would also be God's Word because he allowed you to write precisely what you saw. When you question anything a prophet says that appears in writing in the Bible, the premise is that you are questioning the very

CHAPTER 6

Word of God.

God's will and His plan for all things are sovereign. God directs all events in keeping with His will— all things that fulfill His purpose. Regardless of what man does, God is moving everything along according to His timetable and His sovereign plan. God knows exactly what will happen tomorrow, next year or in a lifetime of lifetimes. God is omniscient, which is to say that He knows all things—those things that will or will not take place in the future. The prophet Isaiah relates God's declaration,

> "I foretell the end from the beginning, And from the start, things that had not occurred. I say: My plan shall be fulfilled; I will do all I have proposed."[6]

If we know the future, the scope of God's plans by what His prophets have told us then it stands to reason that what the prophets have said was divinely inspired. If the Bible is the very Word of God then the Bible itself is divinely inspired. In addressing the prophetic messages of the Bible, the messages themselves would render those prophecies to be divinely accurate. Inspired does not mean word for word but rather a picture or a snapshot of what God is telling us. God does not leave the course of human history and the future of mankind to chance but rather His divine will is the supreme factor in the fulfillment of all things under heaven and within heaven as the prophet Isaiah declares. No promise of God can fail, for there is nothing that a prophet has said that has not been fulfilled except the end times prophecies.

There are hundreds of examples of God's inspired prophecies, all recorded in Scripture and are now a matter of record within the very history of mankind. My point is how can we the Jewish people who God has charged with being His emissaries, his light to the world not know and understand what God has said regarding specific prophecies that will affect the world? His prophetic declarations that tell us precisely what the future holds for mankind should surely, at the very least, be known to we who God has called "His chosen people." His power and His glory have been manifested for thousands of years, set to the written word within the pages of the Bible, every prophecy, every covenant and every promise, but do you have the faith in all that God has said? Can you tell an agnostic to believe in our God and when he asks you to give him a reason for your beliefs the only answer you have for him is to *"Have faith!"* I encourage you to heed these simple facts and rather than ignoring the promises— the prophecies of the Bible, embrace them and know the wisdom of God's Word. Seek and you will find wisdom, for if one does not pursue the answers of life then one will not have those knowledge to support their own faith— let alone have the ability to share that faith with others. Not seeking the understanding and the knowledge that awaits us in God's Word, the Bible, is like walking up to a closed door that has wondrous blessings on the other side and you stand there and never knock!

Notes

1 Jeremiah 20:4-6

2 Genesis 8:21-22

3 Genesis 9:8-17

4 Genesis 12:2-3

5 Jeremiah 31:31-34

6 TANAKH, Jewish Holy Scriptures, Isaiah 46:10-11

Chapter Seven

The Prophets of Israel

Who were those men whom God chose and called to devote their lives to declaring His will and His thoughts to the people of Israel? They were the Prophets of Israel and throughout time, none of the religions of the world have given such a valuable gift to mankind as the prophetic Word of God. Prophecy enables us to know the future, including all that will take place during end times. It provides us with God's plan for mankind through the prophecies of those simple men He chose and anointed to do His work. There are respected, classic works on religion by brilliant theologians, and the book "Beacon Lights of Prophecy" was no exception. In this book published back in 1914, Dr. Albert C. Knudson said of our Jewish prophets and prophecies, in essence, that "No one contributed so much to the permanent moralization and spiritualization of religion as did the prophets of Israel."

Why God used the most common of men to be His prophets is not a mystery. The prophets were Israelites and were chosen by God from among the people so that they would be relatable *to* the people. However God's messages, especially those of things to come were not just for the Israelites but for all of mankind. God's desire was that everyone would come to Him so that He could be their God and they would be His children. This was the foremost reason that He created man in the first place. God wanted fellowship and a personal relationship with all of His people. When God created man and a woman to be his helper and mate,

The Final Prophecy

God created them in His image.[1] This does not mean a physical image but rather an inward image, one of love and the desire to fellowship with Him. This is an example of God's desire for all of mankind to have a personal relationship with Him. This is shown in Genesis where God is walking in the Garden of Eden in the cool of the day seeking Adam for fellowship with Him. Unfortunately Adam and his wife Eve were hiding from God because they had sinned.[2] It is also unfortunate that our ancestors did not really understand that they, the chosen people of Israel were to be His emissaries to the rest of the world— a walking and talking example of God's love. God desired that it was He that people turn to for their needs and not to false gods who were worshipped by pagans. God wanted mankind to love Him by choice and not because they had to out of fear. God also left no room for any misunderstanding about what He would not tolerate –namely any and all types of sin.

One of the primary duties of the prophets was to provide sufficient warning to the Israelites when sin was prevalent. God wanted there to be no question that He is holy, loving and just and that eventually God would have to punish the sins of His people— although His patience seemed to be more enduring than we deserved. The more our people sinned the more they became separated from God which was totally opposite of what God planned for His beloved Israel.

In the Old Testament, there are seventeen Books of the prophets. I have listed them according to their position in the Bible and not according to their importance or prophetic content.

1. Isaiah
2. Jeremiah
3. Lamentations (Jeremiah)
4. Ezekiel
5. Daniel
6. Hosea
7. Joel
8. Amos
9. Obadiah
10. Jonah
11. Micah
12. Nahum
13. Habakkuk
14. Zephaniah
15. Haggai
16. Zechariah

CHAPTER 7

17. Malachi

However, in the Tanakh, according to the revised edition that was printed after the 1917 edition, (The New JPS Translation or the Jewish Publication Society- 1985) the prophets, or NEVI'IM are separated into the categories of "The Prophets" and "The Minor Prophets" that include Joshua, the Judges, 1 Samuel, 2 Samuel, 1 Kings, 2 Kings and has positioned Daniel, Ezra and Nehemiah in the category of "The Writings" or KETHUVIM. I note this in the event you are referring to a "Revised Edition of Tanakh" and not the older translation. In either case, be it Tanakh or a standard Holy Bible, I have sought to pursue clarity and correctness.

There were many others who were Biblically declared as having the gift of prophecy but only the Books of the prophets who are in the Bible are named above. Those who were also referred to as having the gift of prophecy included Aaron, the brother of Moses, [1] Abraham, [2] Ahijah, [3] Balaam, [4] Eldad,[5] Gad, [6] Hannaniah,[7] Iddo, [8] Medad, [9] Nathan, [10] Oded,[11] and Shemaiah[12]

Also within the prophetic order were Prophetess', holy women of God who knew what it was to be "lifted in the Spirit" of God and receive that which God desired to convey to them. Some of those women were: Deborah, [13] Huldah,[14] Miriam,[15] and Noadiah.[16]

Let's take a written snapshot, if you will, of the seventeen prophets who spent their lives in God's service— delivering His messages and His warnings to our people. Knowing some of the background of the prophets such as when they were called into God's service, how they were called, why they were called and where they came from should provide you with a deeper insight into their lives and the prophecies they declared in the name of God. These were men who gave up everything to answer God's calling so when I read about some soothsayer of modern times predicting something that makes newspaper headlines the first thing I ask is, "What do they have to gain? What are they personally looking for—money, fame or both?" These are self-professed psychics and not

The Final Prophecy

prophets, for God has been silent and has not chosen a prophet for over 2,400 years. As for what the ancient prophets had to gain, they surely did not do it for the glory, the esteem or the recognition. The prophets called by God were scorned, jailed, beaten, stoned and often had to perform almost inhuman tasks of sacrifice and courage to deliver the words and the visions that God wanted to deliver to the people of Israel.

Knowing the Prophets

Who were the prophets and what were their individual roles in prophecy? To truly know the detailed history of all the prophets of Israel one would need to read an entire book on the subject. For our immediate purpose, here is a simplified, overall snapshot of the seventeen prophets of the Old Testament with some basic details about each of them.

Isaiah °Tanakh, Pg. 615

- His name means *"The Lord is salvation."*[1]

- His name is similar to Joshua and Elisha.

- In addition to his sixty-six Chapters in the Biblical Book of Isaiah, he is quoted over 65 times in the New Testament and mentioned directly by name over 20 times—which is more than any other prophet is referred to or spoken of.

- He was the son of Amoz, and served primarily four kings in Judah. They were Uzziah (Azariah) Jotham, Ahaz and Hezekiah.

CHAPTER 7

• Isaiah was not unknown in the region of Judah, in fact he was rather well known. The Bible shows that he had full access to go before the king.[2]

• Isaiah was a contemporary of Hosea and Micah.

• His death was a brutal one, being cut in half with a wooden saw under King Manasseh.

Historic:

Isaiah served as a prophet at the time of the divided kingdoms but the majority of his messages were for Judah. He spoke against the ritualism and the idolatry that was being practiced by many of God's chosen people. His prophecies were numerous and as some of them came to pass, the people of Israel clearly saw that Isaiah's warnings and prophetic declarations were assuredly made known to the prophet by God. In Isaiah Chapter 37, the prophet states that Sennacherib's efforts to takeover Jerusalem would fail and Isaiah was precise and correct. In Chapter 44, Isaiah names the new King of Persia as the one who would deliver the Jews out of captivity to return to their homeland. History shows us the exacting fulfillment of that prophecy. More than anything else, Isaiah provides us with vivid, prophetic declarations concerning Messiah and the future Day of the Lord. Even the Revised Tanakh lists Isaiah as a Major Prophet yet the majority of our Rabbis continue to deny the prophecies concerning Messiah that were spoken by Isaiah.

Jeremiah ° Tanakh, Pg. 763.

• Jeremiah was a prophet who was quite verbal, much more than all the other prophets and mostly about his own life. The most noticeable note on Jeremiah was that his life and his service to God were one and the same. If you know his prophetic life you know his personal life. He too is listed in Tanakh as a Major Prophet.

The Final Prophecy

- Jeremiah was the son of the priest Hilkiah, who discovered the Book of the Law. The Book had been lost for several centuries as a result of disuse.

- Jeremiah was from a village about three miles NE of Jerusalem, called Anathoth and now called Anata in modern Israel.

- Jeremiah remained unmarried, which was analogy for Judah as the bride of God. You can explore this in Jeremiah 16:1-4.

Historic:

Jeremiah was known as the "weeping prophet." He was quite sorrowful over his predictions of the Babylonian captivity. Much of his weeping and outwardly expressed anguish for Jerusalem and its people was conducted at the top of a small mountain within a cave. The small mountain is called Golgotha, (skull) and overlooks Jerusalem. The two openings in the cave that faces the city of Jerusalem seem to appear as the eyes of a skull looking up at it from below. Jeremiah surely did not become a prophet for the glory of it all as during his ministry he stood trial for his very life, was placed in stocks, was forced to flee from Jehoiakim and was humiliated publicly and thrown into a pit. His ministry was during the time that Judah was sinfully practicing idol worship. In fact the Israelites were not even hiding their sin of idolatry, performing pagan, ritualistic acts right out in the open! His messages to the people were mostly about their sins and his strongly warning the Israelites of the impending invasion of the Babylonians. Jeremiah warned the idolaters repeatedly of their subsequent captivity if they did not cease their worship of idols and return to the Lord. God gave repeated warnings through Jeremiah over the course of a year but to no avail and the consequence of their failure to repent was the destruction of Jerusalem, the Temple and most if not all of their properties.

CHAPTER 7

Ezekiel ° Tanakh, Pg. 893

- His name means "Strengthened by God" and he is not mentioned anywhere else in the Bible except in his Book by his name. He is also listed as a Major Prophet in Tanakh along with Isaiah and Jeremiah.

- Ezekiel's prophecies were told with visions, parables, signs and symbols to proclaim the Word of the Lord.

- His ministry began about 593 B.C. and he served the Lord for twenty-two years. He and his wife, along with approximately 10,000 others, were captured and taken to Babylon in 597 B.C.

- Ezekiel was a contemporary of Jeremiah who was about 20 years older than Ezekiel and was also a contemporary of the prophet Daniel.

Historic:
Ezekiel utilizes extensive symbolic language in his prophetic pronouncements and was both a prophet and a priest as Jeremiah also was. As such, Ezekiel was very familiar with the details within the Temple in which God also utilized his services. His ministry could be defined best in three types of service and pronouncement which fit into the four major sections of the Book of Ezekiel.

- Condemnation— (the sin of the people of Israel)
- Retribution, (prophetic visions of what was to come from their enemy Babylon)
- God's call to Repentance
- Future Restoration and Consolation.

The Book of Ezekiel contains the prophecies of the destruction of

The Final Prophecy

Jerusalem in Chapters One through Twenty-Four, the retribution on the neighboring nations in Chapters Twenty-Five to Thirty-Two, the final calling for Israel to repent of its sin in Chapter Thirty-Three and God's future restoration of Israel in Chapters Thirty-Four through Forty-Eight.

Daniel ° Tanakh, Pg. 1469

- Daniel was the prophet who provided us with the most vivid picture of end times and all the events that would occur—including **The Final Prophecy.** His prophetic visions were historical, prophetic and informational as well as some of the most lyrical prose included in Scripture. In addition to this introduction of Daniel and the other prophets, you will find more of a study of this prophet in a later Chapter for his vivid prophetic pictures of the course of history was shown to be precise in every prediction that Daniel made as well as those in his interpretation of the dreams of the King of Babylon.

- Daniel bridges the entire 70 years of captivity in Babylon and along with his three friends that were chosen for the king's service, Daniel demonstrates incredible faith, wisdom and plays a most critical role in outlining the future— not only of Babylon and the reigning powers to come but of the future of mankind— visions given by God of the end of days.

- Daniel's name means, "God is my Judge." His prophetic pronouncements come through dreams and visions, verbally painting an apocalyptic picture in the Old Testament—somewhat the forerunner of the Book of Revelation in the New Testament. Modern times now look back to the fulfillment of Daniel's visions of the ruling kingdoms that followed Babylonian rule in that region of the world. Historically, every prediction he made came to pass— precisely as God disclosed and Daniel proclaimed.

CHAPTER 7

- Daniel is mentioned in the Book of Jeremiah and also in Ezekiel.

- The prophets Habakkuk and Zephaniah who, together with Jeremiah, were contemporaries of Daniel and also proclaimed the warnings of Babylonian captivity.

Historic:

Daniel was taken into captivity as a young man, probably in his early teens. He was kidnapped from his royal family in Judah and taken to serve the king of Babylon with other young men of good stature and intelligence. Daniel lived in Babylon until his death. He was approximately eighty-five years of age when he died and during his years in Babylon he always had a purposed heart to make the best of his captivity. He exalted and praised the living God in all things and during every circumstance and all of Babylon knew Daniel and his friends. Daniel's three friends were Hannaniah, who was renamed Shadrach, Mishael, who was renamed Meshach, and Azariah who was renamed Abed-Nego. These were Babylonian names and even Daniel was renamed Belteshazzar. As history records, Daniel was the only one in all of Babylon who was able to describe the Kings dreams. Babylon had its share of sage's and mystics however none of them were able to even guess what the kings dreams were about. God always prevails and at one time when Daniel's three friends refused to bow down to a golden idol and were thrown into a blazing furnace (the declared punishment by the king of Babylon) they walked out of that furnace without so much as even an ash upon them—totally unharmed. However, while they were in the furnace, God's Word tells us that king Nebuchadnezzar saw a fourth person in the furnace with them. It is who the king declared he saw that our Rabbis are, to say the least, quite uneasy about. Although it is a recognized Biblical quote from the Book of Daniel and is in all the original or older manuscripts to support the inclusion of this story itself, the king refers to a "Son of God." The exact verse depicting this incident is, "although they had thrown

THE FINAL PROPHECY

three young men into the furnace there were four in the furnace and the fourth person looked like the Son of God."[21] How the king knew that He was the "Son of God" or depicted the fourth image that way is hidden in the mysteries of God's Word however I will leave this to your own spiritual discernment and perhaps further study. Another event that was life-threatening to Daniel at a much older age was when he was punished and had to spend an entire night in a below-ground den with hungry lions. (A Biblically based story that has been told for many generations in that the angel of God would not allow the lions to devour Daniel.) Daniel was lifted out of the pit in the morning when king Nebuchadnezzar came to see if he was alive. The King had been restless all through the night, actually fearing that nothing should happen to Daniel. In spite of the Kings obligation to carry out the previously declared punishment he highly favored Daniel and it is indicated that he was duped by a jealous member of his Court. It was when the king witnessed the power of God for having saved Daniel from the lions that the king declared that Daniel and his friend's were free to worship their God as they chose. The king had been a witness of several such miracles but mostly witnessed Daniel's unyielding faith in the God of the Jews. This is a poignant illustration of what it means to be a witness, an example of your faith for all to see— rather than simply talking about it. That is what God had in mind and wanted from all His people Israel.

Hosea: ° Tanakh, Pg. 981

- Hosea's name means just one word– "Salvation."

- Little is known about this prophet and it is believed that he came from the northern kingdom for he knew a great deal about the history and typography of that area. He served during a time when the southern kingdom was heavily engaged in sinful acts and God had him take a wife who was then unfaithful to him. This was to be a symbolic illustration that God used for His purpose. The illustration was that of unfaithfulness of the bride (Israel) to God the Groom. The main themes of Hosea address sin, judgment and God's forgiving love.

Joel: ° Tanakh, Pg. 1005

- His name means "The Lord is God" and he identifies himself as "Joel the son of Pethuel"— a name not mentioned in the Old Testament. We know little about Joel however the theme of his message is The Day of the Lord and that in itself is a powerful message when we are speaking of end times. It deals with a period of God's wrath and judgment, revealing the character of God as being holy, mighty and powerful. Such a day is associated with devastation, darkness and events that far exceed anything man has ever seen in God's previous judgments of sin. You will note that there were several prophets who received this vision or future look into the time that God would determine judgment day for the sinfulness of the world.

Amos: ° Tanakh, Pg. 1015

- His name means "burden" and/or "burden bearer" or "bearer of burdens." He was from a small village about ten miles South of Jerusalem called Tekoa, and he was a contemporary of Jonah.

- Amos worked as a sheep-breeder and did not come from a noble family nor was he a priest. This illustrates, as I previously stated, that God can use anyone [22] for His divine purposes and one never knows when they may be called.

- Amos was called to deliver a message to the northern tribes of Israel. It was under the reign of Jeroboam II who, following the examples of his father Joash brought the Israelites through a time of prosperity.

The Final Prophecy

- This was subsequent to Jonah, sometime after Nineveh had repented for their sins. Although there was a short period where they displayed their repentance by earnestly worshipping God, it did not take long before the people of Nineveh went back to spiritual sin, flagrant corruption and the overall moral decay of the people. Changed times do not necessarily mean grateful times and Amos was to admonish the northern tribes for their ritualistic approaches to worship which were surely not in keeping with honoring God.

Obadiah: ° Tanakh, Pg. 1033.

- His name means "servant of the Lord" and was a prophet with an unknown background. It is thought by the references within his Book in the Bible that he could have been from the southern kingdom. His Book is also the *shortest* Book in the Old Testament.

- It appears that Obadiah wrote his prophecy shortly after the Edomite attack on Jerusalem. There were four invasions of Jerusalem, by Shishak, the king of Egypt around 925 B.C., the Philistines and Arabians around 848-841 B.C., Jehoash, king of Israel in 790 B.C. and Nebuchadnezzar, king of Babylon, bringing about the fall and captivity of Jerusalem. Because Obadiah does not mention Babylon or the destruction of Jerusalem in his Book, it is thought that he served during the invasion of the Philistines and Arabians.

- Obadiah writes of God's judgment on Edom and then on the Nations and the restoration of Israel. There is a great deal of similarity in the style and the parts of the writing itself between Obadiah and Jeremiah.

CHAPTER 7

Jonah: ° Tanakh, Pg. 1037.

- His name means "dove" and the Book is titled after his name from the Hebrew Masoretic text. Both the Septuagint and the Latin Vulgate ascribe the same name. The problem has been that nowhere does the author make reference to himself as in the first person but rather in the third person. However, the autobiographical information points to Jonah as the author.

- Jonah shares the better times of his ministry as in the case of Amos, however he will find himself in a most precarious place for three days! It was a time of spiritual poverty and despite there being a time of peace and abundant luxuries, religion was becoming more and more ritualistic with idolatry once again on the rise. As a result the people had become perverted in several areas of their lives. The peacetime and the wealth had caused the people to turn away from God instead of towards Him. God now intended to bring the Assyrians against His people for the sins that they were warned about during the prior year.

- God instructed Jonah to go to Nineveh and tell the people to repent of their sins. Jonah disobeyed God and ran in the opposite direction for he was laden with resentment and distaste for the people of Nineveh. The rest is history as Jonah spends three days in a giant fish and then finds himself in Nineveh doing what God told him to do in the first place. Of course the fact that two plagues broke out in Nineveh and there was a solar eclipse while Jonah was on his way there surely might have helped in preparing for the repentance of the people! God has His ways of accomplishing His will and purpose even if and when man hesitates or ignores God's callings and admonitions— or tries to run the other way!

The Final Prophecy

Micah: ° Tanakh, Pg. 1041

- His name is a shortened name for Micaiah or Michaiah and means "Who is like the Lord." Although little is known about this prophet his writing suggests a godly heritage. His prophecy was during the reign of Jotham which was 750-731 B.C. He preached of injustice and religious corruption. The northern kingdom under Micah's ministry was about to fall to Assyria. His messages were primarily to the southern kingdom where he resided.

- He primarily preached judgment to a people who continued to pursue evil and presented God's message in what appeared to be "courtroom terms." His message can be broken down into two parts, the first being "Hear" as in "listen to the words of the Lord." He speaks of impending doom because our people had broken the laws given to their forefathers at Mt. Sinai. He then moves to "Hope" because of God's covenant given to our people's forefathers.

- Micah was to Judah what Amos was to Israel, warning them of the impending invasion and the punishment for their sin.

Nahum: ° Tanakh, Pg. 1055.

- Nahum means "comfort" or "consolation" and is a shortened form of Nehemiah –not to be confused with the Nehemiah who oversaw the rebuilding of the walls of Israel after his release from captivity. As other prophets who do not expound on their own personal lives but rather focus on the message from God, little is known about him as he followed that same style of writing. There are no mentions of kings or others in the introduction and since he is addressing Nineveh, his message of judgment portrays strength in its deliverance which would place his message sometime before the fall of Nineveh in 612 B.C.

CHAPTER 7

- It was but ten years later that Nineveh (after they had repented for their sins to Jonah) returned to their old ways of idolatry and violence, displaying a general arrogance concerning any judgment declared upon them. They were in fact boasting that their walls were 100 feet high and they had built a moat that was 150 feet wide and surrounded the city. Nineveh was strong and extremely sinful. Nahum recounted God's mercy preached by Jonah a century earlier and recounted God's wrath and judgment against Nineveh if she did not turn from her ways.

- An interesting point of Nahum's prophecy was that Nineveh would be hidden and after her downfall in 612 B.C. the site of Nineveh was not rediscovered until 842 A.D!

Habakkuk: ° Tanakh, Pg. 1063.

- The name of this Book is the authors name which means "one who embraces." Little is known about this prophet in the absence of the inclusion of any personal information in his Biblical Book. However, as his opening statement is "The prophet Habakkuk," this would imply that he was well known and needed no introduction as to family or social standing. Habakkuk's ministry was served during the final days of the Assyrian Empire and the beginning of Babylonia's world dominance under Nabopolassar and his son Nebuchadnezzar. The father assumed power about 626 B.C. and immediately began to stretch their borders and their influence to the North and to the West. Under his son Nebuchadnezzar their army overthrew Nineveh in 612 B.C. just as Nahum had prophesied.

- Habakkuk's opening verses seem to historically imitate the messages of Amos and Micah in that justice was prevalent

THE FINAL PROPHECY

throughout the land. Violence and wickedness were also highly pervasive. The prophet cried out for divine intervention as the situation continued to worsen and although the prophet received the spiritual awareness of God's intentions it was not as the prophet expected—and just like Job, he began to argue with God. This produced a deeper understanding of God's sovereignty and His character, thereby producing a firmer faith in the prophet.

Zephaniah: ° Tanakh, Pg. 1071

- His name is thought to mean "The Lord hides" and he was a contemporary of Jeremiah. It appears that his ministry precedes the reforms that were made by king Josiah at that time, as Judah was knee deep in idolatry and wicked practices.

- He warned Judah that the final days were near and that Judah would be punished at the hands of Nebuchadnezzar of Babylon. He uses the term The Day of the LORD and also looks ahead to the prophecy of Daniel and the 70th week— which is the final week or the last period of seven years in Daniel's prophecy of end times and the judgment of the Lord—The Final Prophecy.

Haggai: ° Tanakh, Pg. 1079.

- His name means "festal one" suggesting that he was perhaps born on a feast day. He is mentioned in Ezra in conjunction with the prophet Zechariah. Both Haggai and Zechariah were directed by the Lord to hasten the people to not only rebuild the Temple in Jerusalem after their return from Babylon under Zerubbabel but to also urge the people to maintain their spiritual zeal. His message was of the glory of God and for the new Temple to be even more beautiful than the last, with God granting peace to the nation. He spoke out about the indifference towards God

CHAPTER 7

and the rebuilding of the Temple that was beginning to consume them in diverted devotion. It was his ministry to reach the people and encourage them—and that is precisely what he did. The new Temple was rebuilt in less than four years in 516 B.C.

Zechariah: ° Tanakh, Pg. 1083

- His name means "The Lord remembers" or "He who the Lord remembers." As were his counterparts Jeremiah and Ezekiel, he was a prophet *and* a priest. He was also a member of the Great Synagogue which had a counsel of 120 men—originated by Nehemiah and presided over by Ezra. This is the counsel that later developed into one of the most influential groups in Israel, the Sanhedrin. Zechariah was actually born in Babylon during the exile. It is believed that he was still very young when he was called into ministry as a prophet as he is addressed as "naar" which in the Hebrew is "young man" also translated as "boy," "lad" or "youth." We see this also used by Saul in addressing David in 1 Samuel when Saul is telling David that he is a mere "naar" and not old enough to fight Goliath. As the prophet Haggai was encouraging the rebuilding of the Temple, Zechariah took up where he left off, taking on the task of leading the people to a complete spiritual renewal. In his Book we see four divisions. The first being the introductory address calling for repentance. In the second part we have eight visions (shown to Zechariah in just one night) which are followed by a symbolic transaction concerning the last days and God's dealings with Israel which was an answer to the question surrounding the observance of the national fasts by a deputation of Bethel. The fourth is the striking message concerning the coming of the Lord with all His saints. This part will be discussed later in specific detail.

Malachi: ° Tanakh, Pg. 1101.

- This is the last of the minor-prophets to speak just before God closed the Old Testament. As you may recall from previous

The Final Prophecy

discussion, God then remained silent four hundred years. Some have said that the opening infers that the book was to be called "The Lord's Messenger" as opposed to a proper name however it has been identified as Malachi. His ministry appeared to take place during the late fifth century B.C. and just about the time of Nehemiah's return from Persia. Many years had passed since the rebuilding of the Temple and the priests were becoming increasingly corrupt and overly complacent in their spiritual leadership. There were many concerns dealing with marriages to foreign wives, (interfaith marriages) [23] the lack of tithes to the Temple and the usual social injustice practiced by most people of prominence who were becoming stiff-necked[24] from their pride.

Malachi wrote the final message to Israel— the message of God's warning in that they had been delivered from total annihilation by the Lord on many occasions, despite their sinfulness. God sent the people several prophets who rendered many admonitions, giving them ample opportunity to repent and heed the Word of God. The problem was simply that nobody was paying attention. The final message centered on what God said overall, "that in the future, should they repent and follow what was asked of them the Messiah would appear and be revealed. God's covenants (His promises) would be fulfilled."[25] It would be 400 years before another prophet was to arrive on the scene, this time to talk about preparing the way for the coming of Messiah.

These are the prophets of the Bible. The question remains however, why haven't our Rabbis taught us more about the prophets and their prophecies? Why are the prophets almost ignored or skimmed over in religious or Hebrew School teaching? Why wouldn't our teachers embrace the teaching of all the prophetic pronouncements, especially those of Daniel, Zechariah, Isaiah, the prophets whose prophecies of end times all point to Israel? The prophets are our gateways into the wisdom and insight of the messages that God sent to His people Israel. If one-third of the entire Bible is prophecy, that alone should speak of the importance of knowing and understanding the prophets and their prophecies. Nothing brings us closer to the mind of God than the prophets, encouraging us to live and conduct our lives according to God's commandments, knowing that

CHAPTER 7

time is precious and is running out in terms of the fulfillment of the last prophecies. Would we not want to make every moment count?

Now that we have a basic understanding of who the prophets were and prior to exploring prophecy, we need to talk about promises, predictions, prophecies, covenants and what it all means to us in the year 2004 and beyond. What affect does prophecy have on the life of a Jewish person? The first focal point of meaning is that we are not the people of chance but rather the people of choice – God's choice in terms of His affections and His desire for the fulfillment of His plan for us. Most of our problems seem to come from our making the same wrong choices over and over again. Naturally there were separate generations of our people who sinned against God but one would think that within the history of all our consequences we would have come to a place of repentance.[26] God sent seventeen prophets to show us the way to His heart and rather than embracing the prophets and their messages, we ignored them, rebuked them and even killed them.

Now we begin to tie all the pieces of the prophetic puzzle together. We will examine God's covenants (promises) to whom they were made, why they were made and how they affect all things that are yet to come. I believe that to fully understand the vision of what is yet to come we must first learn the validity of all other prophecies. It is important to make known the faithfulness of those who delivered those prophecies so that you, the reader, are prepared to receive the Bible's prophetic insight of the times to come— the final seven years that will change the entire course of the path of man's history. I have also stated that this was a journey, a path of learning that most of us were never taught or attempted learning on our own. Those who read this work will be better prepared to understand how and why the prophecies of the future are all threaded or woven together since time began and are all part of God's plan for mankind. Come and let us continue to reason together.

Notes

1 Genesis 1:26

2 Genesis 3:7

3 Exodus 7:1

4 Genesis 20:7

5 1 Kings 11:29

6 Numbers 24:2

7 Numbers 11:26

8 1 Samuel 22:5

9 Jeremiah 28:17

10 I Chronicles 13:22

11 Numbers 11:26

12 I Kings 1:32

13 II Chronicles 15:8

14 II Chronicles 12:5

15 Judges 4:4

16 II Kings 22:14

17 Exodus 15:20

18 Nehemiah 6:14

19 Name translations for Isaiah and all the prophets going forward from

CHAPTER 7

Isaiah are taken from the accepted Hebrew translations.

[20] Isaiah 7:3 Instructed to go out and meet King Ahaz.

[21] Daniel 3:25

[22] As noted in the opening introduction to the prophets.

[23] We know that this was the reason for the falling away from faith of Solomon.

[24] A term used in rebuke of the Israelites in several places in Old Testament.

[25] Author's paraphrasing from Malachi's message.

[26] Renouncing and turning away from sin, adapted from a military turn to *"about face."*

The Final Prophecy

Chapter Eight

The Promises of God

When we speak of God's promises, the covenants between He and mankind, my thoughts turn to Abraham, the patriarch of one of the most powerful, everlasting covenants. I am naturally referring to the father of Isaac and Jacob. Seldom do I hear any mention of the son that Abraham fathered with Hagar, the maidservant to his wife Sarah. This child, born before Isaac, became the benefactor of another promise given to his mother Hagar, to become the father of the Arab world. It stands to reason that if we are discussing prophecy and the course of man's destiny, it is important for us to understand the promise that was given to Abraham by God and the circumstances under which God sealed this incredible covenant.

> "When Abram was ninety-nine years old, the LORD appeared to Abram and said to him, "I am El Shaddai. [1] Walk in My ways and be blameless. I will establish My covenant between Me and you, and I will make you exceedingly numerous." [2]

If anyone had a heart for God and knew the tolerance, the patience, the love and the providence, power and purpose of God it was surely Abraham. The covenant that was made between God and Abraham in

The Final Prophecy

Genesis Chapter Twelve will be continuously fulfilled as it has been since the day it was made. Note also that Abraham was actually named "Abram" until God changed his name in Chapter Seventeen of Genesis which was noted as "The Sign of the Covenant" that God made with Abraham before Isaac was born. Sarah's birth-name was actually "Sarai" before God changed her name after changing Abram's to Abraham. It should also be noted that while we, the Jewish people, are the physical descendants of that covenant there are also "spiritual" descendants of that covenant who are not Jewish.

> "The Lord said to Abraham, "Go forth from your native land and from your father's house to the land that I will show you. I will make of you a great nation, and I will bless you. I will make your name great, And you shall be a blessing. I will bless those who bless you, And curse him that curses you; And all the families of the earth, Shall bless themselves by you." [3]

This was the promise that God made to Abraham. Was it conditional? Did God say I "might" do this or I will "possibly" do this for you? No, God simply said to "go forth from your native land and from your father's house" and Abraham did as God instructed. That was all he had to do—leave! Of course he could not go wherever he pleased. He needed to go to the land that God "showed him." And was the "basis" of the promise. The great nation that God said He would make of Abraham in verse two is Israel. God made another promise to Abraham in that He would give him a son. It was this son's seed through his wife that would bear the children who would be the establishers of God's plan

So how did Ishmael get into this picture between a Jewish father of nations and Hagar, a non-Jewish servant to Abraham's wife Sarai (Sarah)? After God's promise of a son and time had passed without conception, Sarai grew anxious, actually impatient because she felt she had waited long enough. She was concerned that Abraham might die

CHAPTER 8

without the blessing of a son to carry on his name. Her natural thinking instead of supernatural faith had her wrestling with the reality of her age, Abraham's age and the passing days. She must have thought, "Perhaps I can build a family through Hagar!" It appears that she was relying on the custom of that time that if a woman was barren she could obtain a child through one of her own maidservants. Although God had made the promise (the covenant) and was bound to fulfill it, Sarai reversed her role with God and sought to make herself the initiator rather than the recipient of that covenant. Sarai allowed her flesh (worldly thinking) to interfere with her spiritual discernment. This was no different than unbelief in not having the faith that God would fulfill His promise as God said He would—in His time and not hers. You should note from all of this that the problem back then was very much like the problem that prevails today in awaiting God's blessings—patience. We seem to want it in our time and are not willing to wait on God's timing. The simple truth is that God alone knows our present and our future and He will not fulfill his promises until the right time arrives for every individual. Faith is the substance of believing in not only He who cannot be seen but in His Word and that He wants what is best for us in each, individual circumstance of our lives. What is the condition of your belief and patience today, when it comes to God and your unanswered prayers?

A Decision of Impatience

As the Bible declares, Sarah sent her maidservant Hagar to lay with Abraham that he might have a son before he died and he consented. Shouldn't he have counseled her to wait on the Lord? Abraham knew the custom but God had made a promise. Is giving in a familiar trait when temptation is before us, even though through established worldly excuses or our own justifications we know in our hearts that it's wrong? It is the consequences of giving in that we rarely consider. Do you recall the incident in the Garden of Eden where Satan tempted Eve and she in turn gave Adam to eat of the fruit? Sarah provided the temptation, not the immediate temptation (the woman Hagar) but rather the possibility

THE FINAL PROPHECY

of the outcome of the act, a son. She gave her blessings for Abram to lay with another woman so that Abraham could have the fulfillment of his greatest desire. He could have said no, just as Adam could have said no. Think of the consequences of both those decisions!

Let us also consider this promise, "All the families of the earth shall bless themselves by you" or "be blessed by you."[4] All the family's means "all" and not partial, not a particular group of people but all people. We need to consider this carefully for it is an important part of our overall understanding of how and why these events took place. Our people (Israel) believe that this promise was meant only for the Jewish [5] people, thinking it was the Jewish people who would be blessed. Abram (Abraham) was to be more than simply a man whose seed would literally birth the people of many nations. He was also to be a vehicle for God's divine revelation—the new heaven and the new earth, ruled by Messiah, after the end times.

When Hagar conceived and was pregnant with Abram's child, "Her mistress became despised in her eyes."[6] After consulting with Abram concerning the matter and Sarai being told by Abram, "do to her as you please," Sarai dealt harshly with Hagar who then fled to the wilderness when an angel of the Lord appeared to Hagar "by the spring on the way to Shur" and said;

> "I will greatly increase your offspring. And they shall be too many to count. The angel of the Lord said to her further, Behold you are with child. And shall bear a son. You shall call him Ishmael, For the Lord has paid heed to your suffering. He shall be a wild ass of a man; His hand against everyone, And everyone's hand against him; **He shall dwell alongside of all his kinsmen.**"[7]

As promised, Ishmael was born and from Ishmael would later come Esau and the sons of Keturah, the Arab world, in part, who are also descendants of Abraham. Ishmael actually had twelve sons [8] beginning

CHAPTER 8

with Nebaioth, and they all "dwelt from Havilah by Shur, which is close to Egypt, all the way to Asshur; they camped alongside all their kinsmen." [9]

Isaac was Abraham's fulfilled blessing,[10] the promise God had made to him and the promise Sarah had laughed at when she overheard the promise.[11]

"And God said to Abraham, "As for your wife Sarai, you shall not call her Sarai, but her name shall be Sarah. I will bless her indeed, I will give you a son by her. I will bless her so that she will give rise to nations; rulers of peoples shall issue from her. Abraham threw himself on his face and began to laugh. "Can a child be born to a man one hundred years old, or can Sarah bear a child at ninety?" [12]

With God all things are possible when there is faith. God does not make promises He does not keep. It is man's impatience that fosters a lack of faith for the intent of God within the big picture will allow for nothing to change His plans. The only thing that ultimately changes is the recognition of the blessings that are bestowed upon the recipients of God's grace. Is it any wonder that when Sarah conceived and gave birth to Isaac, one of the first things she said was, "God has brought me laughter; everyone who hears will laugh with me."[13]

A short time after Isaac was born Sarah went to Abraham and asked him to cast out the child Ishmael and his mother Hagar. Sarah was concerned that Ishmael would want a portion of Isaac's inheritance. Ishmael was good enough when he was the only son that Abraham fathered but now that they had a son who was of their own flesh and blood, why should Ishmael receive what should be Isaac's? God spoke to Abraham and informed him that he would make a nation from Ishmael because Ishmael was Abraham's seed and God had already made that promise.[14]

As Jews, we honor Abraham each and every time we declare "The God of Abraham, Isaac and Jacob." We acknowledge Biblically the birth of his son as a miracle unless you personally know of a 90-year-old woman who conceived and gave birth naturally to a healthy child! The birth of Isaac and the sacrifice that God ordered on Mt. Moriah and whom the son

The Final Prophecy

represents in terms of a nation will surface again later in the book and we will explore this in more comparative detail.

Let us put this all in perspective so that we understand that traditional covenants require man to uphold the basis of that promise. When we say that a covenant with God is unconditional it means that God will fulfill that promise in His time and according to His will. That's when the responsibility is lifted and no matter what man does, the sins we commit, the wrong choices we make— if God makes an unconditional promise His word is always upheld. Note that I did not say that God would fulfill His promise according to our expectations. He will not hurry to reward sinfulness and disobedience but someday, in His way and in His own time He will fulfill that covenant. As a simple example we have had thousands of years of rain and God has not flooded the earth as punishment to a sinful world since His covenant with Noah. If you believe that they were sinful in the days of Noah you surely would agree that today's world is even worse. In ancient times it was idolatry and generally unfaithfulness. Today we have murder, robbery, prostitution, idol worship, divorce, child abuse and the list goes on. In Noah's time they did not have drugs, guns to murder each other with, pornography to pollute the minds of young people and adults on the Internet, weapons of mass destruction to annihilate whole people groups, (genocide) terrorists and suicide bombers killing thousands of innocent people and all the things that has made our world anything but close to what God desired for us. However, through it all, God has not wiped out mankind to begin all over again. Make no mistake— God did not say He would not pour out His judgment and His wrath at some future time. Consider also that God's covenant was fulfilled and is continuously being fulfilled in the seed of Abraham and all who came after him. You should also consider that the covenant was partly conditional in terms of any single generation. When God said He would bless those who blessed Abraham, He was referring to those who were of the faith—those who believed in Him. God was not about to bless idolaters and atheists. God said that He would also curse those who cursed Abraham. That would mean the defense of the nation Israel and its Jewish population, seeded by the descendants of Abraham. They are the one's who shall receive God's blessings. For

CHAPTER 8

those who would curse Israel, who attempt to come against her or who try to annihilate her will know the curse of that covenant. Why did God promise Moses that He would lead our Jewish nation out of Egypt and into the Promised Land and then keep our people wandering in the desert for forty years? God promised and after forty years, those of the new generation of Israelites entered the Promised Land. With the exception of three men, the entire original sinful generation had been purged over those forty years with only three of the original generation remaining to cross the Jordan. The rest had perished in the wilderness. Only those of faith were the recipients of God's blessing and received the fulfillment of His promise. Are you of the faith to inherit God's blessings or are you still in sin and holding-out in the desert of disbelief?

To every decision of poor choice there is a consequence. Abraham made some poor choices and the consequence was evident in the lapse of time in which God fulfilled His promise. There was a time of testing, a time of sharpening Abraham's faith, fine tuning it until Abraham's faith was as strong for God as God's promise was to Abraham—unconditional. Abraham had to understand the consequence of disobedience just as the Israelites in the desert had to be made to understand the consequence of not obeying God's commandments. He will surely test you, purify you, and put you through the burning coals (trials) until He has sanctified you to His satisfaction.[15] The ultimate test of faith as well as a silent message for the world was when God ordered Abraham to sacrifice his only son Isaac on Mt. Moriah. This was the son that God had promised Abraham, the son he had waited for his entire life and now God had told him to sacrifice him as an offering to God. Have you ever read this portion of the Bible and simply scratched your head as you paused and asked why God would do such a thing? What would you have done had you been in Abraham's shoes? You will find the entire account of this test of faith in Chapter Twenty-Two in the Book of Genesis and I suggest that the reading of this Chapter is quite significant in understanding God and His ways. Perhaps Abraham concluded that God would surely resurrect Isaac after the sacrifice— after all, he trusted God. The question to be dealt with however is why his only son for a sacrifice? Was this significant of something that God was showing Abraham in addition to unconditional faith?

The Final Prophecy

Was there a message in this for all of us to see and discern? I believe that there was surely more to this request (or demand since it came from God) for quite often the proof of love stated is action itself, one's deeds and not just the statement of love and faith. We are known by what we do, by what the world witnesses and how we react to various trials—our faith and our trust in God under any and all circumstances.

Prior to this incident, Abraham and Sarah did not fully and unconditionally believe that they would have a son. That is not "unconditional" faith. Isn't that why their impatience and disbelief was the very motive behind the conception of Ishmael? When God told Abraham to go to a certain place and Abraham went to Egypt instead because he was worried about food and provisions, wasn't that disobeying God? [16] In fact, it was an insult to God, displaying a lack of faith and trust in God to provide all that they needed. What about the land that God told Abraham to occupy? Did Abraham listen to God or did he exchange the intended land with his nephew Lot in order to keep peace between them? That was sheer disobedience to what God had instructed Abraham to do. What about the consequences when the seed of Abraham went after Jacob into Egypt for hundreds of years? Despite disobedience, God never forgets His promises and despite the times when God seems to tarry in fulfilling those promises, eventually He always keeps them.

"A long time after that, the king of Egypt died. The Israelites were groaning under the bondage and cried out; and their cry for help from the bondage rose up to God. God heard their moaning, and God remembered His covenant with Abraham and Isaac and Jacob. God looked upon the Israelites, and God took notice of them." His word never comes back void.

I have had conversations with many Rabbis over the years and in discussing the prophecies and covenants of the Bible I have heard several variations of their beliefs that they shared with me. Some of the Rabbis stated that they do not wish to debate over what they termed "trivial things" such as why it took so long for God to fulfill His promises. When I attempted to discuss any contradictions relative to the prophecies of the Bible in their having already been fulfilled, there was simply further controversy. Many Rabbis have stated that God gave us the Law and all that

CHAPTER 8

is important to a religious Jew is the observance of the Law. "Moses gave us the Law, and the Law is God's will to His people Israel".[17] This is the root of the belief system of our Orthodox Jews and nothing will change that except the coming of the Messiah. However, according to the Rabbis of yesterday and today, that would be when He comes –which denotes for the first time.[18]

So all of us have been told that it is the Law that is the uppermost constant in our religious heritage from the desert of Mt. Sinai—the Ten Commandments, revealing to mankind what God has declared concerning the moral issues of life and how God wants us to deal with them. I said for "mankind" because The Ten Commandments have since been adapted as the very basis of human morality and ethics for all of mankind and not just for we the chosen people. The most controversial in my opinion are the Religious Ordinances that number [19] over six hundred. They were the very basis of an Israelite's relationship with God—in ancient times. Every Orthodox Jew attempts to follow the Law, just as it was throughout our history. What is my point in all of this? I do not know how any human being could possibly adhere to and uphold over six hundred laws! There is one final point I would like to make about the Law itself. Nowhere within the Law do I see a way to find eternal grace with God. Nowhere within the Law do I see a place to provide the spiritual strength to uphold these laws or any mention of the Law providing eternal assurances, namely our salvation.[20] The Law was not for all nations but for the nation Israel. The question is why and how did the New Covenant (declared by God through the prophet Jeremiah) affect the stringency and practice of all these laws? That is a question we need to explore in great detail for the word "new" as in the "New Covenant" would surely replace the old—would it not? Is it possible that God was sending us a message concerning the fact that He knew we would never be able to uphold over 600 laws but gave them to us so we would realize our inadequacy of attempting to be righteous without Him? The point is that once we realized we couldn't we would turn to Him. Instead of being "under the law" we would be worshipping and fellowshipping with God—as God intended for His people to do, for any righteousness whatsoever is in God alone and no man can be righteous "under the law."

THE FINAL PROPHECY

There is not an Orthodox Jew today who could state that they have kept every law their entire life and stand righteous before God! When I ask an Orthodox Jew if they are indeed keeping all of the six-hundred plus laws the usual answer has been, "We do what we can do and God knows our hearts." The key is have we given our hearts to God in all matters of life or are we simply attempting to appear righteous by going through the motions of the law when in fact we have absolutely no righteousness before God whatsoever. The prophet Isaiah declared that our righteousness is likened to filthy rags so how is this righteousness obtained? We shall also explore this point in more detail in a later Chapter. For now, let us simply leave this as a major point to ponder, consider, reason through and explore more deeply at the appropriate time. How do we obtain the righteousness necessary to stand in God's presence when our predestined time here has ended? What are your thoughts? Have you thought that you were righteous in the sight of God and are without sin? Have you believed that you were a "good person" and worthy of having a place with God eternally? Did you ever think about how the Book of Life was assured to you in Synagogue and did your Rabbi mention anything to you or the Congregation about being worthy or righteous to stand before God on the Day of Judgment? We will soon explore that question and discuss what God's definition of worthiness is when we speak of entering eternal life with Him. If I had my entire eternal destiny at stake, I would want to know what God said and not what man told me. Surely, one is not going to stand before the Lord one day and argue with Him that, "My Rabbi told me I was in the Book—look again, my name *must* be there—I'm a good person!"

Notes

1 "Almighty God"

2 Genesis 17:1-2 Tanakh, Jewish Holy Scriptures

3 Genesis 12:1-3 Tanakh, Jewish Holy Scriptures

CHAPTER 8

4 Different translations

5 Those who have studied the Bible are aware that Ishmael was also of Abraham.

6 Genesis 16:4

7 Genesis 16:6-12

8 Genesis 25:12 Tanakh, Jewish Holy Scriptures

9 25:18

10 21:1-3

11 Sarah was sitting by a tree and overheard the promise of a child by the Angel of the Lord when he related that promise to Abraham from God. Sarah could not help but laugh aloud because she was 90 and Abraham was almost 100!

12 Genesis 17: 15-17

13 See Genesis 18:13-15 also.

14 Genesis 21:13

15 Cleansed of old sins, "cleaned up."

16 Genesis 12:10-13:1

17 Quoted from my personal conversation concerning prophecy and God's covenants, with a Florida Orthodox Rabbi who I knew over the course of some ten years.

18 All Orthodox Rabbis believe that the Messiah has not yet come and His coming would be the first time and not the second time as Messianic Jews and Christians believe.

19 Exodus 24:12-31:18

20 Spiritual life after death

The Final Prophecy

Chapter Nine

Facing Truth

Since ancient Biblical times, the historic accounts of the nation Israel almost seem to be an incredible cinema production— an on-going drama, if you will, of enormous proportions. When Cecil B. DeMille produced The Ten Commandments, a true big-screen epic, the history of our people was relived for the entire world to see. The film depicted a series of wonders and miracles, portrayals of God bringing His chosen people out of Egypt and to this day we seem to yearn-after the events of those times when God spoke to our people through His chosen prophet. The movie also depicted the handing-down of the Law by God through Moses and our forty years in the wilderness until we reached the plains of Moab. It was a journey that began at the Egyptian tip of Goshen, from Ramses and then Succoth to a panic-driven crossing at the tip of the Red Sea,[1] then on to Etham and turning back to Pi-ha-hiroth, camping near Migdol. Moving on through the Wilderness of Shur, the journey continued through Marah, Elim, Rephidim, and into the desert of Sinai.[2] The war with Amalek took place just before arriving at Mt. Horeb and then the giving of the Law at Mt. Sinai. From there the trek angled towards Kibroth where manna fell from the skies, onto Hazaroth where Miriam was struck with leprosy for her stirring up trouble against Moses in the camp and finally on to Kadesh-barnea where the judgment of Korah took place. This accounting of various landmarks and related events are the essence of a journey that brought the Israelites from captivity to freedom. Moses was leading the people but their true guide on this journey was

The Final Prophecy

God. God provided a cloud that covered their encampment by day to shelter them from the blistering desert sun and a pillar of fire by night that would warm the temperatures of the freezing desert nights. We were a people who were dwelling alone and surely not reckoned to any nation. Manna that fell from the heavens that fed a starving people and water, the gift of life in the desert that was obtained from a "smitten" rock.[3] Egypt was now behind them, Canaan was ahead of them and God was always with them. That was the beginning, the settling of a territory granted to us by God that would one day become the nation Israel—a land that God promised would belong to our people "forever." We know historically that it was not that easy— the cost in human life, the suffering and the flowing of millions of tears. Then the Jewish actor Paul Newman played the leading role in Leon Uris' portrayal of the book and movie, "Exodus,"[4] once again bringing to the big screen the story of yet another plight of our people in their quest for religious freedom. This of course was the story of the ship that would never dock, that remained in the harbor with all its passengers willing to die of starvation rather than enter a land that was governed by any other rule but their own, another great dramatization depicting the will of the Jew to be free.

It was in 1948 that we were finally granted self-rule over the land that God chose for His people. Conflict after conflict and struggle following struggle, we as a people have fought for our homeland— that place in the wilderness God not only brought His people to but promised that we would dwell upon that land forever. God did not promise however that we would dwell in peace. Total peace can only come to Israel when Messiah rules from the holy city of Jerusalem and not before. It was May 15, 1948, just one day after our statehood went into affect that the Arabs attacked Israel. Despite her small army and inferiority compared to the masses of Arabs who attacked, God's providence once again brought the Israelites out of this surprise attack as the victors. It was also a time of each nation gathering their misplaced people with Arabs flocking back to their own lands from Israel and Jewish refuges returning to Israel from Arab lands. Neither wanted to be in the way of what was perceived as the start of an all out war between the two nations. Were you aware that over sixty percent of Israel's population today (about three million people) are

CHAPTER 9

Jews who once lived in Arab countries and fled back to Israel because of the severe brutality of the Arab governing armies? Less we forget the history of brutality and inhumanity from the Arabs has long been forged against our people. In the 1948 war it has been stated by neutral journalists and historians that far more Jews than Arabs became penniless, losing all they had when they fled to Israel from the Arab oppression and the accelerated massacres that continued until literally hundreds of thousand fled and returned to Israel— leaving their material goods behind them to save their own lives from the bloodshed between these nations. This is measured as "small" when compared to the oppression inspired by the seventh-century book of the creator of Islam. It was recounted by the PLO, the governing body that the Jews from the Arab states were driven from their homes and shamefully deported after their entire properties were taken from them for literally pennies on the dollar of their value at that time. These were Jews who had lived in the Arab land even before the advent of Islam! Some of the Jewish settlers were there over one-thousand years before the Arabs and they too were ejected, fleeing to Israel with the others. There was no shame, no humanity, no helpful neighbor— just plain and simple persecution.[5] This is not a valid exchange of Arabs leaving Israeli land and Jews leaving Arab land. Our people were driven out and the Palestinians were allowed to leave with their belongings in tact. The United Nations became involved and as it was then and remains to this day, consistently demonstrates a lack of support for our cause. In fact, the knowing Jews of Israel do not regard the U.N. as friends of Israel. It is interesting how the United Nations Headquarters in Israel is located in Jerusalem and sits on the property known as The Hill of Evil Counsel. This is the precise place in history that Ahithophel counseled Absalom on how he should take the kingdom away from David.[6] The U.N. has become a devoted ally of the Arab world, in fact of all the Middle East— except Israel. Perhaps I am not being politically proper however I am surely stating truth that lies within the closed door voting records of the United Nations when it comes to matters for or against Israel. Why am I getting into this political tone? I am not a political person and I mention these things only on the basis of the role that will be played out in the beginning of the fulfillment of Daniel's prophecy—the end of these times.

The Final Prophecy

Am I without fact in these allegations? Read on.

In spite of all that has transpired, Israel is protected by a power so much greater than all the hatred directed against the Judeo-Christian ethic. It is the power of the God of Israel who declared that Israel is *"the dearly beloved of My soul"* in Jeremiah 12:7. Israel exists today because God intends for it to exist and whoever comes against Israel is coming against the "apple of God's eye."[7] Almost every Jew knows about the past history of our own people. However, most of our people are not clear in their understanding of that past and why the political and religious conflicts today have so much to do with the past and will have a great deal to do with our future. God has written, produced and directed this epic drama of thousands of years of trials, repentance, rewards, joy and suffering. People have often asked, "Why can we not find a peaceful solution to all of this bloodshed? Why can't we learn to live in peace in the Middle East?" It is a fair question which many believe is all about land and land alone—but it is not, although the land has been in question for a few thousand years since the Palestinians do not recognize that the entire land of Canaan was given to Israel by God. It was God's covenant to Abraham and from Abraham through Isaac through his descendants forever. Genesis 13:14 is where the land grant was provided but no terrorist or dissident Palestinian is going to recognize God saying, "Lift your eyes now and look from the place where you are—northward, southward, eastward and westward, for all the land which you see I give to you and your descendants forever." If you recall in our discussion about God's promises, His covenants, this is an "unconditional" covenant. In Chapter 15 of Genesis, God reiterates this as a covenant with Abraham and in verse 15:7 God declares once again, "I am the LORD who brought you out of Ur of the Chaldeans, to give you this land to inherit it." So let us not quibble about Israel and all the surrounding land, including the West Bank for it all was granted to Israel and God never goes back on His covenants. The land that was captured by Israel during the six day war is not the source of the hatred and the battles. It is really not about giving back the West Bank or taking a Jewish settlement from the West Bank and moving it to another place. Oh, the land has much to do with it but the underlying reason is hatred, pure and simple. The Muslims and the Jews

CHAPTER 9

are not about to shake hands and walk off into the sunset after thousands of years. A terrorist from the Gaza once stated publicly that "all Jews will be destroyed and the land will revert back to its rightful owners." [8] It's the Koran vs. The Bible and the hatred will continue until the prophecy of the final battle is fulfilled. This is a spiritual battle of evil attempting to triumph over what is just and God's armies stand ready for that final prophecy to do battle with those armies of evil. Every serious Bible student knows that the conflict of thousands of years will one day come to an end but only through the great loss of life, for in this battle the blood will run as high as the "thighs of the horses" that carry the warriors who fight this final battle.[9]

There has always been hope among Jews who live outside of the Middle East and sincerely, with no disrespect intended, most of us do not have a clue as to what is really going on over there. Let's face facts— I too was just as naive until I went to Jerusalem in 1996, spoke to Israelis who had lived there for many years and saw the situation firsthand. I made it a point to engage Israeli soldiers and shop owners on issues of our history. I studied the historical records of the Bible in depth, and the politics of the Middle East by reading books and special reports that came out of Israel and were not watered-down with politics. All in all, ask any citizen of Israel and all they want and pray for is to "live in peace." I personally know of several Group Guides to Israel who have insisted that trips be canceled due to the hostilities and the terrorist attacks. Through it all, God has already told us the outcome, the final days and how it will all occur. All that transpires in between is the attempt to take back more fighting ground and weaken Israel in battleground-acquired possession. It is surprising to me that the enemies of Israel have not yet come to the realization that our God, the God of Israel never loses in any confrontation or in any battle where He has preordained the outcome for His people. No one will ever permanently take the Holy Land from God's people—perhaps for a short time but it forever belongs to Israel. I refer to the day that Satan tries to take the throne from our God in his last, frenzied attempt for world dominance and is cast into the Biblical Lake of Fire for one thousand years.[10] Then the Messiah rules the world in peace and in love from the land that God gave Abraham and his descendants

THE FINAL PROPHECY

forever. No more sorrow, no more tears, no more crying or suffering, just neighbor loving neighbor by a fig tree and the lion reclining side by side with the lamb. That will be the peace that is everlasting and can not become a reality until the prophecies of the Great Tribulation and the Final Battle are fulfilled.

We know about false peace for it has been tried before. For one moment in time, the world almost believed it possible. It was through the efforts of three men and three nations; America, Israel and Saudi Arabia. I personally will never forget the headlines of Tuesday, March 27, 1979, when those three men stood before the cameras of the world and the headlines read "LET THERE BE NO MORE WAR"[11] and another newspaper announced, "EGYPT AND ISRAEL SIGN FORMAL TREATY, ENDING A STATE OF WAR AFTER 30 YEARS; SADAT AND BEGIN PRAISE CARTER'S ROLE"[12] while the Jewish Exponent (Jewish Newspaper) carried the pictures of the three men on their front page with only the words, "SALAAM – PEACE – SHALOM."[13] Three words of peace that represented three Countries and from three men who took the steps, made the attempt and the world wept at the thought of peace—except those who knew Scripture, who understood the prophetic truths of the Bible and knew that this was a temporary abatement and not a permanent solution. It was a striking statement when the Daily News portrayed on page 3 of that Edition, three words that are actually related to the New Heaven and the New Earth after the Great Tribulation—"No more war, no more bloodshed, no more bereavement (crying) (mourning)" Some writer must have thought that the promises of the Book of Revelation would be usurped and this was the cure – and President Jimmie Carter, Egyptian President Anwar Sadat and Israel's Prime Minister Menachem Begin appeared before the world with hope written all over their faces. But wait—it was Sadat who planned and ordered the invasion of Israel in 1973 on the holiest day of all Jewish observed Holidays—Yom Kippur, the Day of Atonement. Perhaps he realized after this small war that Israel was not about to be taken down. Although the Israelites were outnumbered and were attacked by surprise, the Arabs lost many men and arms and Israel again came out of it as the victor. Without belaboring the point, what happened to two of these men in the days after this historic moment? In 1979, the very same year that peace was declared, the PLO leader Yasser Arafat announced of this Peace Process, "Sadat should understand that he will be struck down. It is his destiny." Arafat knew that *Sadat* would be killed—and he was. We surely know what happened to Menachem Begin. What has never ceased to amaze me is the killing of Sadat. For the first time in Egyptian history, the people of Egypt murdered their pharaoh!"[14] If you were to go to Israel today and question any true citizen of Israel who has lived there for any length of time and who were current on the news from the Islamic forces, Saudi Arabia and Israel, they would admit to you that within their hearts they are convinced that we are now, in this present time on the countdown to all-out war which will bring to fruition the horrors of Armageddon. Some of us strongly believe that the declaration of war on Iraq, coupled with all the other slow-burning events and terrorism events in the world signaled the true countdown to The Final Prophecy.

Notes

1 See the Book of Exodus, Chapter Fourteen

2 This is an overview of the journey and not a precise encampment record. For precise details on the journey across the desert to the Jordan, read the Book of Numbers beginning in Chapter Thirty-Three.

3 This was the rock in Rephidim where God instructed Moses to strike but once for water to flow from the rock for the Israelites. It was the second time that Moses disobeyed God's instructions and in anger against our people complaining and bickering, struck the rock twice—the sin that would never allow his feet to cross the Jordan River.

4 Not to be confused with the Biblical Book "Exodus."

5 As related by a Jewish Journalist living in Israel.

6 2 Samuel 16:21, 17:2

7 Zechariah 2:8

THE FINAL PROPHECY

8 From a former CNN news broadcast from Gaza, a matter of record on file at CNN

9 Book of Revelation

10 Book of Revelation

11 Daily News Front Page, Tuesday March 27, 1979

12 The New York Times, Front Page, Tuesday March 27, 1979

13 Jewish Exponent Vol. 165, No. 13 2 NISAN 5739 March 30, 1979

14 A quote from *Sacher, A History of Israel, Vol 11, pg. 135*

Chapter Ten

Glorifying God

The fanatical, suicidal terrorists who "call" themselves Muslims[1] do not and will not recognize the sanctity of human life any more than they recognize the God of Israel—and it has never changed throughout history. They believe only in suicide bombings, terrorist activities and hiding behind the name of Allah. Kill a Jew or any American capitalist and great rewards await them in Paradise. Their hatred began during the formative years, instilled by their parents and their schooling. Their parents were taught to hate by their parents and right back through history to their ancient descendants. There are no men that I am aware of who have the Spirit of God within their hearts and are able to do the things that a terrorist does. What do you think would have happened if we had fulfilled the mission that God purposed His chosen people to fulfill? It was a single mission, to transform the sinful world by demonstrating our unyielding faith in the God of Israel. This was not by words but by living among the ungodly men and women who did not know the God of Israel and demonstrate the nature and the character of His love to these heathens—totally by the way we lived, worshipped Him and our devotion in keeping His laws. Why do you think that God placed us right in the middle of it all? Why did God promise us the land and we find ourselves today, fighting for every precious inch of what was once a desert? The children of Israel actually served as a rather poor witness for God, seemingly prone to the world's sinfulness and allowing themselves to be

The Final Prophecy

influenced rather than influencing others— certainly not attracting heathens to our way of life. We allowed ourselves to become the world rather than attract the world to our God. In a religion that looks upward to God, our people surely failed to realize that in seeking heaven our hearts must renounce the things of the earth. It is heaven where we are to seek recognition and fulfillment and not from man or the things of this world. So it was and so it is and time after time God forgave us, re-gathered us and provided us with further opportunity to be His light, His witness to those who did not really know or understand the true, living God of Israel. That light never grew bright for it was nothing more than a flickering flame that seemed to go out at the slightest stirring of the wind of discontent. We could not seem to fulfill our mission and to this day we ask why peace has not come to Israel. There were profound, prophetic warnings, time and time again yet those warnings were never taken to heart—not by enough Israelites to make a difference. Although God demonstrated loving patience with His people for a longer time than was deserved, He eventually grew tired of waiting on our people to fulfill the task of illuminating His glory throughout the world. He gave that job to another group of people, but only after He had given us every opportunity to fulfill His purpose. I believe that our people never truly understood the whole picture or the mission itself, and instead of pronouncing His glory, used every opportunity to glorify the sinful attitudes of the world. Not only did we blatantly ignore the admonitions of God's prophets, but in some instances we even killed them! Here is the shorter version of several thousands of years of a story that the majority of Rabbis are unwilling to tell or to teach. You see the more we read, examine, study and apply every method of interpretation to the word of the prophets, we see an all together different story than what we may have been taught or assumed. Those who read and study Scripture for any length of time see the truth and the realities of our past and the prophetic predictions of our future. Some of those predictions even now taking shape and ready to come to fruition—for it is in that fulfillment that God will indeed be glorified and all the truths of the Bible will become the light to all mankind.

    Being a prophet in ancient times was not an honor or a privilege, even if you view prophetic ability as being unique or exciting. It might have

CHAPTER 10

been that way had the people heeded the admonitions of the prophets and changed their sinful ways in favor of godliness. Being a prophet was a very lonely calling, for not only did the prophet stand up against sin, he was also against the ungodly and the rebellious. The prophet had no other weapon with which to face them, except words. History shows us our rebellious and stiff-necked natures when it came to glorifying God. The Prophets words however were not human words of influence but rather the inspired words of God. To a man who has been called by God and been given the gift of prophetic vision, who hears the voice of God in his mind and in his heart, everyone else appears as though they are deaf and blind. Once you have experienced divine presence and that presence has left you, one can only imagine the void it leaves and the loneliness that must follow.

God's Word determined the lifestyle of man but man was not ready to live compatibly with God's presence. Living in an acceptable coexistence with God determined the course of history for we Jews. Living outside that compatibility altered the course of history for us. The path of our history had already been set, before the prophets spelled it out clearly. It was our choice to follow or reject, for although God had shown us the way, He also gave us the freedom of making the choices. I believe there is an old adage, "Give a man enough rope and he will eventually hang himself." Surely not pleasant but so very appropriate to what our ancestors actually did, in a symbolic way. Remember that God did not want puppets He wanted mankind to love and fellowship with Him because they wanted to. Due to the callousness of our people and their outright disdain for the prophets, the prophets often lived a life of scorn and reproach by their own people. It is truly amazing how our own came to us, and we did not recognize or listen to them. Isaiah cried out, Jeremiah wept, and each had a way of dealing with the disappointment and the frustration of God's words going unheeded. The terrible thing they had to live with was that they knew the consequences of rejection! They were the one's who announced God's judgments against the sin of the people, and warned the people to follow God's admonitions or perish. They watched the people disobey their admonitions from God and go their own way, often becoming a part of the misery of the consequences.

The Final Prophecy

Remember, the prophets were right there when our people allowed themselves to be influenced by the heathens in the lands they conquered, the lands that God gave to them when He made the very promise we just discussed to Abraham.

The prophet Jeremiah declared,

> "For twenty-three years the word of the LORD has come to me, and I have spoken persistently to you, but you have not listened. You have neither listened or inclined your ears to hear, although the LORD persistently sent to you all His servants the prophets, saying; Turn now, every one of you, from his evil way and wrong doings. Yet you have not listened to Me says the Lord."[2]

If you were asked to warn a person or a group of people about an impending danger if they did not change some things and follow some instructions, and you did this for twenty-three years, would you become frustrated? Can you even imagine carrying the Word of God to our people and being ignored, time after time? It matters not, for the prophet had a grave responsibility. His absolute duty was to speak to the people as God had instructed the prophet to do, whether they listened or not. The prophet speaks, the prophet warns, the prophet has done his job.

> "If I say I will not mention Him, Or speak any more in His name, There is my heart as it were a burning fire shut up in my bones, And I am weary with holding it in, And I cannot. [3]

CHAPTER 10

THE MEN OF GLOOM AND DOOM

The prophet cannot win, for if he remains silent he dishonors God because he represents the Word of God. If he speaks of impending punishment or danger he is scorned and rejected. He has to be in opposition of all— from the people to the priests, the judges, and even go up against the false prophets. There were many false prophets in Jeremiah's time, men who claimed to carry the word of God on their lips. These were seekers of recognition and of money, for they were infiltrating not only Judah but were even infiltrating the Temple in Jerusalem. Often the false prophets would say one thing and Jeremiah would contradict what they said and accuse them of falsely carrying a word to the people that was not of God. At times, it appeared to be a better idea to keep quiet, withhold the word and let the people find out for themselves. What or whom have you been listening to concerning the things of God—one who claims to know or the Word of He who knows all?

> "If the watchman sees the sword coming and does not blow the trumpet, so that the people are not warned, and the sword comes, and takes any one of them; that man is taken away in his iniquity, but his blood I will require the watchman's hand. So you, son of man, I have made a watchman for the house of Israel; whenever you hear a word from My mouth, you shall give them warning from Me."[4]

The chief job of the prophet then, was to proclaim to Judah their transgressions and to Israel it's sin.[5] It is actually quite remarkable that the prophets were not slaughtered in the middle of any given night! When you really think about their public position, they were the voice of doom and the chastisers of sin. Nothing passed by them that they did not know and their words were often sharp and spoke of destruction. Those that did not believe the prophets were mostly the pious ones or the priests,

The Final Prophecy

who called the prophets blasphemers. To the people who did not understand the prophets, they were called crazy and disregarded as one who lost their wits. To those who carried the power of being in charge, they regarded the prophets as seditious. To many who have studied the prophets in depth, they were the mouthpieces of God to a generation that God could not even gaze His eyes upon because of their sinfulness.

"This people's failure was most serious. The beloved of God worshipped the Baalim."[6] "The vineyard of the Lord yielded wild grapes"[7] "My land made My heritage an abomination."[8]

These were all accusations against us, the chosen people of God. They were not simple rebukes, but rather our God telling us that He was most displeased with the people He chose to do a job and that job was to save the world. Perhaps we as human beings might look upon ourselves and try to rationalize that we're really not that bad but I believe God, who finds even angels imperfect, totally disagrees.

> "Can mortal man be righteous before God? Can a man be pure before His maker? Even in His servants He puts no trust, How much more those who dwell in houses of clay. Whose foundations are in the dust, Which is crushed before the moth…What is man that he can be clean? Or he that is born of a woman, that he can be righteous? Behold, God puts no trust in His holy ones, The heavens are not clean in His sight. How much less one who is abominable and corrupt, A man who drinks iniquity like water."

If you had read the Biblical Book of Job, you would see that man has had some rather misguided notions about his overall standing with God.[9] Solomon said that; "Surely there is not a righteous man on earth who does good and never sins."[10] The Biblical Book of 1 Kings declares; "For there is no man who does not sin."[11]

King David declared; "Enter not into Judgment with Your servant; For no man living is righteous before You."[12] The prophets duly point out

CHAPTER 10

that when it comes to disobedience in preserving a state of morality, few men may be guilty but we are all responsible in the eyes of God.

Can you meet His requirements today? Can you answer to the admonitions of Scripture, such as:" "You will seek Me and find Me, when you seek Me with all your heart?"[13] Do you recall the new covenant God gave through the prophet Jeremiah? God wanted His laws and commandments written "upon their hearts and not upon tables of stone." Why should God make a new covenant that deals with our hearts? Because the old covenant was not working, not being adhered to and was first written to show man that he could not possibly do it all on his own. How could we ever think of standing before a holy and just God and declare; "But Lord, I am a good person!" It is not for man to judge man and the prophets did not judge mankind from the viewpoint of societal norms but rather from God's standpoint. Although we were chosen by God we should not mistake that "chosen" is divine favoritism. In fact, God expected a lot more from us rather than less. There is a saying today that goes, "Don't mistake my patience and generosity for weakness." There was no immunity granted against being chastised just because our people were "chosen." The consistent chastisement by God's prophets was the order of the day, in the midst of consistent sinfulness. That meant more serious rebuke, and the prophets were the ones to carry it out.

> "Hear the word that the LORD has spoken against you, O people of Israel, against the whole family which I brought up out of the land of Egypt. You only have I known Of all the families of the earth; Therefore I will punish you For all your iniquities.[14]

So stated by the prophet Amos, he was called into service at a time when there was much material wealth and prosperity in the land during the rule of Jeroboam II who reigned for about thirty years. When Amos came on the scene in the North, the cities were elegant and showed the pride of the people— especially those of financial means. They adorned

The Final Prophecy

their summer and winter dwellings with ivory, sporting fancy couches with pillows of damask which were used for reclining during the feasts. They had plentiful vineyards, and anointing oils were used without much discretion. They were also very much into, if not addicted by plentiful supplies of wine. Sounds wonderful, doesn't it, however the poor were exploited, afflicted and were even sold into slavery.[15] Enter the prophet Amos, working at the time as a shepherd of sheep and a dresser of sycamore trees— that is until the LORD chose Amos to be a prophet. God called him to speak against the North, against Samaria, against Bethel and especially against the corrupt judges and rulers. The LORD spoke to Amos in a vision, saying; "The end has come upon my people Israel"[16] Amos called upon the people of the North to "seek the LORD and live"[17] Amos spoke his words in a voice tone of rage, proclaiming God's words of literally loathing our ancestors deeds.

> "The Lord roars from Zion, And utters His voice from Jerusalem; The pastures of the shepherds mourn, And the top of Carmel withers. [18]

The tone of this declaration would drive a flock of sheep to panic. The Lord was angry over the absence of loyalty and the absence of pity. Syria had tortured and slain the people of Gilead. Amos instantly recalled how Philistia had ruled from Gaza, carrying an entire population into captivity and selling them off into slavery. The Ammonites took women who were pregnant with child and literally tore them into shreds— just to gain some land. Moab burned the bones of the king of Edom into lime. On top of all of this, God's own people rejected the Torah and had not kept God's statutes.

CHAPTER 10

What's Different Today?

Bring your thoughts forward to today and allow me to show you some similarities. Is there an absence of loyalty and pity in America? Do foreign countries show apathy towards the United States? The world is filled with bombings, civil wars, guerilla warfare, ethnic cleansing, religious persecution, abortions and the list goes on. Did you follow the war with the Serbs a few years ago? Were women with children not ripped apart in the name of ethnic cleansing? Do you weep for what is happening in Africa, uprisings that are killing women and children and their bodies being piled up in the streets? How about the Supreme Court ruling that came down in which sodomy was declared legal? Did you know that if pornography was outlawed from the Internet that it would go bankrupt and cease to exist? Do you know that charitable donations are way down and support of Gay rights is way up! Do you know that 92% of the teenage girls who took vows of chastity in 2002-2003 have broken those vows already—but the statistical bookkeepers say that at least they are having sex with less partners than two years ago! Did you know that sexually transmitted diseases and Aids are on the rise? Did you know that 52% of marriages failed and ended up in divorce in this country last year? Did you know that the homeless population is increasing by the day throughout the United States? Do you think that God approves of the condition of this world today? Is the God of Israel being glorified?

Sin or Blessing

Whether we are referring to the failures of the Israelites in the promised land, the temptation that caused Eve to sin in the Garden of Eden, or the prevalence of sin in this modern day and age, we see that the problem is not about people considering the consequences of sin but rather _not_ appreciating their blessings! Stop and think for a moment of the scene in the Garden between Eve and the serpent. Adam and Eve had the beauty, the blessings and the broad line of privileges within the Garden of Eden. They did not want for anything and had plenty of time on their hands to do anything they wanted and to know each other well. Satan strongly pointed out the negative, what they could not do and phrased it as though that one prohibition against eating the fruit should be the most important issue on their minds. Surely they could be like God if they ate and would gain all that knowledge. What Satan did not point out nor did Eve recall at that moment of temptation were all the comforts and the blessings that God had already granted them. Nor did she consider God's love and care for them and trust that He knew what was best for them. The "can't do's" become the focus, the challenge, appealing to the free-will of the human spirit, the nature of man that wants more and pushes further— just as a child pushes the limits in search of how far they can go or how much they can do and get away. Adults and teens alike always seem to cave-in, except for a few who are spiritually strong, who have reached the point of satisfaction, counted their blessings and would do nothing to hinder those blessings— especially their relationship with God. They know what they really have and do not consider wants in places of temptation.

So why do people continuously fall into the trap, the snare of temptation? The five senses of a human being are connected to the inability to resist temptation, as our senses are often mislead into thinking that we need it instead of understanding that the senses have tempted our reasoning by wants instead of needs. "Wants" are selfish and self-centered. "Wants" are self-fulfilling. "Wants" are about us and not about others, unless you actually want something for another who has real needs. How many people do you know, including your own family who are not usually wanting something?

Accountability

The one major problem that I see over the course of the history of our people Israel was that there was a lack of accountability. For a reason that has created some speculation, many people seem to believe that their accountability is to themselves, as in, "I did it, I have to live with it." For

CHAPTER 10

the most part, we as a people are a moral and responsible society. Our life is usually centered on our families, our traditions, the Synagogue and our professions. We are hard working people who know how to live and enjoy life. But here is the underlying issue that causes me to speak of accountability. Accountability is the awareness of being answerable to someone or something for every action and deed in your life. Are you? Many are not since most of my life everyone I knew who were Jewish had a code of ethics that were a make-up of who we were as moral Jews. We were accountable to doing what was right and good and that made us good people. The rest we would take care of on the Day of Atonement. God would forgive us as though it was a shoe-in and all we had to do was show up at the Synagogue, ask and we were cleansed and ready to start the year all over again with a clean slate. I was there, arriving in Synagogue when dawn broke and staying until the sun set. No food, a few sips of water and a whole lot of prayer. I actually left the Synagogue to break fast in high spirits, believing that I was in the Lambs Book of Life. I was righteous, forgiven and was going to heaven if I died. Then I studied the Bible, the prophets and what God said about my righteousness! Is that what you truly believe? If you are like most, you don't think about it. You have responsibilities to yourself, to your family, to others and there is no time to wallow in regret for wrongdoing. It's time get on with it, make a living, have some fun. Will you go back to your business the next day after Yom Kippur and lie about the quality of your product to someone? Will you measure less than a pound in your store and charge the full pound price? Will you substitute inferior materials for the proper grades to save on the cost of production? Will you tell a little lie in representing what a product can do for someone? Will you give bad advice or none at all when someone needs it? Will you get angry and curse a man within your heart? Will you loan someone money and then charge them a rate of interest that is usury? Will you look at a beautiful woman with lust in your heart and desire her? Women, will you look at a handsome man and desire him if there are problems at home with your marriage? You are right back where you were before whatever time you spent in the Synagogue and you are in sin again. "But our ancestors sinned over and over and God forgave them" you say. Yes, God did, but God also punished them for their transgressions and punished them heavily. We are a nation caught up in sin and we can't seem to help ourselves get out of it—we are not strong enough on our own to ward off the temptations of this material world we now live in. We are not accountable in terms of a moment –by- moment accountability, being covered for our sins and able to render true repentance for the sinfulness in our hearts. That would provide for God seeing our attitudes and our attempts to do what is right in His sight— a demonstration of repentance by our deeds and not just our words. When is the last time that you heard words that shook the foundations of your very being and drove you into a state of absolute repentance for every sinful thing you have ever done? If you believe that these are words that are reserved for our forefathers, you are gravely mistaken. The fact is, that without being held accountable and without consistently recognizing your deeds of sin, you will become complacent and overly secure in your life, especially when things are going well for you. The wisdom of repentance and accountability is not in whipping yourself or being constantly down on your self for your ill-fated decisions or wrongful deeds. Being accountable and being reminded is for the sake of awareness. After a while, man becomes complacent in his sinfulness and sin becomes the norm rather than the exception.

Proverbs tell us that "the beginning of wisdom is the fear of the Lord."[21] This is fear in terms of respect and not a physical trembling or a fear of being harmed. The respect for His awesome power, His mercy, His kindness, His love and His Word as it is written. A few prayers here and there amount to nothing more than lip service because there is no follow-through with actions and deeds. Actually seeking-out what God thinks about a situation from the Bible and then applying that wisdom and counsel to your situation by following it, makes evident your respect for God. Second, if someone tells you that you are doing wrong, shows you or points out God's Word to you in a loving and caring way by rebuking your sin and showing you how to correct it, that too will lead you to wisdom for "a wise man listens to counsel and a fool does not." Why is this so important? Why am I literally harping on the absolute necessity for our people to return to daily worship and unconditional love and respect for God? Because we have strayed just as the Israelites did and time is

CHAPTER 10

not on our side. We have lost the awareness of that spiritual connection to our Creator through apathy and through our ignoring the signs of the times—the end of the times, and we will be left holding the proverbial bag of accountability and punishment for every action we now perform that is outside of God's will and His instructions for the way we are to live our lives. No this is not a popular thing to say, however I try to say what is right and not what is popular! You can't get to heaven on a popular quotation—just on repentance and doing what is right and just before God. Yes, I am crying out for you to repent, to see the handwriting on the wall, the signs of terrible times to come, the truths that have been ignored and honor the Lord your God. True peace within the depths of your soul will not come to you until you do, just as peace will not come to Israel until the final prophecy has been fulfilled. If you are here when that prophecy comes to pass, I truly pray that you have found God for anyone who has not by that time, will not want to be on the face of this earth when God's judgment is cast upon it.

Notes

1 This is to say that not all Muslims are fanatical however authoritative, Muslim officials here in the U.S. have stated on several News programs that about fifty-percent are fanatical and want to see the United States and Israel destroyed. Let's keep in prayer the other peace-loving fifty-percent.

2 Jeremiah 25:3-7

3 Jeremiah 20:9

4 Ezekiel 33:6-7

5 See Micah 3:8

6 Hosea 11:1-2

7 Isaiah 5:2

8 Jeremiah 2:3,7

The Final Prophecy

9 Job 4:17-19, 15:14,16.

10 Ecclesiastes 7:20

11 1 Kings 8:46

12 Psalm 143:2

13 Jeremiah 29:13

14 Amos 3:1-2

15 Amos 2:6-8 and 5:11

16 Amos 8:2

17 Amos 5:6

18 Amos 1:2

19 Proverbs 19:20

20 Proverbs 15:31-33

21 Proverbs 1:7

Chapter Eleven

Daniel

Author's Personal Notes on Daniel

Daniel's prophetic declarations of the future of the world and of mankind, if printed in today's newspapers would likely be regarded as "unbelievable." However, Daniel's prophecies were not printed in a newspaper. They were printed in the Word of God and dealt with both the events of that day as well as future times. The first part, now the "past" to us, has come to fruition—precisely as Daniel predicted. The extent and the depth of his prophecies are far greater than can be properly portrayed and explained in a single chapter. However, without covering at least the specifics of Daniel's life and the prophecies he declared, I would not be doing justice to your understanding nor to the historic events that took place before, during and after the life of this prophet.

BABYLON

The Babylonians were Amorites, a Semitic people who had migrated from Arabia and settled on the site of Babylon along the middle Euphrates and Tigris rivers. This was an excellent geographical location and ideally suited to become the capital of Mesopotamia. By its geographical location, Babylon dominated the trade along the Euphrates and Tigris rivers. All commerce that existed between Sumer and Akkad had to pass by

The Final Prophecy

Babylon's walls. (The wealth and power of Solomon show similar traits in the geographical location of his land through which all merchant caravans needed to pass). The merchants of Babylon followed the Tigris north to Assyria and Anatolia, while the Euphrates took the merchants to Syria, Palestine and the Mediterranean. I point out these geographical positions so that you can see how the city of Babylon grew in commercial importance and political power. From about 1792-1750 B.C., Babylon had a king who possessed foresight as well as a strong ruling ability. His name was Hammurabi, the sixth king of the First Dynasty of Babylon. His goals are historically clear, for there were three specific ones that history shows us that he set. First, make Babylon extremely secure, the second was to unify Mesopotamia and the third to win the Babylonians their place in Mesopotamian civilization. Culturally he encouraged and promoted the spreading of myths, explaining how Marduk, the god of Babylon had been elected the king of the gods by the other Mesopotamian deities. It surely worked for in the belief of this myth that spread throughout the region, Babylon became the religious center of Mesopotamia. The conquests of Hammurabi along with the activities of the Babylonian merchants spread the Babylonian culture north to Anatolia and west to Syria and Palestine. One of his most noted accomplishments was the law code that related to daily life in Mesopotamia. This became known as the "Code of Hammurabi" and had two striking characteristics. First, the law differed according to the social status of the offender, and second, that the punishment fit the crime. It called for "an eye for an eye and a tooth for a tooth" if you have ever wondered at the origin of that saying. In this case it was more than a saying, it was the law. A person of higher social status who was accused of destroying the eye of a commoner or a slave could pay a fine instead of losing their own eye and once a Judge rendered a verdict, it could never be changed. So much for our modern appellate systems. The code obviously attempted to provide a fair trial and a just verdict. The subsequent rulers to Hammurabi saw the realm of the Amorite Dynasty diminish and in 1595 B.C. the Hittites sacked Babylon. This was the world into which Daniel came and eventually rose to have great prominence and influence.

CHAPTER 11

JERUSALEM & JUDAH FALL - THE CAPTIVITY BEGINS

In 589 B.C. Nebuchadnezzar, the reigning king of Babylon marched on Jerusalem. Jehoiakim (reigning king of Israel) died at this time and his son Jehoiachin surrendered the city to Babylon in 597 B.C. Most Judeans including the royal family were marched off to Babylon as depicted in 2 Kings 24:6-12. Nebuchadnezzar appointed Zedekiah over Judah who revolted against Babylon in 589 B.C. Judah was ravaged and Jerusalem besieged. Although Pharaoh Hophra in an aborted campaign provided a brief respite for Judah, the city fell in the summer of 587 B. C., Zedekiah was captured, Jerusalem was burned to the ground and the Temple was destroyed. Many more Judeans were taken into captivity (see Jeremiah 52:12-14, 2 Kings 25:1-21). Daniel was a mere teenager when his captivity began (it is thought he was taken captive during this second round-up) and spent the rest of his life in Babylon. In 2 Kings 24 and in 2 Chronicles 36, you can read the Biblical account of his life prior to and including his capture from his hometown in Judah.

Daniel and three other Judean youths who were also carried away to Babylon with Daniel, remained together and connected in friendship from the first day that the king ordered them to eat of his table and they all politely refused. But let us not forget that Daniel's refusal was not his character. He had to have a reason that always pointed to his obedience to God. Daniel purposed himself not to be defiled (Daniel 1:8-10) and the meals served at the king's table included meat from forbidden animals as well as food that had been offered-up to the Babylonian gods, therefore Daniel found a "diplomatic way" for he and his three friends to uphold the Mosaic laws. You will also find a close parallel should you wish to pursue the historic account of Daniel, in the book of [1] Tobit, 1:10-11 RSV, that declares, "When I was carried away captive to Nineveh, all my brethren and my relatives ate the food of the Gentiles: but I kept from eating it because I remembered God with all my heart." In the Biblical Book of Daniel we see the obvious influence of Daniel's refusal to deny God's laws and to trust in his "deliverance" in all circumstances.

Daniel was an Ambassador for God, not a title he wore on his sleeve, but a conviction he retained within the essence of his very being. God's

The Final Prophecy

hand was surely on Daniel as well as his friends, somewhat obvious upon examining their names. Daniel and each of his three friends had names that referenced a form of the names of God. Abbreviations for God in the Hebrew are "el" for Elohim and "Yah" is an abbreviation for Yahweh or Jehovah. Daniel's name means "God is my Judge." As for Daniel's friends, Hananiah is translated "Jehovah is gracious." Mishael is translated "Who is He that is God" and Azariah means The Lord is help." It is obvious that Daniel and friends were strongly linked to God and God's will. But what happened to Daniel and his friends in their young lives that brought the love of God to their hearts with such a devotional strength? The answer is that there had been a revival, one that I wish I could see in this land among our people. All a revival of faith takes is one person and then a handful of people to illuminate the darkness of stagnant faith hiding in the shadows of despair and disbelief. You see, under the leadership of the very young king Josiah who ruled at the time of young Daniel's life, there was a complete revival of faith and worshipping God, along with the help of the prophets Jeremiah and Micah—another role for the prophets beyond doomsday sayings and punishment proclamations! So Daniel and his friends went off to Babylon filled with renewed strength in their absolute, unconditional faith in God. That's how they made it through those times and that is how Daniel was able to be a light to the Babylonian people, a witness for the God of Israel. He never faltered—not once. Now that represents the character of a political figure that I prayed would be running for national office. The Babylonians could change Daniels address, his name and his lifestyle but never change his heart for God. This was the Daniel in the Bible that most of us only make reference to in the stories we tell to our children, "Daniel was in the lions den!" Daniel is symbolic of the way our children should grow up. Perhaps we might pay more attention to teaching them the Bible, for when it comes to a heart like Daniel's, I reference Proverbs 4:23, "Keep the heart with all diligence, for out of it are the issues of life." I submit to you that each of us should purpose our hearts to live each day as though the Lord will pour out His judgments tomorrow at sunrise. Then each day will have meaning and purpose to be all that you can be—with a heart purposed towards following the Lord.

CHAPTER 11

We have examined the validity of prophecies by looking into the details of the fulfillment of the prophecies themselves and into the life of the prophet. Based upon all the historical accounts, his character was without flaw though no human is without sin. How many scandals have you heard of, watched on television or read about in the newspapers that rocked this nation concerning political leaders in this country? It seems that those holding public office today have more in common with public offenders than public servants. Where are the leaders that we can look up to? Now look at the life of a man who was captured in the beginning of his youth and rose within that foreign nation to become a leader and public figure—without ever renouncing his former life or turning from God. One cannot find a single thing in the historic and Biblical record of his life that even resembles wrongdoing, political injustices, scandals or publicly defaming another man's character. Daniel not only interpreted dreams but also attained a high, political position within the nation that once held him a prisoner. Through it all, he demonstrated that his faith was unyielding, unconditional and unquestionably loyal to God.

Babylon stood for sixty-six years and upon the death of Nebuchadnezzar, Evil-Merodach, his son, succeeded his father and reigned for eighteen years. It is the accuracy of Daniel's prophetic statements, the timetable that Daniel predicted for the rise and fall of nation after nation that the famed British historian, Sir Rawlinson once referred to Daniel as a sort of "Manual of Ancient History" and some later history as well, having prophetic value all the way to the 19th Century in fulfillment credibility. Chapter Eleven of the Book of Daniel is known as the longest prophecy in the Bible, demonstrating that all of Daniel's prophecies cannot be taken in a figurative sense but must be read and accepted in a literal sense because they cannot be denied. Going forward with the person, the personality and the prophecies of this young man of God, how would you act and feel if you had received all this ability from the visions of interpreting dreams and gaining the favor of your employer, being number one in the workplace and getting raise after raise and promotion after promotion? Daniel received these types of personal elevations related to those times but never stopped being a humble and respectful person. Humility is a virtue that Daniel surely displayed. In his humility he prayed about every

The Final Prophecy

decision he made, making sure that God would have him do whatever he would do. 1 Samuel 2:30 tells us, "Them that honor Me, I will honor."

Daniel – Interpreter of Dreams

The prophetic starting point in examining the accuracy of Daniel's prophecies begins with the first dream that Daniel interpreted for the king of Babylon. Let's focus on the dream itself, what it depicted in terms of the future of Nebuchadnezzar and Babylon and the miraculous fulfillment of the dream precisely as Daniel explained it. At this historic time we know that Daniel had become well-known as an Israelite with great power that was fully derived from "his God." This was surely understood by king Nebuchadnezzar when Daniel told him of the huge statue that was comprised of varied substances. "The images head was of fine gold, its chest and arms of silver, its belly and thighs of bronze, its legs of iron and its feet partly of iron and partly of clay."[2]

The dream describes the succession of world powers that impacted the people of Israel. The term world power is not one that we are familiar with today, having almost 140 democratic nations alone. However, in ancient times the rulers of these vast empires controlled the fate of much of the known world. The dream that Daniel describes shows a progression of empires as symbolized by the strength of the material that formed each part of the statue. The head of gold represented the kingdom of Babylon for gold is more valuable and so much stronger than silver and also considering that at the time, Babylon was the ruling power. The silver is divided into two portions of the body which represented the succeeding empire that would conquer Babylon—the Medo-Persian Empire. The belly and the thighs of bronze was the next succeeding power as bronze is more powerful than silver and that represented the Greeks. The legs were of iron which I see as the "iron will" of the Roman Empire, the fifth kingdom of the ruling powers and not to be confused with the feet and toes for although they were of iron content they were mixed with clay. This final "mixture" arising from the prior Roman Empire could represent a confederation of power occurring in the future and has been

CHAPTER 11

likened to a possible form of the "European Confederation" which originally had 10 member nations and may again in the End Times when this prophecy is finally completed.

Let us go back to the silver portion of the image and begin looking at the incredible details of this history foretold by Daniel. The breast and arms of silver, as stated, symbolized the initially divided Medo-Persian Empire. There was Cyrus, the king of Persia and Darius the king of Media until Persia swallowed up the Medes to become the Medo-Persian Empire that stood for 208 years. The initial seed of the Persian Empire was a small kingdom that had formed in the region of Anshan around 700 B.C. The ruler of that kingdom was Achaemenes who was the great-great grandfather of Cyrus II, the Great. When Cyrus II came to his father's throne in 559 B.C., his kingdom was part of a larger Median kingdom. The Medes controlled the territory northeast and east of the Babylonians. In 550 B.C. Cyrus rebelled against Astyages who was the Median king. His capture of Astyages gave Cyrus control of an area from Media to the Halys River in Asia Minor. Soon thereafter, Cyrus challenged the king of Lydia, giving him (Cyrus) a victorious rule over the western portion of Asia Minor. In 539 B.C., Babylon falls to Cyrus, the fulfillment of Part One of Daniel's prophecy regarding the fall of Babylon and those after her until the iron feet of Rome trampled all about her for total power. At this time politically, the Persian Empire was the best organized of all those the world had ever seen. By the time of Darius I, 522-486 B.C., the empire was divided into twenty satrapies of various size and populations. The satrapies or political units, as they were known, were subdivided into provinces. Here is where reading the details may bring you one of the "eye-openers" I referred to. Initially, Judah was a satrapy of Babylon. The satrapies were governed by Persians who were directly responsible to the Emperor through three governors— one of whom was Daniel.

During this time, roads were improved, new ones built and merchant goods moved hundreds of miles. The Empire grew and became wealthy and the use of minted coins was promoted and the development of a monetary economy aided their identification with a larger world. The coins of the Emperor were handy reminders of the privilege of being a part of this Empire. The administration of Persian law had significance to

The Final Prophecy

our people the Jews, in allowing us official support for keeping the Law. The authority of the Law was given to local laws and this allowed us to maintain our customs and our traditional laws of which there were about six hundred and thirteen! Biblical history and our people were affected greatly by the Persian Empire. As we know and are about to delve into, Babylon had conquered Jerusalem and destroyed the Temple in 586 B.C. When Cyrus conquered Babylon, he allowed our people to return to Judah and actually encouraged the rebuilding of the Temple.[3] The work had begun but was not completed and was not dedicated until the sixth year, supported by Darius.[4]

The Grecian Empire was represented by the brass belly and thighs which appropriately provides for a starting reference of The Bronze Age [5] of Greece which was about 1500-1200 B.C. It was in the late part of this period that the mainland absorbed the civilization of Crete. By 1400 B.C. the Achaeans were in possession of the island itself thus becoming dominant on the mainland. The Trojan War [6] began about 1200 B.C. which was but one of a series of wars during the 12th and 13th centuries. Historians believe that this was connected with a northern invasion that brought the Iron Age to Greece. The Dorians left their mountainous home area located in Epirus and pushed their way down to the Peloponnesus and Crete, using iron weapons to fight against and expel the previous inhabitants of that region. They overthrew the Achaean kings and settled in the southern and eastern part of the peninsula. Sparta and Corinth became the chief Dorian cities. By 750-550 B.C., a series of natural events ranging from food shortages to the rise of trade produced a great colonizing movement and colonies were established from the eastern coast of the Black Sea to what is presently Marseille, France. By 650 B.C. (Hellenic Period) many of the Hellenic oligarchies are overthrown by tyrants. Then we have the Persian wars era where the Greek colonies in Asia Minor are overthrown by Cyrus the Great and nearly all the Greek cities in Asia and the coastal islands became part of the Persian Empire. In 499 B.C. Ionia along with Athens revolted against Persia. King Darius I, as you may know, squashed the revolt in 493 B.C. and by doing so reestablished total control of the area. War after war was waged and we move directly forward to Alexander in 344 B.C., who, succeeding from his father Philip[7]

CHAPTER 11

went on a conquest lasted about ten years and spread Greek influence as well as the Greek civilization and language throughout a Macedonian empire. By the time Alexander died in 323 B.C., Greek culture had spread throughout most of the ancient world. The Greeks were rising in glory but while they were celebrating, the Romans were building-up enormous power to the west. As we know, the Greeks were at their best when it came to art, literature, science and philosophy. The Romans, as our ancestors soon would learn, were their best when it came to warfare. Rome rose to power slowly, gradually and we find them historically, dominating the world—including Israel.

DANIEL THE PROPHET

From the first written page I have strived to provide you with a balanced view (Biblically and historically in varying degrees) of the prophets of Israel— prophets whom God called into His service to declare His Word. Most of the prophets played a critical role in providing God's warnings to our ancestors, mainly concerning their sinfulness and their future punishment if they did not repent (turn from sin) and return to the God of Israel.[8] Sin abounded and God's warnings of punishment were unheeded. One would think that seventy-years of captivity in Babylon would discourage the worst of sinners to repent! Daniel declared the prophecies concerning the Messiah, how and when He would come, why he would come and under what circumstances He would come—declarations of the sovereignty of God's will as opposed to human expectation. Daniel foretold the prophecy concerning the day that God will pour out his wrath upon mankind— those who have not declared Him LORD but choose to declare the things of the world as their gods instead. Doesn't it stand to reason that after several thousands of years of spiritual wisdom and Biblical facts, mankind would recognize that every prophetic event that was predicted has taken place except the last one?

The Integrity of the Prophets and Their Prophecies

Of the prophets who provided us with the most extensive prophetic words relating to the critical subjects of the Bible (the coming of Messiah and the Day of the Lord) I would personally look to Isaiah, Daniel, Ezekiel, Joel and Zechariah. The prophet Zechariah's Book in the Bible (Zechariah is referred to as the prophet of hope and glory) is steeped in visions of God's wisdom, containing specific prophetic declarations in the last Chapters (his Biblical Book) of the "end of this age."[9] Chapter Fourteen of Zechariah declares, "Behold, the day of the LORD is coming, And your spoil will be divided in your midst. For I will gather all the nations for battle against Jerusalem......(verse 1-2a) In verse six the prophet further declares, "there shall be no light." That would relate to the day of God's judgment. Then in verse seven, "It shall be one day- Which is known to the Lord." There is not a living soul on earth who knows the day or the hour when God finally declares that man has crossed the line of His patience and grace for the last time. It is then that tarrying will give way to the living nightmare of the reality of the judgments— for those who have not given their hearts to the Lord. However it is not just certain men that will come to the reality of Messiah, but entire nations will as well, for in verse sixteen, Zechariah declares that the very same nations that went against Israel in the prophesied events of the end times shall, when it is all over, come up to Jerusalem once a year to "Worship the King, the Lord of hosts, and to keep the feast of Tabernacles."

The continuity of the writings of the prophets and the prophecies we have studied to this point should now begin to provide you with some semblance of clarity and order with respect to the prophecies of end times. This would also include the end of this age, the judgment day of the Lord and finally the rule of Messiah—the Messianic Kingdom of God. As a further example of continuity the prophet Joel declares the judgment of the nations in Chapter Three of the Biblical Book of Joel, illustrating that just about all of the prophets have had visions given to them by God

CHAPTER 11

of this future Day of the Lord.

> "And I will show wonders in the heavens and in the earth: Blood and fire and pillars of smoke, The sun shall be turned into darkness."[10]

The verses continue on to describe "great wonders in the heavens," a look at the supernatural events that herald in the Great Tribulation and the Day of the Lord. The prophets Isaiah and Daniel provide us with some of the most extensive Messianic declarations that foretell the prophecies concerning the rule of Messiah and the events that will herald-in the end of days

THE PROPHECY OF THE SEVENTY WEEKS OF DANIEL

This prophecy is a matter of history, precise in its detail and recorded as it occurred—passed down to our modern civilization of today so that we might see the pattern and the entire picture as a whole. There is a "final week" that we have referred to previously as the time frame of the Final Prophecy. The prophecy of Daniel was 70 weeks and each of those weeks represented years. History depicts sixty-nine of those weeks having been fulfilled as Daniel predicted. Now we enter into this seventieth or Final Week of Daniel in which the prophecy of this last week or seven years is divided into two separate, three and one-half year periods. The wrath of God known as The Great Tribulation[11] would occur at the start of the second half of this period. There is really no motion picture that could accurately depict the horrors of this time and the question I pose to you is will you be there? Once the judgments have been fully issued, God's Word declares that Messiah will step foot onto Mt. Zion and from that day forward He will rule the world from Jerusalem. The Messianic Era— the final prophecy will have been fulfilled. It is then that peace will prevail, no more war, no more terrorist bombs, no "ethnic cleansings" and

161

The Final Prophecy

no religious differences as the world becomes united as one in Messiah. All the dispersed Jews from every corner of the world, the "remnants" of our people will be gathered to the Holy Land. The Temple will be reestablished and the entire world will know and worship the God of Israel. This is a belief that has strengthened us and sustained us through every trial and all the suffering of our history on this earth. Although the coming of Messiah is portrayed in Jewish thought as a coming event, it influences all of Judaism, past and present. The promise of Messiah also influences all the countries of the world and those who believe in and practice the Judeo-Christian traditions of faith. In that day we will be united in faith for all Tyranny will cease, all Dictatorships shall fall and every last man, woman and child shall be as one— free and worshipping He who stands upon this new earth, the Prince of Peace—the Messiah. This is a time honored promise that has been given to us without question, Jew and Christian alike, prophetically declared and not only believed in but awaited by the world—all who love the Lord. As the great Rabbi Moses Mamonides stated, "money and possessions will no longer be the favorite goal of mankind, for greed will become generosity." All the earth will worship the one, true and living God, both Jews and Christians alike. Those who did not believe in Messiah previously will surely become believers. All faces will be turned towards Israel and all prayers and worship will be offered towards Jerusalem. The world will be at total peace. The biggest question in all of this hope and all of these dreams is when—when will this finally happen and bring this fallen world to peace? We have waited for thousand's of years and yet Scripture declares that a thousand years to us is but a single day to the Lord.

Truths of the Past and the Future

It was world peace that spurred the creation of the United Nations when free nations of the world first came together in San Francisco in April of 1945 to form this global organization. What it has become is another story for nothing can be or remain pure in motive or existence in this fallen world with the exception of God's Word. My point however

CHAPTER 11

is that at the U.N. headquarters in New York City, in the Plaza of Nations there is a Wall of Peace. It is made of stone and upon its surface there is a single writing that stands alone with no other beside it, telling the Judeo-Christian world of believers the hope that is echoed and shared by all free nations; "Swords shall be beaten into plowshares—- Nation shall not lift up sword against nation, neither shall they learn war anymore."

These are the words of God, once spoken by the prophet Isaiah[12] and are the words that the Rabbis of the Jewish community declare is the one verse in the Bible that will announce the reign of the true Messiah. Isaiah declares,

"The word that Isaiah son of Amoz prophesied concerning Judah and Jerusalem. "In the days to come, The Mount of the Lord's House Shall stand firm above the mountains And tower above the hills; And all the nations Shall gaze on it with joy. And the many people shall go and say: 'Come, Let us go to the Mount of the Lord, To the House of the God of Jacob; That He may instruct us in His ways, And that we may walk in His paths." For instruction shall come forth from Zion, The Word of the Lord from Jerusalem. Thus He will judge among the nations And arbitrate for the many peoples, And they shall beat their swords into plowshares And their spears into pruning hooks; Nation shall not take up sword against nation; They shall never again know war.[13]

There was another prophet who echoed those words almost as though he and Isaiah were speaking as one. His name was Micah, and in Chapter Four of his biblical Book you will find these very same words. Seeing as Micah was a younger contemporary of Isaiah, we can only assume two possibilities. The first, that Micah received these words directly from the Lord or second, he received these words directly from Isaiah who received them from the Lord. Both prophets speak of the same outcome— the Messiah's reign and Israel becoming the Messianic Kingdom where Jerusalem literally becomes the capital of the world. In the first verse, "the days to come" are interpreted from the Hebrew as the "latter days" that are used in other translations. These words are prevalent in the deliverance of a vision that was spoken of by the prophet Ezekiel. In most of the Jewish accounts of the coming of Messiah, one of the elements that I have noticed to be missing and not spoken of is the time prior to

The Final Prophecy

the coming of Messiah—the period directly connected to the prophecies of Daniel. All accounts of the reign of Messiah are exciting, however we must also be very much aware that the Bible beyond Torah, tells us much more than our Rabbis have been teaching.

Daniel's prophecy specifically states that the first half of the final week of Daniel would be totally misrepresented and will trick Israel during the first half or three and one-half years of the seven year period. It is said that we will be totally and thoroughly misled by the one who will claim to be Messiah. The circumstances surrounding the false claim of he who will pose as Messiah will appear to be as we Jews have always believed—Isaiah's declaration of world peace by the "laying down of the swords of man." For three and a half years, prosperity will reign throughout the world, appearing to be a time of jubilation, as all nations declare this "false Messiah" as the true Messiah! What is it that will also impress and gain Israel's favor? Peace in the Middle East and the rebuilding of the Temple. If there is now a point of confusion and you are thinking, "if this man is not the Messiah, who is he?" "Does the real Messiah come? When and how will the world know he's a fake?" The answer to these any other questions is that the entire world looks to Israel, for she is the setting of the final scenes before the curtain comes down on the most terrible time the world has ever known. Just as the world seems to be falling apart and so much more worse-off than before this all began, good vs. evil will come to that moment of truth, of Divine providence, of prophetic fulfillment and Messiah's reign will begin— as the Spirit of God flows throughout the world as living water to the souls of all mankind. You see, there are many stories, many accounts, but we must only rely upon and trust the words of the prophets of the Bible for God alone inspired their truths. These were set down in Scripture to enlighten us as to what God said He is going to do and not what man thinks or predicts will happen. These prophecies are in essence, the revelation of God's sovereign power and purposes. Each and every truth simply leads to a choice, your very individual choice. Believe or be here when it all begins.

CHAPTER 11

Daniel's Dream

Daniel's vision occurred during the night, while lying on his bed[14] and out of a dream he saw four winds of heaven churning up the great sea. He then saw four beasts, coming out of the sea. Daniel describes the first as, "one like a lion with the wings of an eagle," and its wings were torn off as Daniel watched, and it was lifted up onto two legs and given the heart of a man. The second beast was one like a bear, raised-up on one of its sides and had three ribs in its mouth, being told, "get up and eat your fill of flesh."[15] Then there appeared to Daniel the third beast, one like a leopard, and on its back it had four wings like those of a bird. The beast had four heads. The fourth beast was apparently very frightening. One would say that a creature having large iron teeth, crushing and devouring its victims, then trampling whatever was left of them under its feet would make anyone think they were deeply involved in a nightmare! This beast however, was quite different—it had ten horns.

The interpretation of this dream is given in the Bible by Daniel in the second half of Chapter Seven. Daniel saw these beasts emerge from the sea and in the Bible the sea is representative of the nations of the world. The winds "upon them" would represent these nations being in turmoil. The term great sea would mean the Mediterranean Sea. However, our focus is on the eastern end of the Mediterranean where Palestine is located. This is the central point of attention as it will become the focus of the entire world. According to the Bible, Palestine geographically is just about at the very center of the globe. It is also the center of the Old Testament as well as the New Testament for everything in prophecy and all that is of God's promise to Israel. When anything in the Bible refers to the North it is referring to the Northern part of Israel and the same reference for the other directions— South, East and West. It is the site of the final struggle between good and evil and the site for the coming kingdom of God on earth. The beasts that Daniel envisioned in his dream seem to have a similarity to the dream that Nebuchadnezzar asked Daniel to interpret. There were four main parts to the great statue and four beasts that came out of the sea. The Mediterranean Sea has had its history in just about all of the world's empires, for either

The Final Prophecy

they initially held positions on the coastline or eventually, over time in their dominion of power grew to the coastline of the Mediterranean. In ancient times, as the "Gentiles" moved westward, the sea was most important to them strategically—that is, until the rise of the Roman Empire. After their conquests the Sea soon seemed to be no more than a lake in strategic power to anyone. Rome ruled and it mattered not where you we.

The first beast, the lion, is the nation of Babylon. Although Babylon itself was far from the Mediterranean, the eastern and southern shores were conquered by Babylonians. As the Euphrates was the eastern boundary of the promised-land, the Mediterranean was its western boundary.[16] The second beast, the bear raised-up on its side is Medo-Persia. The third beast, the leopard, is the Greeks. Here again we see the significant demographics of the Mediterranean as Persia, even further from its shores than Babylon was, came to the Mediterranean to fight against the Greeks. The last which is the one most feared is the one who was trampling them all—the Roman Empire. We have studied in great detail the prophetic fulfillment of the first dream of Nebuchadnezzar but now here is a dream also referencing these kingdoms and it is Daniel's dream and concerns much more than simply the fall of Babylon and successors to kingly power. The lion (first beast) had wings like an eagle reflecting the historic fact that Babylon had conquered and became mighty in power and that it occurred unusually fast. Yet the wings were seen "plucked" as though the power of the beast had been taken away and lifted above the earth before its destruction. As you may recall, Babylon's conquests were vicious and swift (the wings) conquering all of Syria and Palestine and then Babylon invaded Egypt and took ancient Tyre. The Bear, Medo-Persia, lifted up on one side as a representation of its power and the three ribs in its teeth are the three powers it has overthrown—including Babylon. The leopard with the four wings and four heads is the prophetic vision of the Grecian army, commanded by Alexander. Leopards are very swift, signifying the speed in which the Grecian army accomplished their conquests. The interpretation of the four heads of the beast might have been guessed by any history buff for we historically know that the kingdoms that were conquered by Alexander upon his death were divided-up between Alexander's four generals until these lands were conquered by Rome. The prophecy of the first, three "beasts" or "kingdoms" are now a matter of historic record or known as "textbook events"—having been fulfilled precisely as they were predicted. That fourth beast also had ten horns and that is symbolic of the nations that will arise out of the Roman Empire (Europe or Western Civilization) and will unite in a confederacy that will strive to accomplish a unilateral government as we previously discussed. The significant question at this juncture is how? How to unite, how to bring all into one ideal and accomplish one common goal? The little horn that emerges is the key to the answer, the one who will rise into worldwide notoriety and when he emerges in Daniels vision, three of the first horns are plucked up by this little horn having eyes like a man and a mouth saying great yet boastful things. Who is this little horn? He is the evil that has permeated earth and has been permitted to walk to and fro about the earth seeking out victims to devour— to bring down in sin. It is more than obvious that he did not have a difficult time finding victims as we view the condition of this world today. It did not all happen in one day but rather a steady decline in morality and values over the centuries. This is Satan—not Satan in the flesh but he who has been inhabited or possessed by Satan and now is fully controlled by the evil of Satan. This man will be a man of great power with all the shrewdness and trickery that has been in Satan's court for thousands of years— the very same cunning and trickery that swayed Eve in the Garden of Eden and the very same shrewdness that manipulated the minds and perished souls of millions who chose not to resist his temptations. This has been Satan's ploy for all-time, the exchange of your eternal soul for the temporary rewards of fame and fortune or the pleasures of sin after which you will have the rest of eternity in Sheol to regret that choice.

Daniel then had a vision of a ram and a goat.[17] He saw the ram with two long horns, standing beside the Ulai canal nearby to Daniel. The ram charged in different directions, North, West, and so forth and no other animal could stand against this mighty ram. As Daniel considered this vision, "he saw a goat with a prominent horn between his eyes come from the west, crossing the whole earth without touching the ground."[18] It was then that the goat attacked the ram, charging at him furiously,

The Final Prophecy

striking the ram and shattering his two horns. The ram was now powerless to stand against this goat and the goat knocked the ram to the ground and trampled it and the goat became very great. However, just as his power had grown significantly, his large horn was broken off and four prominent horns grew up towards the four winds of heaven. There can not be the slightest bit of doubt that Daniel's prophecies and all that transpired were of Divine inspiration—directly from God. Daniel foretold of the entire world's historic process and there is not a word that was not part of the facts of exactly what history brought forth.

The Vision of the End Times

"Out of one of them came another horn which started small but grew in power to the south and to the east and toward the Beautiful Land. It grew until it reached the host of the heavens, and it threw some of the starry host down to the earth and trampled on them. It set itself up to be as great as the Prince of the host; it took away the daily sacrifice from him, and the place of his sanctuary was brought low. Because of the rebellion, the host of the saints and the daily sacrifice were given over to it. It prospered in everything it did and truth was thrown to the ground. Then I heard a holy one speaking, and another holy one said to him, "How long will it take for the vision to be fulfilled—the vision concerning the daily sacrifice, the rebellion that causes desolation, and the surrender of the sanctuary and of the host that will be trampled underfoot?" He said to me it will take 2,300 evenings and mornings; then the sanctuary will be re-consecrated."

The interpretation went on, as the Angel Gabriel made clear this vision and all that was to come. Strange interpretation for the prophet Daniel

CHAPTER 11

to receive when he had spent most of his life interpreting visions for others!

"And I heard a man's voice from the Ulai [19] calling, "Gabriel, (the Angel Gabriel) tell this man (Daniel) the meaning of this vision."[20] As he came near the place where I was standing, I was terrified and fell prostrate. 'Son of man,' he said to me, 'understand that the vision concerns the time of the end.' While he was speaking to me, I was in a deep sleep, with my face to the ground.[21] Then he touched me and raised me to my feet. He said, "I am going to tell you what will happen later in the time of wrath, because the vision concerns the appointed time of the end. The two-horned ram that you saw represents the kings of Media and Persia. The shaggy goat is the king of Greece, and the large horn between his eyes is the first king. The four horns that replaced the one that was broken off represent four kingdoms that will emerge from his nation but will not have the same power.[22] In the latter part of their reign, when rebels have become completely wicked, a stern-faced king, a master of intrigue will arise. He will become very strong, but not by his own power. He will cause astounding devastation and will succeed at whatever he does. He will destroy the mighty men and the holy people. He will cause deceit to prosper, and he will consider himself superior. When they feel secure he will destroy many and take his stand against the Prince of princes. Yet he will be destroyed, but not by human power. The vision of the evenings and mornings that has been given you is true, but seal up this vision for it concerns the distant future."[23]

The distant future, but how distant or how long will it be until the beginning of the last days are actually upon us? Distant future was at the time that this vision was given to Daniel. That period of time was surely quite a distance in the past—around 525 B.C. towards the end of the 70 year period of Babylonian captivity. We know that Babylon was conquered by Medo-Persia as Daniel predicted in 539 B.C. so there are specific time references that place our present overview of the distant future at more than 2,500 years since Gabriel told Daniel to seal up the book." What that means is that "distant future" can mean tomorrow, a week, a month or next year. No man knows and only God Himself will begin the countdown. However, we need to remain sharp and vigilant because this

The Final Prophecy

is one prophecy that the Bible encourages us to "remain in a state of constant expectation," making ready for that day by our lifestyle changes, by faith, by our deeds and by recognizing the truths of the Bible— the truths of Biblical prophecy. Be ready as though tomorrow, God could say that the world has crossed His line of grace and it is time to fulfill the final prophecy. All eyes are on the Middle East and the struggle with Palestine and with the terrorists, as well as all the battles being fought in the Middle East with United States involvement. One would view this as a "powder keg," just awaiting God to allow it all to be ignited.

To provide some insight and summary into what you have just read, it is of no surprise that Daniel was quite disturbed by this dream. He could relate a portion of the dream to that of the dream of Nebuchadnezzar but this dream had some new twists to it and that was what disturbed him the most. Daniel knew that Babylon was actually somewhat benign when it came to the overall prophetic picture, comparing Babylon to the heartless treachery of those who were coming to power when Babylon would eventually be defeated. Daniel knew within his heart that the time of the "Gentiles" had come upon the world.[24] I also believe that Daniel knew that Persia was coming to defeat Babylon not only through his vision but by the fact that he was privileged to a great deal of political information as a statesmen in the Babylonian Empire. The vision however of the four beasts were not exclusively related to Persia but rather pointed to the coming iron willed forces of the Roman Empire. It had to have been a new and disturbing realization to Daniel that Persia would eventually fall to a western power. Look at the visions presented to Daniel and think about his time in history. Daniel did not have a library of theological and historical research materials. He did not have the completed Bible to examine and interpret when comparing the creatures of the dream to forthcoming events. Imagine his confusion, as intelligent and as informed as he was. And through it all, Daniel never lost faith and never gave up his hope. I believe that somewhere in Daniel's mind he looked ahead to the end of the time of captivity and imagined a gathering of all God's chosen people returning to Israel and re-building the Temple. He undoubtedly believed that this could also be the time for the coming of Messiah and that all of these atrocities, the human suffering of the world and the conquering of

CHAPTER 11

nations would cease. However, let us not think for a moment that the captured Jews in Babylon could be compared to the captivity in slavery of our people in Egypt. It's not as though our people were tortured or forced to make bricks and build the Babylonian kingdom to the sky! After some initial years, our people blended in very well with the Babylonians and many achieved privileged lives, businesses, political positions (such as Daniel) and were doing rather well for themselves. The problem was in maintaining their beliefs and their faithfulness to God. In the desert of Sinai it took only forty days of Moses' absence to turn our people to commit pagan acts. Here we had seventy years!

Coming from Jerusalem, the Israelites were used to narrow, winding streets and shabby housing. In Babylon, Nebuchadnezzar was quite the persistent builder and the city was like a palace to our people. The streets were broad and the homes were huge and some two and three stories high. The downside was that our people lived among the fifty-three temples of the chief gods, over fifty-five chapels that were dedicated to Marduk the mythical king of the gods, about three-hundred chapels for the earthly deities, six-hundred for the heavenly deities and one hundred-eighty altars for the goddess "Ishtar." There were one hundred-eighty altars that were divided between the gods Nergal and Adad and a dozen or more for other gods that were possibly "missed!" Try living in the midst of this for seventy years and be as faithful and pure as Daniel remained. There were so many temptations for our people that they became a fixation in their minds while polytheism ruled their everyday surroundings. Would you deny a deity of a foreign power that you were subject to when the known consequences were to be thrown into a den of hungry lions or a blazing furnace? Every single day of that period of seventy years, our ancestors faced the enticements of a pagan world. It is short of a miracle that during an entire lifetime, Daniel remained a true and faithful servant of God.

The Final Prophecy

Daniel's Prayer

Chapter Nine of the biblical Book of Daniel is Daniel's prayer, where Daniel sees the consequence of sin and the people's denial of the words of the prophets, admitting that our people are "covered in shame." Daniel prays for God to turn away His wrath against the people of Israel, appealing to God's merciful consideration, asking forgiveness and stating that the city of God's people would bear God's name. Daniel does not exclude himself from the sins of the people although he has remained pure and faithful to God. Daniel knows that no man is free of sin and his prayer is one of repentance for the sin of the people and himself. He does not claim to be righteous, important or anyone other than who he and what he is, confessing his sin, coming before God in sackcloth and ashes, fasting and asking God for forgiveness. He had been called to be a light, a witness for God and biblically we see that he was, yet Daniel was humble and confessed his own unworthiness.

This is critical to your understanding of end times. It is this chapter that has been called by many Bible scholars as the very backbone and skeleton of all Bible prophecy. It contains the framework around which all other prophecy is built. It is here, from the confession of Daniel to the revelation of this "time-line" that we see the roots of understanding God's plans for Israel. Prophecy is God's own method of proving His truths to the world and Daniel's vision of the future of this world was no exception. When God declares His will in the Bible, He will show men of average intelligence the fulfillment of His prophecies. That is His Divine "Seal," if you would, by demonstrating that this "Seal" can never be counterfeited and is affixed to the truth which it attests to. God has the foreknowledge of the actions of His agents— the prophets who recited and recorded His intentions as they were divinely inspired. Only God will declare "new" things before they spring forth.[25] The glory of such, He will not share with anyone.[26] Only God can foretell the future with absolute accuracy.

CHAPTER 11

SUMMARY

- Daniel was captured from what was a good life at the age of fifteen.
- He never once showed himself to be disheartened or void of unyielding faith.
- Daniel gave us the prophetic visions of the rise and the fall of Empires in those times, just as they occurred within the time frames that Daniel prophesied.
- Daniel's prophecies are some of the most powerful in the Bible and the preciseness of those prophecies could only have come from God.

We know that in the Book of Ezekiel, the prophet, Daniel was three times referred to and compared with Noah and Job.[27] Some Rabbis have argued that there were two Daniels, just as Rabbis argued there were two Messiahs—Ben Joseph and Ben David which we will surely address in the Chapter, "Who is Messiah." I am speaking of the Ras Shamara poem in the fourteenth century, known to most Rabbis, where this highly respected Jewish priest was referring to a "Daniel" by name alone--it is highly unlikely that an ultra conservative Jewish priest would refer to one who was not mentioned in any of the sacred books. Also, would a holy man of God, a Jewish priest refer to a hypothetical Daniel in the same breath as he referred to Job and Noah?. Daniel was taken to Babylon several years before Ezekiel the prophet. Both prophets were contemporaries in Babylon and one would surely think that Ezekiel knew Daniel's reputation. Ezekiel also referred to Daniel's wisdom[28] and some Rabbis have argued that Daniel was far too young to have been referred to as "wise." The Hebrew word used in this reference in the original manuscripts is "yeled" which denotes "youth or youthful one." In the Biblical Book of Genesis, Joseph was called a youth[29] with the same Hebrew word. If we dig a bit further we find that in the Book of Ruth the same "yeled" was used in referencing the two sons of Naomi (One of whom was married to Ruth) who had died.[30] The Book of Maccabees cites the events that happened to Daniel in Babylon as established facts.[31] Additionally, Daniel's

The Final Prophecy

writings were found as fragments among the Dead Sea Scrolls dating back to 165 B.C. The famed Jewish historian Josephus (A.D. 37- A.D.100) wrote our Jewish history from the reign of Antiochus Epiphanes to the fall of Masada in A.D. 73.[32] Josephus was the son of a priest and named Joseph ben Matthias. He was highly educated and respected in the Jewish community. He joined the Pharisees at the age of nineteen. The English edition of his works first appeared in 1736 and has been used as an authoritative source of Jewish history by Theologians, Rabbis, History Writers and History Teachers. Josephus includes Daniel and his prophecies are recognized as absolutely factual. In any event, let us now go into the final prophecies of the end times and the seventieth week of Daniel. We have covered a great deal of in-depth analysis of Daniel's life and the history before, during and after him.

Notes

1 A reference for Rabbis and learned Jewish brethren

2 Daniel 2:32-33

3 Ezra 1:1-4

4 Ezra 6:15

5 Compton's Historical Commentaries, Greece, Ancient Civilizations, (GR)

6 Described by Homer and the Iliad

7 Philip was assassinated

8 The word "repent" in the original ancient language was actually a military term which meant "retreat"

9 It is said that we are in the age of God's grace for each day that passes before the Day of the Lord is another day that God will welcome another soul to Him and another soul to find eternal refuge in His kingdom we know as heaven

CHAPTER 11

10 Joel 3:30-31a

11 *The Great Tribulation, The Day of the Lord,* when God pours out His judgments upon the earth for the sins of mankind.

12 Isaiah 2:4

13 Isaiah 2:1-4 Tanakh, Jewish Holy Scriptures

14 Daniel Chapter Seven

15 Daniel 7:5

16 Numbers 34:6-7 and Joshua 1:4

17 Daniel 8:1-14

18 Daniel 8:5

19 A river East of the Persian city Susa.

20 It is believed that this was God's own voice speaking to Gabriel.

21 This was a common physical reaction to a heavenly visitation, as it also happened to the prophet Ezekiel in the first Chapter.

22 To keep things understandable, the *four* horns represent powers such as the Syrians under Seleucus which will lead eventually to Antiochus Epiphanes as the *little horn* who is now deemed to be the Antichrist who will reveal himself and persecute our people Israel.

23 Daniel 8:16-26

24 Remember that *Gentiles* in those times were those who did not believe in God but had pagan gods and pagan beliefs. Please do not confuse the word *Gentile* with the word Christian.

25 Isaiah 42:8-9

26 Isaiah 42:8

The Final Prophecy

27 Ezekiel 14:20

28 Ezekiel 28:3

29 Genesis 37:30 and 42:22 when he was about seventeen years old.

30 Ruth 1:5

31 1Macabees 2:57

32 Masada is a mountain top fortress built for a battle against the Romans. Ever Jew involved gave up their lives rather than be captured by the Roman soldiers. I stood at the top of this fortress and wept when I considered the will of our people and their sacrifices to be free of Tierney.

Chapter Twelve

The Final Prophecy: Digging Deep

The coming of Messiah is instrumental to God's plan for the Nation Israel and for His people. However, Messiah will not step foot upon the Mount of Olives as was promised[1] until after the Great Tribulation, also known as the Day of the Lord.[2] The Great Tribulation begins this final period in the seven year prophecy. This is the seven-year period referred to in the Bible as "The Revelation of the Seventy Sevens of Israel," also "The Seventy Weeks of Daniel." (See Leviticus 25:1-3 and 25:8).

> "And while I was speaking and praying and confessing my sin and the sin of my people Israel, and laying my supplications before the Lord my God, on behalf of the holy mountain of my God—while I was uttering my prayer, the man Gabriel, whom I had previously seen in the vision, was sent forth in flight and reached me about the time of the evening offering. [3] He made me understand by speaking to me and saying, "Daniel, I have just come forth to give you understanding. A word went forth as you began your plea, and I have come to tell it, for you are precious; so mark the word and understand the vision. Seventy weeks have been decreed for your people and your holy city until the measure of transgression is filled and that of sin complete, until iniquity is expiated, and eternal righteousness ushered in, and prophetic vision ratified, and the Holy of Holies anointed. You must know and understand. From the issuance of the word to restore and rebuild Jerusalem until the time of

The Final Prophecy

> the anointed leader is seven weeks; and for sixty-two weeks it will be rebuilt, square and moat, but in a time of distress. And after those sixty-two weeks, the anointed one will disappear and vanish. The army of a leader who is to come, will destroy the city and the sanctuary, but its end will come through a flood. Desolation is decreed until the end of war. During one week he will make a firm covenant with many. For half a week [4] he will put a stop to the sacrifice and the meal offering. At the corner of the altar will be an appalling abomination until the decreed destruction will be poured down upon the appalling thing." [5]

In Hebrew, the angel Gabriel would be translated as "the servant," "the strong one of the strong God." We know this from the Hebrew root words, *"gebher"* that means man, as in "the strong one" and the second root *"el"* which means *"the strong God."* All Biblical scholars who believe in the authenticity of Daniel believe that each of these weeks represent years and not literal weeks. That would leave the last week or the last seven-year period of this prophecy to be fulfilled at some future time. What do the years imply? If you take each of the weeks as years, you would have approximately four-hundred and ninety years. This is considering that our Hebrew year at the time of this prophetic revelation was three hundred and sixty days and adjusting the time for the longer months (extra days in the Julian calendar) that number would stand correct. This would be initiated at the time that the command was given to rebuild Jerusalem as contained in verse twenty-five. The conclusion is four hundred and ninety years later as found in verse twenty-seven. This is specifically for the people of Israel as God addresses other people groups in Daniel Chapters Two, Seven and Eight. Those chapters refer to the Gentiles.[6] This does not involve any other group, not Christians, not the church, but specifically God's intent to restore Israel and our Jewish people to the redemption and full possession of the land of Israel.

It is important that we note that our God has always dealt with His people Israel in seventy-weeks increments or four-hundred -ninety years. The classic examples of this are:

CHAPTER 12

▶ The establishment of the covenant with Abraham to the coming of the people to Canaan was four hundred - ninety years.

▶From the time that Joshua led the Israelites to the possession of the land until they actually established the kingdom of Israel in Palestine, was four hundred-ninety years.

▶From the time of establishing the kingdom to the day of their captivity was four hundred- ninety years.

▶From the time the Israelites return from captivity to the time that God has dealt with the Israelites, according to Daniel 9:24 will be another four hundred-ninety years.

In this present timeframe in the history of our world, so many men have asked why God waits so long to set-up His kingdom on earth and remove sin from the world. Christians and Jews alike ask to be rescued from the plagues of sin, all wanting to see the fruition of the Seventieth week—the final piece of Daniel's prophecy in place. Why has it taken so long? God is merciful and has declared a season of grace[7] so that as many as are led to forsake sinful lives and return to the Lord may do so—"Whoever calls upon the name of the Lord shall be saved." [8] That is the reason that the end of days has yet to occur. God is merciful and desires all who would not perish to come to Him— to give up their ways of sin and return to the Synagogues and the Churches of the world and live a godly life. Then when the Great Tribulation occurs, those who have turned away from sin and returned to the Lord will all be spared from the horrors that will beset those who have chosen evil over good , sin over righteousness and hate over love. Do you realize that the Bible tells us in the Book of Revelation that while the Judgments of God are being poured out on the earth there are people who still refuse to accept God and accept what is going on about them! They actually stand in the midst of the turmoil and shake their fists at God!

If you study Scripture you will also see that all of Biblical history is

The Final Prophecy

actually in segments of time that God has designated for things to occur according to His will. Even the reference to the Old Testament and the New Testament shows time segments, the older segments and the newer ones— including those to come. It appears that all divine revelations are of successive ages. All things that occur are for the sovereign purposes of God and each of those time frames has been told to us—if we only looked and cared enough to read them. Time segments are not always defined with an actual date, just as the Seventieth week has never been defined. Key words are when and so many days and latter days an example of which is Deuteronomy Chapter 30, "It shall happen *when* all these things…" Daniel 2:40, "Because you saw that it was cut out of the mountain without hands, and that it broke in pieces the iron, the brass, the clay, the silver, and the gold; the great God has made known to the king what shall happen *hereafter*; and the dream is certain, and the interpretation of it sure." Hosea 3:4, "For the children of Israel shall abide many days without a king," Verse 5, "shall come with fear to Yahweh and to his goodness in the latter days." I have selected these verses as they are obviously *without* time frames (according to man's perception of time). However in God's perception of time, that would be of God's choosing and of man's waiting. The Bible is also filled with specific time frames, those that deal with God's purposes and how and when they shall occur. The evil one being "cast into the lake of fire for one thousand years"[9] which occurs after the Great Tribulation is one specific example. The period of captivity was also given to the people of Israel who were taken to Babylon for "seventy years." This time frame was given as it was of divine purpose. God needed to purge the people from their sins and that was the number of years it would take to do so, passing through a generation and raising up the next to godliness instead of sinfulness. It seems to me that God did the very same thing to His children when they come up out of Egypt. Forty years in the desert to purge away the sinfulness and allow the next generation to be raised up and return to the righteousness of God.

God's time frame for the end of days shows signs that are also referred to in the Bible— signs that concern world financial power such as the Euro-Dollar and the European Confederation. The Eurodollar is gaining strength every day and the value of the Eurodollar will soon surpass the

CHAPTER 12

American Dollar if it has not already done so by the publication of this book. How close is it to an all out war in Israel? It is difficult to say with any certainty what will occur next in the Middle East as the climate is not only volatile but appears to be focused not only on Israel but also on the war in Iraq, the organization of the terrorists, nuclear capabilities of Iran and elsewhere. The prophecies of end times are beginning to sound like Fox News summaries and panel discussions and yet it all funnels down to one topic—God. Are the events that are stacking up in the Middle East a forerunner to the beginning of the countdown to the fulfillment of the Final Prophecy? It is most curious how hardly any of our people seriously read the prophecies yet just about every person has heard the terms Armageddon and The Day of the Lord. The prophet Joel told us sometime between 835 B.C.— 796 B.C.,

> "Blow the trumpet in Zion, And sound an alarm in My holy mountain! Let all the inhabitants of the land tremble; For the day of the Lord is coming, For it is at hand;

Those who are Biblical scholars believe we have begun the countdown towards God setting into motion the final seven-year period. Some say the invasion of Iraq triggered the countdown and others look to Israel and what will happen with Israel's bordering neighbors (the Arabs) and the Palestinian issue. We are close enough to the fulfillment of the Final Prophecy that it is imperative that you understand it and identify with the final days and what will occur. Would you prefer to begin learning about it all when the horrific events of the Great Tribulation first begin?

It is very clear that not every prophecy in the Bible can be explained to everyone's satisfaction and complete understanding. No human being has that capability to know but every person has the capacity to believe or disbelieve. There are the prophecies from Daniel and other prophets that one cannot deny. One example where we can examine these verses

The Final Prophecy

for their fulfillment is Daniel 11:23. If we are to discuss and reason over specific Bible verses and their place in history, past or present, here is where we go through a short exercise in doing so—before we get to the final Chapters of this book where diligence to every word of every Bible quotation will be imperative in understanding their links to prophetic fulfillment—especially our reasoning concerning Messiah. One example of this is *Daniel 11:2-3* which I have previously mentioned but did not interpret for you, knowing we would later examine these verses and the circumstances for their fulfillment. You be the judge if this was not exactly as history shows us what actually happened. Daniel states that there would be three kings and then another in Persia and that the fourth "shall be far richer than all of them". In these verses Daniel is referring prophetically to Alexander the Great. Let's look at the very history that God provided the visions of to Daniel. Three kings followed Cyrus and the fourth was Xerxes, the richest of them all. In response to all of this among the threat of conflict, Philip of Macedonia begins making plans to launch a great war against Persia but never carries his plan through himself because he dies. But Philip has a son whose name is Alexander and he takes his father's plan and goes ahead and invades Persia. Alexander went up against the Persian army in 333 B.C., known as the "Battle of Issus." The final battle that brought Alexander to power was in 331 B.C. and was the Battle of Arbella. The first battle was foretold by Daniel in Daniel Chapter Eight and the second battle that defeated Persia was foretold in *Daniel 11:2-3* as previously noted. And what about Alexander, this great and mighty warrior who would sweep across the battlefields like a locust eating everything in its path! *Daniel 11:4* declares, "And when he has arisen (referring to the fourth king, Alexander) his kingdom shall be broken up and divided toward the four winds of heaven, but not among his posterity nor according to his dominion with which he ruled; for his kingdom shall be uprooted even for others besides these." Alexander died in 323 B.C. just eight years after the decisive battle of Arbella. Alexander had four generals that were loyal to him and were always with him as history depicts. His four generals divided up his empire upon Alexander's death. First, Ptolemy (Soter), took Egypt and part of Syria, Judea. Second, Seleuscus (Nicator) took Syria, Babylonia and the territory east to India.

CHAPTER 12

Third, Lysimachus took Asia Minor. Fourth, Cassander took Greece and Macedonia. In this prophecy coming to Daniel from God and God alone, two of the four generals, Egypt—Ptolemy (Soter) and Seleuscus (Nicator) who are the king of the south and the king of the north—begins the historic passing of the Holy Land between these two divisions of kingdoms with wars mainly fought over Judea and the possession of that territory. Some would now say that the last page has been historic trivia but it has all been shown to you because it is historic fact. (Another good example of prophesy fulfilled is in Ezekiel 24 which describes the destruction of the fortified city of Tyre 150 years before it occurred and exactly how it occurred (scraped off the face of the earth.) How could anyone doubt the incredible "mountain" of detailed-proof facts that the prophets of God gave the world in foretelling the future? It was all God's plan, each and every step, time frame by time frame— the rise and the fall of power, the details of births, of lives and of deaths. There is an old saying that goes, "He who does not learn from history is doomed to repeat it."[10] God will often use an historic figure to illustrate something that will occur in the future. If you want to know when the right time would be to make sure that your proverbial house is in order it would be when you hear of plans to rebuild the Temple in Jerusalem! That's when we will know that the time has been shortened to the final events. The final events— what exactly are they and how do they line up? Here is a brief overview[11] listing the order of things as they are predicted to occur along with the Biblical verses that support them so that you may refer to your Bible and confirm them on your own. After all, there is a little work you should invest into this journey!

1. The believers in Messiah are *removed* from the earth—all believers in Messiah. Revelation 3:10

2. God releases His restraining grip on the evil of this world. (Removes His Spirit) 2 Thessalonians 3:7

3. A man whom we refer to as the "Anti Christ" reveals himself and rises to power under false promises and pretenses to the world—but the world believes him because he has the power to make peace. Daniel 7: 20, 24

THE FINAL PROPHECY

4. The Antichrist rises to power over the Romans. Daniel 7:20, 24.

5. The Antichrist befriends Israel and makes a pact or covenant with Israel. Daniel 9:26-27

6. This begins the first three and one half year period and we re-institute the sacrifices at the Temple which has been rebuilt. Revelation 11:1-2

7. The world church dominates religion and the Antichrist seeks to destroy the remaining church.

8. Satan is cast-down from heaven and provides the power to the Antichrist. Revelation Chapter 17

9. Palestine is invaded from the north by Gog. Ezekiel 38:2, 5-6, 22

10. God's army destroys Gog in this fierce Biblical battle.

Ezekiel 38:17-23

11. The Ten kings under the Antichrist destroy the world church. Revelation 17:16-18

12. The Covenant (promise) that was made between the Anti Christ and Israel is broken. Daniel 9:27

13. 144,000 Israelites are saved and sealed upon their foreheads. Revelation 7:1-8

14. The second half of the seven year period begins with the Great Tribulation which we shall cover in detail in another Chapter so that all the details are fully explained and you will have a fuller picture of the devastation we have been speaking of that occurs during this period.

15. There will be the mark of the beast, the scattering of Israel as she is invaded and overrun by Gentiles. The world is deceived by false prophets and deceived by this Anti Christ as well and the Trumpet Judgments begin.

16. The king of the north and the king of the south fight against the Antichrist. (Daniel 11:40)

17. The armies of the east and the north head towards Palestine and Jerusalem is ransacked. (Daniel 11:44, Revelation 16:12 and the prophecy of this very event was foretold by the prophet Zechariah 14:1-4)

CHAPTER 12

> "Lo, a day of the Lordis coming when your spoil shall be divided in your very midst! For I will gather all the nations to Jerusalem for war: The city shall be captured, the houses plundered, and the women violated; and a part of the city shall go into exile. But the rest of the population shall not be uprooted from the city. Then the Lord will come forth and make war on those nations as He is wont to make war on a day of battle."[12]

The "end times" is not a fable out of a story book. They are promises of God from His own Book. Just like ancestors, we disregard the prophets and the accounts of this time that God provided for mankind in the Book of Revelation. We have disregarded this because it was a New Testament Book, and wasn't for us. We are the people who do not know the Bible (in its entirety—all 66 Books) because we were not brought-up to study the Bible but rather our traditions, our Holidays—that was and is our religion. It is time for change, beginning with you who should ask the questions, get the answers and then intellectually and spiritually not be able to deny prophecy. God alone gave us these prophecies and they will come to pass as surely as your children and grandchildren will bear witness to them when God sees fit to begin the countdown. You will soon have choices to make, especially in the Chapters of *"Who is Messiah"* and *"The Great Tribulation"* where I will explain to you in exacting detail what will occur upon this earth and specifically what will happen in Israel. Come and reason with me and reason within yourself for it is all Biblical truth. The world must come to this for life to go on and for man to be right with God and not in sin before God. To unite us in loving Him and not being divided in our understanding of whom Messiah is.

The Final Prophecy

Notes

1 Zechariah 14:4, Tanakh

2 Zechariah 14 – Tanakh

3 There were two offerings each day at this time in history and this one thought to be about 3:00 P.M. Also the prophet Ezra confirms evening offerings in Ezra 9:5

4 Three and one-half years

5 Page 1487 of Tanakh— Jewish Holy Scriptures— KETHUVIM DANIEL. Chapter 9, verses 20-27

6 All who were not Jewish during the times of ancient Israel.

7 Unwarranted, unmerited, undeserved favor.

8 Biblical Book of Romans 10:13 NT

9 Book of Revelation, NT

10 Published as a quotation from a noted, secular philosopher named Santayana.

11 Several *phases* and much detail has been omitted from this illustration as they are provided in other Chapters ahead.

12 NEV'IM ZECHARIAH – The Tanakh, Jewish Holy Bible, Page 1098

Chapter Thirteen

Who is Messiah?

If you were to mention the name "God" in a conversation among several people, the reactions would likely be a smile or perhaps a nod of affirmation or someone might have a theological question or introduce a related discussion. However, mention the name "Messiah" and you will usually find a varying degree of reactions. These "reactions" might include the start of a debate, an argument, lot's of opinions, speculations and unfortunate divisions—especially within the ranks of our own people. Questioning will likely come from our seeking teens and young adults, while debates and challenges from our older generations. Years ago we would simply accept and retain the traditions of our Judaism, just as we were taught. We believed because most of us were brought-up to respect our Rabbi and if we were fortunate enough to have them with us, the teaching handed down by our grandparents. For example, when was the last time you even thought about the name "Messiah" before reading this book? You would have no reason to unless you were a theologian, Hebrew School Teacher or student of the Bible or someone engaged you in a conversation on the subject. Factually however, there are a great number of Jews who can authoritatively answer the question—"Who is Messiah?" The last time that I checked on the statistics of practicing Messianic Jews there were 1,208,000 who finally found the truth. Coming to a place of understanding and belief is not something that comes easy for many of us as we have been a people who have kept very much to our own theology and traditions throughout history. However, once a Jewish

The Final Prophecy

person reaches a point of seeking a greater understanding, our spiritual needs are never quite the same. The inner, spiritual joy that was lacking before not only becomes full but is usually overflowing. Real joy knows no boundaries. They (Messianic Jews) have completed their search for spiritual fulfillment and nothing changed in their Jewish lives except that they are now "completed" Jews. By "nothing changing" I am referring to our Jewish heritage, our customs, traditions and our daily normal lives. The joy of knowing Messiah is the "addition" and the only "subtraction" or what we wind up losing is the uncertainty of life after death and the lack of inner fulfillment because we never had that assurance.

There have been hundreds if not thousands of books, pamphlets, leaflets, movies, television programs, radio shows, tapes and CD's that have, for the most part, portrayed the same message concerning Old Testament prophecies and discussions about Messiah. It has been rationalized, reasoned through, argued, debated and fought over in just about every way for thousands of years. It is a question that raises eyebrows and begins to extract comments from some of my Jewish friends such as, "Religion in itself is a big business" to which, in some cases, I wholeheartedly agree. However it is not difficult to spot those who use God for their personal agendas, nor does it invalidate the holiness of God, but rather shows us how sinful human nature corrupts everything it touches. For most of my younger adult life I attended one of the oldest, strict Orthodox Synagogues in the U.S. The largest attendance we ever had was of course on Yom Kippur.[1] It was interesting that just before the afternoon prayer for the deceased which we know as the "Kaddish,"[2] the attendance practically tripled. It was a matter of a few more hours until we concluded the Day of Atonement and went home or to a neighbor's to "break the fast." My point is that from the early morning hours just after sunrise, only a handful of people would be there to spend the "entire" day before the Lord. It is but one day a year and yet most people can not even spend more than a couple of hours to repent and cleanse themselves of their sins.

Some have said that religion is simply a means of "social control" and in some ways that opinion has some merit to it if you can picture a world without God's Ten Commandments! There would be total chaos in the world and there might not even be a world that resembles this one without some degree of religious beliefs and the morals that stem from those beliefs. The problem has always been that our heritage, our birthright, our designation as a chosen people and all of our Jewish traditions, do not provide for eternal life with God. What do our people really gain by putting down Biblical truth before we really understand what we have rejected? Make no mistake, end times is not a fantasy. Eternal life is not some control factor to scare people into believing in God's Word. We are headed towards the time of judgment in which every human being will stand before God—whether you believe it or not. We spent a considerable amount of time on the subject of covenants and promises (Chapter Nine) that were made between God and others in the Old Testament. Don't take the "conditional" ones for granted. They were exactly as they were presented—conditional. Through His servant Moses, God gave us the Mosaic Law. Where within the "Law" is there a promise of heaven? It was not meant to provide heavenly assurances but it does provide us with God's assurances. Within His Law God declares that if we are both of the faith and faithful, we are assured of the covenant between God and Abraham. That brings us to another truth that we have neglected to accept and that is the covenant God made with Abraham was not meant for the Jewish people alone. God has seen fit to reveal Himself to the entire world and not just to our people. We were to be the light of His blessedness, the witnesses of His love but we failed miserably in ancient times and failed as badly in modern times. Most of us do not even have an understanding of the Bible, our own history and our own Messiah. It is mostly due to our lack of knowledge and too much invested time in our traditions rather than pursuing God's biblical precepts. The world is heading towards God's promise of the Messianic Age and we know very little if anything about it. Do we actually believe that God will wait for us to be the example of His love forever? God saw fit to reveal Himself in another way and through other people than His chosen ones. We didn't take into account that the non-Jewish people of this world are all descendants of Abraham! How can they love a God whose own people make no effort to share His love with anyone outside of the Jewish faith?

The Mosaic Laws are not our salvation and the Law itself is not our

The Final Prophecy

"promise" of that salvation. We have been told by our Rabbis that our souls live on after us and yet most of our people that I have spoken with over the years believe there is either nothing or there is some supernatural, spiritual existence but discount "heaven and hell." The Law actually is divided in to three parts and I would assume that any Rabbi would support this simple teaching. First, there are the "commandments" as we see in the Book of Exodus 20:1-26. These are "moral issues" and were given to guide us in that sense of knowing God's will when it came to matters of morality. Then there is "God's Judgments," the second part which actually is about Israel as an entirety and not us as individuals. It deals mainly with social and civil life and can be found and read in Exodus 21:1 to 24:11. The third part would be the "religious ordinances" that God gave us and was to be the foundation for Israel's moral relationship with God. You may also find these and read them for yourself in Exodus 24:12-31:18. These verses cover over six-hundred laws that God set before us, the Jewish people and not anyone else in the world. We know from history that this Law, as it were, actually created a theocracy in which the heads of our governing bodies were prophets, priests and then kings. So the question again is that if God intended the Law only for we Jews, what about the rest of the world? Wipe them out? Smother Christianity? Put down all Muslims? Smite the Buddhists! Eradicate the Hindus? Strike down the atheists and the agnostics! What absurdity! If they are "of the faith," descended from Abraham having sincere beliefs in God and have called upon the name of Messiah for their forgiveness and eternal salvation, they are of the faith as well. They will be blessed with the very same blessings that any Jewish person can receive if they too are of the faith. That's where we seem to lose the idea and the implications of exactly what the faith is. The Law was meant to draw God's "line in the sand" between sinfulness and obedience to Him. Just because we are called a "special people" by God does not prevent us from slipping away from Him, becoming separated from Him and living for the world. There is no power to support our adhering to the laws within the Law. There is no justification[3] provided within the Law. Do you not know how many times our ancestors broke most if not every one of the laws handed down by Moses? Over and over they strayed from God and even under the

CHAPTER 13

Law, God gave our people grace by providing us with literally years to repent and return to Him. If they did not, then He gave forth His judgments and punishment. Moses gave us the Law, however only Messiah can offer us the grace and the revelations of truth that will set us free from the Law that God knew we could never keep. The Law was intended to draw us to a moral closeness until the New Covenant was given and a period of grace began before God's prophecy of end times came upon us. God knew we could never uphold 633 laws and in that weakness we would need Him and depend upon Him even more. The Law was for a time and was never intended to be forever. Only the Ten Commandments were and that was all the law we and this world needed.

It is said that before the heart can accept something beyond our present beliefs or understanding, the brain must have a basis of intelligence for that acceptance. Discovering the truths to the answer of "Who is Messiah" provides us with God's promise of eternal life and a hope so profound that no man or circumstance in this world can take it away from you. In our continued quest of reasoning and finding the truth, we will explore historic evidence and examine many of the prophecies that were passed down to us from the prophets of ancient times. We will touch briefly on the discovery of the Dead Sea Scrolls and the evidences uncovered in the archeological digs in the Middle East over the years. Then you will have the information, the truths to make an intellectual decision as to "Who is Messiah" There are also basic facts that today are historic reality. We need not guess or attempt reasoning through piles of documentation. The prophets provided the predictions, history provides the fulfillment and we now have the results. Picture a scale with two sides, similar to the one depicted on Court House buildings, although you need not be blindfolded. That was not humor but rather reasonable reality. When it comes to weighing the facts of history, those that are plain and true, one does not need to weigh through too many facts before it becomes quite clear who Messiah is.

For one thing, prophecy declares that Messiah must be from the "lineage" of David. The prophet Jeremiah declared, "Behold the days are coming" 'says the Lord, That I will raise to David a branch of righteousness; A King shall reign and prosper, And execute judgment and righteousness in the earth, In His days, Judah will be saved, And Israel will dwell safely, Now this is His name by which He will be called: THE LORD OUR RIGHTEOUSNESS. The "branch" is symbolic for "offspring" from the "line" or "seed" of David, just as David was the seed of Abraham. We know of course that David's first child died as a result of sin. The heir to David's throne was Solomon. From David, through the lineage of his son Solomon, the true Messiah of Israel one day would be "born" and not appear supernaturally. This is a biblical fact of absolute clarity and one you should place on the "True Messiah" side of the scale. This shows us that Messiah would come to us in His "humanity" from "the seed of a woman" as Genesis 3:15 declares in God's own Words. Of all the Books of the prophets in the Bible, Isaiah provides the most profound predictions about the birth of Yeshua. In the Septuagint, there was no doubt by the ancient translators that this child— this "Prince of Peace," the Messiah of the Jews would be born of a virgin, the "almah." This would be our "Immanuel," the name stemming from the Hebrew roots "Im" which is translated "with" and from the root "El" which we know to be one of the names we use for God. Scriptures tell us that God will "come in the flesh" and "redeem" mankind from their sins. The Bible does not say He would come and conquer but rather He would come and sacrifice Himself once and for all for the sins of the world. Once not twice, in terms of "sacrificial" for His second coming would be to claim His own and judge the rest. Let us tip the "True Messiah" scale even more by examining his lineage.

His lineage must be of the bloodline of David through Solomon. To trace one's bloodline in ancient times was not a problem—everyone kept records of their lineage and the records were the legal entitlements to deeds for the passage of land and other goods from one heir to the next. These records were closely scrutinized and kept in the towns or villages of the family. 1 Chronicles 9:1a declares, "So all Israel was recorded by genealogies, and indeed, they were inscribed in the book of the kings of Israel." For you who have labored through the Bible pages of the "begot," you know exactly what this refers to! You will also recall that God promised David that his heirs would sit upon the throne of Israel, forever. One would then conclude that Matthew, a Jewish tax collector began the

CHAPTER 13

Book of Matthew in the New Testament with the entire "begot" list from Messiah back to David and to Abraham. This is a critical point that you may add to the scale and not a Rabbi in the world can attempt, in truth, tipping the scale any other way. The genealogy is precise.

A noted Rabbi and Jewish scholar, "Dr. Shmuel Himelstein" in his book "The Jewish Primer" was asked a question, concerning the Messiah. The question was; "What is the Jewish view of the Messiah?" I can only assume that this question was asked by a non-Jew, for all of us know that the Messiah is He who will come and redeem Israel and our people and peace will be secured throughout the earth. But the question was about the Jewish "view" of Messiah. The Rabbi answered and I quote; [4] "Judaism, basing itself on the prophecies of its prophets, sees the advent of the Messiah as bringing with it an eternal era of peace, with men, 'beating their swords into plowshares'. No person can be accepted as the Messiah unless he personally fulfills that mission." I found this answer quite interesting as the learned Rabbi is referring to the second Chapter of the prophet Isaiah where this is actually a resulting condition of His arrival rather than His authenticity and that in itself has complications. To quote Scripture;

> "He shall judge between the nations, And rebuke many people; They shall beat their swords into plowshares, And their spears into pruning hooks; Nation shall not lift up sword against nation, Neither shall they learn war anymore."

This is speaking of a condition of the world only after the Messiah has been recognized by the world and is seated on the throne of Israel. In Isaiah Chapter nine, the Messiah is called "The Prince of Peace"[5] and naturally, one would expect that as the Messiah, once He is seated on the throne of David, He will bring peace to Israel and to the world and war will be no more. But there is another problem that presents itself when

The Final Prophecy

you consider that way of thinking. According to the respected Rabbi's statement; "Judaism itself is based on the prophecies of the prophets." If we are to take this statement at absolute face value and apply literal translation, we get, "He who claims to be Messiah and promotes peace throughout the world will be recognized as the true Messiah by the Jews." The "prophecies of the prophets" is what the famed and respected Rabbi stated. That is what Judaism is based upon—in his own words, yet the prophets are rarely taught from the Pulpits of American Synagogues and we need not ask "why." If you were to study every prophet and every prophecy, the conclusion to "Who is Messiah" would be simple, indeed and that might have changed the very face of our history and our traditions. Is hiding truth justified by traditional protection? I have always opted for what was true.

When it comes to backing up that which is Biblical, we have original manuscripts of the Bible and the Dead Sea Scrolls, all supporting the prophets and their prophecies. (See Chapter Five) That includes the original manuscript of Isaiah, which I emphasize because he is the prophet whom our Rabbis have steered us away from because Messiah fulfilled every prophecy that Isaiah recorded. Comparing the original manuscripts with the documented historical records will verify every prophetic fulfillment. When something has been substantiated as having been written, 400 years in the past and describes in precise detail something that is happening right now, one can be sure it was of God. One may infer chance prediction however one cannot ignore the details of the prediction. One or two occurrences perhaps, but a series of precise predictions that are fulfilled in the time frame and the circumstances described hundreds of years ago is not chance. It can only be of God. You will also note that the predictions of Psychics or those claiming to have clairvoyance, usually contain one or two particulars and are expressed in a general or ambiguous way. Do you realize that there are three hundred and thirty three prophecies that are contained in the Old Testament concerning Yeshua. The probability of chance fulfillment according to mathematical measure (The theory of probabilities) is one in 1,125,000,000,000,000 and those numbers are for 50 of the 333 prophecies coming to fulfillment as predicted! Add but two more predictions being

CHAPTER 13

fulfilled to the 50 and the numbers of chance jump to where they cannot be expressed with any sensibility. These are the prophecies of Messiah, prophecies that one would be hard pressed to arrange or any of them being fulfilled by coincidence.

Who Is We & Us?

It was many years ago that I was reading through the Book of Genesis with the intent of learning more about Creation. There was so much controversy over Evolution and the fact that it was being taught in Public Schools that as a Jew, I wanted to have more knowledge so that when someone said something about Evolution or Darwin I had some Biblical facts behind my retort and not simply an attitude of disagreement. In the very first Chapter, I came to verse 1:26 that stated, "And God said, "Let **us** make man in *our* image, after *our* likeness." I remember staring at that verse for some time and then re-reading it a dozen or more times thinking, "Us, we, our—that's plural so who is God talking to?" Something was missing and I didn't know what it was but I simply knew there was more—there had to be. You know what I am referring to, it's when you get a gut feeling that something is right or something is wrong. I asked my Rabbi and he told me that God was "talking to the angels." That made sense to me for after all, God created all the angels so that must be the answer. Then, as I continued studying about Creation days later, it struck me that God did not use angels to create the earth or create man. I read it again and each time I saw the words "our" and "us" I realized that God was speaking to someone but surely not the angels. Surely the Rabbi was joking with me as it had to be a person, perhaps Moses or Elijah but then I began to think, "Wait a minute, Moses and Elijah were not around when God created the earth!" Becoming somewhat frustrated and not wanting to go back and ask my Rabbi a second time I made a terrible personal mistake by choosing to read-on and leave the explanation for another time. Isn't that what most of us do when we face questions that perplex us?

It was indeed many years later but this time supported by years of

THE FINAL PROPHECY

studying the Bible and its prophecies, I found myself once again addressing the question of Genesis 1:26. However, this time I had already found the answer and the question was not from within me but from another Jewish friend who now had the same question. Allow me to share the answer with you as I now quote this verse directly from Page 4, Genesis, 1:26 in the Tanakh, the new JPS Translation "According to the traditional Hebrew text."[6] If you were able to read Hebrew, (perhaps you can confirm this with someone who is able to) the word in the original ancient Hebrew text for "And God said" at the beginning of the verse, referencing God is "Elohim." So now we come to the difficult question. God is obviously speaking to someone and that person would have to be someone who can speak directly with and in the presence of God. "No man could see God and live." Even the Israelites trembled with fear over 3,500 years ago as God ascended upon Mt. Sinai. Not only could they not see Him, they were warned not to approach or touch the base of the mountain or they would surely die. God cannot be seen or touched by finite, human sinners but He allowed His glory to been. Even Moses was ordered to kneel and not to look but could catch a glimpse of the passing back of God.

> "You shall set bounds for the people all around saying, Take heed to yourselves that you do not go up to the mountain or touch its base. Whoever touches the mountain shall surely be put to death."[7]

In Genesis 1:26, He whom God was speaking to would logically have something to do with the Creation of all that was created for He was there, He was with God. He could not be there with God to create man on the sixth day of Creation and not have been with God for the other five days! By God's Words, He would also have something to do with creation of man, simply because God refers to "our *image*" and that means this man will be a "likeness" (obviously not physically) who will be formed and be capable of many of the attributes of God—and He whom God is speaking with. Surely God is not speaking to an angel. Surely God is

CHAPTER 13

not speaking to another human being! If your Rabbi tells you that God is speaking to an angel ask your Rabbi to show you where in the Bible it declares that an angel can create a man or create life! Angels are ruled out and there is more. If you take the verse of Deuteronomy 6:4, a verse we recite in Synagogue many times, "Hear O' Israel: The Lord is our God, the Lord is one!"[8] If the Lord is one, who is God speaking to in Genesis 1:26? God is speaking to Messiah.

The Bible never disputes itself but rather supports or confirms itself. In other words, when I want to confirm a passage in the Bible, I find another passage with the same or similar subject matter and check the original Hebrew or Greek for that passage. In this manner of study, I will always find support and not contradiction. We know and recognize that Moses wrote Genesis, Deuteronomy, Exodus, Leviticus and Numbers. We know that Moses was not there for the Creation and that God gave Moses these visions that were set down or recorded by Moses, exactly as God gave them to him. If you believe in Moses and you believe in the writings of Moses you would believe that Moses wrote those words that were told to him by God and that would include Genesis 1:26. When Moses wrote the verse, "Let us create man in our image" I wonder what he must have thought, knowing that God had given him a "plural" reference to a monotheistic Jew or did Moses actually know whom God was speaking of and was told never to disclose his knowledge? Could it be that this was one revelation that God wanted man to discover on his own—or until God sent Messiah to us? The Bible of course is not clear on the thoughts of Moses but is very clear on the thoughts of the prophets. So, in the same way God gave the prophets their prophecies for the future, here we have God telling Moses what happened in the past.

In Deuteronomy 6:4, "Hear O' Israel: The Lord our God, The Lord is One, the "One" is "echad," the same translation as was used in Genesis 1:26 in the original language, quoted from the 1917 edition of Tanakh. Why two separate translations from two different editions? Because the later edition (the one printed in 1985) was changed. It only took a "few words" that resulted in changing the "original" meaning in the "original" Hebrew text. This verse was one of the changes, replacing the word "One" with the word "alone" and here is why many scholars agree it was

The Final Prophecy

done. Alone means "one" in theoretical translation, however "one" in the Hebrew, in the "original" writing was "echad" and exactly translated as "one" which is singular. As such, it would be interpreted or understood in that light to anyone reading it who could not read Hebrew nor had researched the original translation. The Hebrew "echad" is derived from the root word "ached" which literally means "to collect together" or "unify" as more than one but being as one. In literal translation of the Hebrew context, it means "united" and that is why the Rabbis changed it in the later edition. I believe the point is well made. How else would the Rabbis be able to explain the original writing if it were left in the original Hebrew context? They could not, so it was changed. Want a support verse? Look up Genesis 11:6 in the original text where it says, "And the Lord said; They are *one* people and they have all *one* language." Here again we see the word "one" in referring to all the people and the Hebrew for "one" in this verse is "echad" And God is referring to the people— plural, as "one" and the same original Hebrew word, making "more than one" united into "one" as in "one people." "Let us make man in *our* image." If the original Hebrew was "yachiyd" then and only then would it mean one and only one in the singular—but it was not, at least until a group of Rabbis re-translated it in the later 1985 Edition of Tanakh. Did they do it to hide this truth from the Jewish people so that we would not question Genesis 1:26? A verse that would have led us to many more verses and then to truths that would shatter the Messianic theory? Here is an example that might give you your own conclusion to that question. Ultra-religious Rabbis are telling the world that the Messiah has already come! They are advertising this hoax on billboards all over Florida. They are running advertisements in many Jewish newspapers and periodicals, showing this false Messiah and telling people he is buried in Brooklyn. If a group of Rabbis can do something like this to the Jewish people then they are certainly capable of changing a few words in the original Scriptures. This is what I say to this ultra-Orthodox group. If the Messiah is buried in Brooklyn, why are your followers guarding his grave site and casket filled with his bones? He shouldn't be there! As for the Rabbis who changed some of the words in the Tanakh, they surely did not heed Solomon's Proverb 30:5-6.

CHAPTER 13

Every word of God is pure, A shield to those who take refuge in Him. Do not add to His words, Lest He indict you and you be proved a liar."

These two verses were taken from the Tanakh, the 1985 edition. Some will answer to God for changing or adding to His Scriptures and replacing His original words. Perhaps much of the hidden truths would not have been veiled from us as long as they have if we had some type of overall Doctrine between our divided ways of observing Judaism.[9] Please understand that I am only stating that the original transcripts of the Bible contain God's truths. The subsequent changes, translations and newer editions are often (not always) mans thoughts, mans words and mans agenda. I certainly subscribe to man acting through the Spirit of God however God would not contradict Himself when He declared that "not one word should be changed or added to the Bible." I believe that when God said "we" and "us" and the original Hebrew text was in the plural, that is precisely what God meant and we do not need a modern translation to tell us that God meant something else!

The very first statement about Messiah came from God in the Garden of Eden. He was rebuking Satan for what he had done, his deceit of Eve and subsequently Eve tempting Adam. God's statement shows without any doubt that Messiah would not come from the framework of some miraculous cosmic event that would suddenly come to earth in a giant fireball! Messiah would be born, just as you and I would be born but this birth had one major difference—her husband would have nothing to do with the conception. According to the strictest of Orthodox traditions, her husband would not even "lay with her"[10] as she would have to be a virgin until her wedding night. This woman would conceive a male child and He would eventually fulfill God's prophecy to Satan for all his wrongdoing. God said to Satan, "I will put enmity, Between you and the woman, between your seed and her Seed. He shall bruise your head and you shall bruise His heel."[11] The point is God said "her" seed and "he" shall strike "his" heel. If you recall I was very specific in pointing out the verses from the Old Tanakh and the changes made in the 1985 Edition. The point is

The Final Prophecy

that the 1917 Tanakh reads as the New King James Bible reads, and here are the very same verses from the 1985 Tanakh. I ask that you read them carefully to clearly see my point. "I will put enmity between you and the woman, And between your offspring and hers. They shall strike at your head. And you shall strike at their heel." From an encounter that would occur in the end of days between Satan and Messiah, cleansing the earth of his evil for a thousand years, the panel of Rabbis sought to "slant" this verse as well as Genesis 1:26 and many other verses in the Torah. The Rabbis sought to eliminate the singular translation of "he" and change it to the plural of "their and they." Why, I ask, would this change be made to God's Word if not for the very same reason Genesis 1:26 was changed to plural from the singular verse? It is because the singularity of that original verse points directly to Yeshua.

Rabbis Reasoning

Many Rabbis have a theory that has been used in an attempt to "explain away" Messianic implications in the Old Testament. The Rabbis state, "just because the original translations of Genesis 1:26 says "our" and "us" it simply means the plurality of God's glory or majesty or He is speaking to all the heavenly creatures!"[12] Bible scholars who know the original Hebrew text and subsequent Greek translations that were transcribed word for word do not agree. The Bible states what God has declared and I personally view this as another side-step, avoiding the truths of the Bible that have faced Rabbis for thousands of years. By that time reference, I submit to you that it was no different in the days of the Pharisees and the Sadducees over 2,000 years ago, as well as the Temple priests. The predicament back then I believe, was, "How do we explain away all these things, even if they are from God so as not to lead our people away from our traditional beliefs? We revere the Word of God but we must protect our people—we also must protect the entire Judaic foundation for we are not about to explain away any radical changes in what we have been teaching. After all, we ARE the answers, the explanations to all things that our people ask us when it comes to God!"[13]

CHAPTER 13

The time setting is about 2,000 years ago. The place in Jerusalem and the rulers of our people were the Romans. Every Jew hoped and prayed for the Messiah to come, however their reason for that hope was very misguided. They were praying for the "conquering Messiah" and not the soul-freeing Messiah of salvation. They were looking for a Messiah to suit their political agenda and not one who came to save us from the "religious mafia" the Pharisees had become. They never thought about eternal destinies, just the present one that was under Roman rule. They were looking for the Messiah to come in the clouds on a white horse with an army of angels behind him. They longed for Messiah and His army to free them from Roman rule, giving their Jewish freedom back to them. The people did not want some Gentile power over them. They wanted their King—the one who would sit upon the throne of David and rule the people fairly and traditionally, not pagan Roman soldiers who did not even understand their laws.

Bear with me through this thought and I ask that you would try to ignore emotional reactions that will only serve to cloud your power of intellectual reasoning. If Messiah did come at that time just to fulfill all that was anticipated in those days, what would have likely occurred was first the Romans would fight against the Messiah and His army of angels and lose. There is a similar battle in end times depicted by Ezekiel[14] to be fought in the future—the great battle between evil and good in the Middle East but [15] not against the Legions of Rome! This was not the time for the final prophecy but rather a time for the world to have a "Prince of Peace." It was He who would bring the message of salvation and not engage in the bloody battles of an all-out war. If "bloodbaths" were the order 2,000 years ago, then it would mean that God's intention was to annihilate the rest of mankind and just leave the people of Israel on this planet! I do not believe for a moment that even a hardened heart would find that intellectually plausible. Coming in the clouds with an army of angels was a little before its time, but the people had no idea of how close their desires then, resembled future prophecies.

Yeshua would have to be the Messiah of righteousness and peace that filled men's hearts with godliness so that men would worship God out of love and not fear. After all, would you love God if you were forced to wor-

THE FINAL PROPHECY

ship Him because He just wiped out the entire Roman army? You would fear Him and never know what it was to love Him for all the reasons He would physically and spiritually soon provide. If God wanted us to love and revere Messiah because He wiped out the enemy in one supernatural swoop, God would have created robots instead of human beings! God was and is about love and not hate or bloodshed. Think back to the Old Testament when God would not even allow David to build His Temple because there was so much bloodshed on David's hands from his battles. Blood was the sacrifice that God demanded as atonement for sin— from an unblemished lamb and not man's blood. The "unblemished lamb" (Messiah) was not what the Pharisees or the Israelites expected and I am sure that Isaiah 53:6 was readily available to them in the old manuscripts of God's Word. "All we like sheep have gone astray; We have turned everyone to his own way; And the Lord has laid on Him the iniquity of us all." No man can change what God has already declared.

THE REJECTED MESSIAH

The Messiah came and when He was about thirty years of earthly age, He rode into Jerusalem on a donkey and not on a white horse. He had palm leaves laid before His path but did not have an army of angels. Both of these facts are recorded in the Old Testament. He left the angels in heaven, watching, waiting and of course knowing all that would occur. Messiah had a mission to fulfill and it would indeed require blood. It was the very mission and purpose that He was born for. His mission was to die—although just temporarily. That is why the prophets declared that He would be "cut - off" or killed before His years. This was the Messiah that the prophets declared would come, their predictions taking place more than four hundred years before God sent Him, without a single detail of those fulfilled prophecies that were left out. So how did the Pharisees explain Messiah away? How would the Rabbis of the years to come explain all of these events, the predictions and the reality of their fulfillment in Yeshua? It would not be too popular, you would agree, to acknowledge a Messiah who taught that "turning the other cheek" was

CHAPTER 13

better than revenge! Or a Messiah that taught you should love your neighbor— regardless of what they do to you or how they behave towards you! Yeshua preached "peace" not war and "love" not hate. Messiah called for repentance and forgiveness instead of sin and damnation— all very much contrary to what the leaders in those days were teaching. Zealots wanted to create a civil uprising and this "Messiah" comes and preaches, "Blessed are the poor in spirit, For there is the kingdom of heaven. Blessed are those who mourn, for they shall be comforted. Blessed are the meek, For they shall inherit the earth. Blessed are those who hunger and thirst for righteousness , For they shall be filled" and those were but six of the eleven points that Yeshua spoke of on the Mount of Olives.

The Pharisees were the voice of the law but it was Roman law and not Judaic law. They possessed so much political and social influence that after their outspoken accusations against Messiah, the people were swayed in their convictions and submitted to the Pharisees influence, condemning Yeshua to "hang on a tree." Even the Roman Governor professed that he could find "no sin or wrongdoing in Yeshua" whatsoever. So Rabbi, tell me how we explain-away the sinless life of this Messiah, a life that was witnessed by hundreds and perhaps thousands who knew Him and watched Him portray His supernatural love for mankind. Sinful is surely not teaching love and forgiveness, or going about healing the blind and the lame--even raising two people from the dead on two separate occasions. His friend Lazarus who was resurrected from a burial tomb in front of hundreds of witnesses after having been dead for several days and the daughter of a Jewish Synagogue ruler.

His name was Jairus who was alongside Yeshua while Yeshua was teaching multitudes of people and someone came from his home to grievously inform him that his daughter, who had been very ill, had died. She was about twelve years of age. Yeshua followed Jairus to his home and witnessed the tumult of the professional mourners in the bedroom of the child. Yeshua asked that they be removed. Why didn't Yeshua have them remain as witnesses— more people to attest to His Divinity? Because He wanted no witnesses and did not want that many people to see these miracles. He never intended to prove who He was to anyone by supernatural acts of healing or raising people from the dead. After all, Messiah

The Final Prophecy

had a date with a tree. He did what He did in His humanity and in showing the love of God for His children. Yeshua had a mission and it did not require a million witnesses—just enough for there to be those that knew that they knew who He was. It was the plan and all the prophets foretold these things that would occur. All Yeshua had to do was to take the girls hand and in the presence of many witnesses she was raised-up as He said to her, "Talitha, cumi" which is translated. "Little girl I say to you, arise." Immediately she rose up and the people were astounded, amazed and Yeshua advised them to keep this matter between them and He left.[16] It was said in ancient Israel that when a person died they went through the "chambers of death" as depicted in Proverbs 7:27, "the gates of death" Psalm 9:13 and trapped in the "snares of death" Psalm 18:5. There was in fact an understanding and a hope in those times of life after death and that would rest with one's understanding of the Hebrew word "Sheol" which is a Hebrew synonym for death. Deuteronomy 32:22 declares, "For a fire it kindles in My anger. And shall burn to the lowest hell, It shall consume the earth with her increase, And set on fire the foundations of the mountains." Sheol exists in the mind of the Jew and it is the hell of the Evil One and the furthest place from heaven a man can go. Amos 9:2 also reiterates, "Though they dig into hell (Sheol) from there My hand will take them. Though they climb up to heaven, From there I will bring them down. " If a man were to go to Sheol he is in hell, shut off from God and unable to worship as supported by the prophet Isaiah 38:18, "For Sheol cannot thank you, death cannot praise you, those who go down to the pit cannot hope for Your truth" and in Psalm 6:5, "For in death there is no remembrance of You; In the grave, who will give You thanks?"

Sheol is also called the "pit" and there is no doubt in anyone's mind, even in those days that there is indeed a heaven and a hell. The prophet Ezekiel in Chapter 32:17-32 provides us with some vivid descriptions of the activities of the "pit." Here Ezekiel is talking about the nations that Israel shall conquer and where they will go—to hell! Verse 21 declares, "The strong among the mighty, Shall speak to him out of the midst of hell." You can also read Isaiah 14:9-17 which describes the fate of the Babylonian king in Sheol.

The question is, what is the Resurrection of the dead in the Old Testament if not the hope of heaven, the hope of resurrecting the dead from Sheol that they may spend eternal life with God. We are told that only the New Testament speaks of resurrection, that of Yeshua in three days after He is killed. Without the resurrection there would be no Yeshua and we would still be waiting for the identity of Messiah. This is one of the most critical points in the fulfillment of prophecy that Messiah would be "cut-off" and then resurrected. He would rise from death and descend to "free the captives" who had not known Messiah in Abraham's Bosom. He would then return to Jerusalem and be seen by over 500 witnesses before ascending to heaven. Yeshua made the promise to return and take the throne of Jerusalem after the Day of the Lord—when The Final Prophecy has been completed. "That he should continue to live eternally, And not see the pit."[17] "Your dead shall live, Together with my dead body they shall arise. Awake and sing you who dwell in dust."[18] The Old Testament points to the resurrection of the dead without question. No Rabbi should point to the resurrection and proclaim it to be a theory or a fable of the New Testament. If you did not know the verses that dealt with resurrection and you were told there was none, than that is what you would likely believe. So once again I ask the Rabbis who deny Yeshua, how do you explain Him away since the "scale" of truth has no more room on which to "pile on" the facts!

THE TWO MESSIAH THEORY

There was at this time in Israel a Rabbi who was known by all. He was not just a Rabbi but also somewhat of a zealot in wanting to do battle with the Romans. The Pharisees and the Temple priests in 1 A.D. made it known that he was the true Messiah! (This reminds me of the one whose bones are still in the grave in Brooklyn!) The problem was that he one day went into a battle—and he was killed. How could that be? The Messiah is slain just like an ordinary man and is not getting up after three days! The Rabbis had to find reasons to explain the death of "Bar Kokhbah," especially after they had encouraged everyone to follow him! So, they came up with "Mashiach [19] Ben Joseph" and "Mashiach Ben David." The theory was that the Bible talks about "two" Messiahs,' the first who is supposed to suffer for our sins and give His blood for the final sacrifice. The first who was likened to Biblical Joseph and the second who would be likened to King David, bringing back to Israel those wonderful, times of worshipping God under David's reign. If you have never read this portion of the Bible, there is a real-person comparison being made between a suffering servant and a victorious servant. First, Joseph of Genesis was rejected by his brothers (the suffering Messiah was rejected by the Pharisees) and thrown into a pit to die. However instead of leaving him in the pit, his brothers saw a Caravan coming so they lifted Joseph out of the pit and they sold him into slavery. Joseph was taken to Egypt, locked in the dungeons because he was falsely accused of an incident and did, in fact suffer a great deal through his entire ordeal— but he was guilty of nothing. Joseph was his father's pride and joy and his "favorite son" for whom he hand-tailored a coat of many colors. His brothers were obviously more than jealous! So out of this concocted story, the Rabbis contend that whenever a Jew reads Isaiah 53, we should think of Joseph— "Messiah Ben Joseph" as this was the official title the Rabbis referred to. Of course, the conquering Messiah who would be compared to King David was Messiah "Ben David" –who naturally was yet to come!

There was to be one Messiah however here we have two Messiahs that had to be explained away—and explained it was! The Rabbis reasoned that, "the two Messiahs both have their respective roles, one to suffer and the other to conquer—but although they are two, they are one in the same!" There exists not a single cohesive word much less a whole verse for this story. It is impossible to find any reference of validity to this except for one, the Talmudic Tractate SUKKAH 52: A and B (Rabbis will be familiar with this reference) which serves the attempt to interpret the verses from the prophet Zechariah that declares, "They will look on Him whom they have pierced; and they shall mourn for Him as one mourns for an only son." This Talmudic interpretation goes on to tell the Jewish people that Mashiach Ben Joseph, the one Messiah who suffers, is going to fight against two kings who represent the evil nature in us, namely Gog and Magog and he is subsequently defeated, suffers and dies. But

CHAPTER 13

then Mashiach Ben David who is the conquering Messiah comes on the scene and here is where their story becomes even more absurd. Again, according to this Talmudic interpretation, written by the Rabbis, they state, "Mashiach Ben David, the conquering Messiah, goes up to God and said, 'Lord, you promised that you would not allow your chosen one to see corruption so let me have the body of Mashiach Ben Joseph. So the Lord grants the favor to Ben David and gives him the body of Ben Joseph! Ultimately, Messiah Ben David will defeat Gog and Magog.' For the critical eyes of the Rabbis who may be reading this, I also refer you to YALKUT, vol. II, paragraph 359 that interprets Isaiah 40. I would also respectfully ask any Rabbi to show me the Biblical grounds for this story, because none exists. It is fabricated and done so to perpetuate the other stories in order to explain away the true Messiah. Not surprising is the fact that as quietly as this story came into existence is as quietly as this story disappeared! Some Rabbis may very well still be teaching this theory but if you recall, I earlier made several references to your possibly being "misled" or were simply not aware of the truths of Messiah. I believe that the truths are beginning to be revealed to you and I simply ask that you continue to discern these facts and to conclude what you will from them. Messiah suffered and died. He was executed by the Romans but was literally sent to His death by our Jewish, Pharisaical leaders, although it was God's intended result. The Pharisees influenced the will of the people by "stirring them up" and because the people in Jerusalem feared the Pharisees and Temple priests. After all, the people did not have a Bible full of prophecies to study, intellectually and spiritually reaching a conclusion that was based on historic truth! If you are yet confused because we are of this modern age of Jewry and simply cannot relate to all of this, let me state some facts about Jewish belief which should help to clarify.

Judaism does not have specific doctrines nor is there some type of creed from which to base our beliefs. The fact is, Judaism basically declares that man can believe whatever he is led to believe as long as that belief is within certain parameters. This tells me that Judaism tells us what we ought "to" believe and then tries to tell us what we cannot believe! To my knowledge, the most sound teaching of any sort of doctrine or teachings can be found in the "Thirteen Articles of Faith" by Moses Maimonides. Aside from these "Articles of Faith" we have nothing of substance or anything that is definite and taught definitively. What we are taught is our customs is that Messiah will come—"someday." "Then we will know everything that He wants us to know. Until then, keep faith."[20] The problem we have as Jews is that our Rabbis have no clear interpretation for the biggest thorn in their Rabbinical side—the prophet Isaiah and specifically, Isaiah 53. Judaism asks, "How do we deal with this?" You see, they could not "shuffle" Isaiah to the end of the Bible as the Rabbis did with Daniel. "Too much prophecy and truth here—let's bury it in the back of the Bible." Daniel is never read aloud or taught by the Rabbis in the congregations of the Synagogues of the world. It is because these prophecies cannot be explained away. Daniel's prophecies were far too exacting and his predictions were historically precise in their fulfillment—each and every one of them. There is but one of Daniel's prophecies that has not been fulfilled and that would surely represent the "end" of his prophetic declarations.

So how does a Rabbi explain the prophecies of end times, the "taking-up" of God's faithful before the Great Tribulation begins and when it's over, the reign of Messiah? Rabbis and Jewish religious leaders cannot explain Isaiah 52 as well, for on one hand Rabbis preach that Messiah is for the Jews alone and on the other hand we see that God's Word declares that Messiahs glory shall reign throughout the world.

> "Behold My Servant shall deal prudently; He shall be exalted and extolled – and be very high. Just as many were astonished at you, So His visage was marred more than any man. And His form more than the sons of men. So shall He sprinkle *many nations*. Kings shall shut their mouths at Him; For what had not been told them they shall see, And what they had not heard they shall consider."

CHAPTER 13

This is Isaiah 52:13-15, the verses that lead into Isaiah 53 which is the bone of contention of all Rabbis. You see, Isaiah 53 depicts the prophetic truths of Messiah –all the way to His death. The words of Isaiah 53 depict His suffering for the sins of mankind, for the blood atonement that could not be achieved after the destruction of the Temple..

Israel-The Suffering Messiah Theory!

This was the next theory that was conjured up and put in place by Rabbis who were concerned that the Ben David and Ben Joseph story did not have enough credibility. The newer interpretation states that the first interpretation might be without merit as the modern Rabbis subscribe to Israel being the suffering servant of the Lord! This translates into their conjecture that Israel is the "suffering Messiah! If we follow this conjured-up line of thought it would mean that when the prophecy speaks of a "conquering king," it is referring to the person of the "Messiah." However, when prophecy refers to a "suffering" Messiah, the prophecy is referring to the nation Israel! There are some plausible statements that one could "almost" believe—except God's Word disproves it. That's why I always look there for the truth in all things. I agree that Israel indeed suffers. Israel has suffered in the past, all through modern time and will suffer in the future— until the Messianic kingdom is established. I again would rebuke this "suffering Israel" theory as a fallacy and here is why. In Isaiah 53, the passages of this Chapter show "three persons" and not two. There cannot be one Messiah who conquers and then all the suffering is passed on to Israel. That would be "two" but God's Word declares a "trinity" and not a duality. If the Rabbis who wrote this were going to come up with a new theory, they should have checked the Bible! First, He—the Messiah, is one person. Then, He was rejected because of "our" iniquities. So we see God, the Messiah and then "us" which is one more entity than just God and Israel. Here is another important observation to assist you in clarifying these facts in your mind. If we were to look at Israel's spiritual condition and the suffering Messiah, the noted difference is that Messiah was without sin. He could not otherwise have been our "atonement sacrifice." Israel is not without sin and Israel can not be a "once and for all" sacrifice! Let's return to the authority on truth which of course is the Bible and Isaiah 1:4. In this verse God appears to be a bit disappointed in Israel and she is surely not without sin.

> "Alas, sinful nation, A people laden with iniquity, A brood of evildoers, Children who are corrupters, They have forsaken the Lord, They have provoked to anger The Holy One of Israel They have turned away backward."

In contrast to these verses, the Messiah is perfect and innocent of any wrongdoing. He is spotless and guiltless and there is no sin in Him whatsoever.

> "And they made His grave with the wicked, But with the rich at His death Because He had done no violence, Nor was any deceit in His mouth."

Rabbis and religious leaders may continue to mislead us and attempt to keep us in the darkness of not knowing truth, but God's Word stands forever and will always support itself. Hence, I believe this concludes the problem with the theory that Israel was the "suffering Messiah." The question has been asked, "Then why did Messiah suffer so much? If He was without sin as the Bible claims, why did God punish Him so severely?" Now that is an appropriate question and God provides the appropriate answer in His Word.

CHAPTER 13

> "Surely He has borne our griefs ,And carried our sorrows; Yet we esteemed Him stricken, Smitten by God, and afflicted. But He was wounded for our transgressions, He was bruised for our iniquities; The chastisement for our peace was upon Him, And by His stripes we are healed.

A great deal of explanation should not be required to interpret these verses. Yeshua was the sacrifice, the Lamb of God who bore the burden of the terrible sins and the consistent iniquity of our people. Short of destroying Israel, something had to be done to pay the debt, the price of sin, the wages of sin, which are death—spiritual death and eventually physical death. Only Yeshua, in His humanity, could have given his earthly-self to suffer and "by His stripes" were the thirty-nine lashes He was subjected to. Roman punishment declared "forty lashes less one for mercy." He was beaten with a whip that had pieces of glass and slivers of metal embedded in its strands. As the punishment was delivered, every lash wrapped around His body and as the lash was pulled back, the embedded strands tore the flesh from the body. This was done 39 times and Yeshua did not cry for mercy or utter a single word of pain from His lips. Isaiah 53:7 declares, "He was oppressed and He was afflicted, Yet He opened not His mouth; He was led as a lamb to the slaughter, And as a sheep before its shearers is silent, So He opened not His mouth." So we see that it was not just the crucifixion Messiah was subjected to as we all have believed. The overall brutality and suffering was inhuman. No mortal man could have endured such affliction without uttering a word of protest or pain. There were more beatings from clubs held by the Roman soldiers. They taunted Him and placed a crown of thorns on His head that dug deeply into the flesh of His forehead sending streams of His precious blood down his beard and onto His garment—a purple robe that they hung upon Him to mock His being "King of the Jews." There is one, critical point in all of this. Yeshua "gave" His life—it was not taken. It was by "His" choice that He hung on that Roman cross. It was because He loved us, more deeply and more supernaturally than we could ever understand—until we are literally with Him on the other side of this life.

How much did He love us, besides suffering and giving up His earthly life for us? Yeshua cried out from the cross just before he died, "Father, forgive them for they know not what they do." Perhaps we might one day know and fully understand the sacrificial love that launched a faith that nothing of this world has ever been able to put down.

How do we know that we know? How does one assimilate all of this information? Although it is all truth from God's own Word, how do we go against the grain of what has been our belief system for thousands of years? Are there other choices? Practically and intellectually, there are not too many choices. In the timeless book, "More Than a Carpenter" the Author challenges the reader to come to an understanding that after studying every available fact, interpreting the Scriptures and the accounts of the prophets, we are left with very few choices of determining just who Yeshua was. The Author points out, that either Yeshua was a "lunatic," a "liar" or the true Messiah. There are no other choices that one is intellectually left with. Was He crazy? I believe that if you read just a few Chapters recounting eye-witness testimonies of His words, His parables, His verbal exchanges with the Pharisees and His miracles, one would never come to the conclusion that Yeshua was crazy or was a liar. Yeshua never once said anything that He did not mean or promise anything that He did not deliver on. How does one explain the biblical facts that Yeshua fulfilled 332 of the 333 prophecies? Can a lunatic or a liar pull that off? There really is but one conclusion you are left with. Yeshua is Messiah. Yeshua was the Lamb of God and because of our early denial of Him, the Gentiles of the world found God through Him and Christianity was born. Every one of the people who initially followed Yeshua we're Jewish. Pharisaical-promoted persecution became so intense that they had to find another way. It was He who drew the heathens of the world to God when the people of God failed to do so. Let us not forget for a single moment in all of this deliberation that Yeshua is the Messiah of the Jews and the heir to the throne of David.

CHAPTER 13

Prophetic Conclusions

Let us not forget that all the work of redemption [21] was to be accomplished by Messiah and by Him alone. Our people surely needed to be redeemed from the debt of their sins and find their salvation in Messiah. God has warned us in so many ways and by so many prophets, that sin unchecked and un-repented will lead a sinner to death. God has declared that "the wages of sin are death."[22] Some may ask, "Is God going to strike me with a bolt of lightening because of a few indiscretions?" No, for the death spoken of is not "physical" death but "spiritual" death. The more we sin, the more we become "separated" from God for God is Holy and will not— can not, look upon sin. At the very moment that Yeshua took the sins of all mankind upon Himself while being crucified, He called out to the heavens asking why He was being forsaken for He knew that God turned His eyes away from Him. It was at that moment when He bore our sins that God looked away from Him. For that one moment, Yeshua was separated from God for the very first time— in all of time. (Remember Genesis 1:26)

"Debt" in the Old Testament could be forgiven every seven years. A man could redeem himself from being a servant every seven years or could choose to stay with the family he served. In any case, there was a "debt" to settle. When you place your trust and the devotion within your heart in Messiah, your debt, your pile-up of sinfulness, your transgressions and iniquities are forgiven in "one clean sweep" and your sins are no longer in the mind of God. Your debt will be paid—in the blood of His sacrifice. You can be redeemed from the course you were on that did not lead to heaven and eternal rest with God. You need to be cleaned up and must realize that you are a "sinner in need of a savior" and being Jewish has nothing to do with that fact. Your sins have to be justified before God, covered, and then you need to be sanctified, washed clean from the sins of the past before God could look upon you and pass you into His heavenly domain when your time arrives. There is no other way to heaven but through Messiah. By His sacrifice He symbolically offers you the ticket to heaven, a free gift based on your willingness to recognize who He is. The decision to accept that gift of His salvation must be your choice

The Final Prophecy

alone. God does not want "coerced" brethren in heaven— complaining forever!

The prophets foretold every detail of Messiah, His life and His earthly death in exacting detail. There could be no validity to any other accounts or stories about Him. A Rabbi doesn't have to place himself in the position of denying the details of what God's Word declares. He does not have to come up with any stories to contradict prophecy, especially in this modern age. All he or anyone has to do is to not teach it to their congregation! I submit to you that the majority of the Rabbis "topical messages" from the Pulpits of our Synagogues need to be replaced with eternal issues. Our Jewish faith does not need topical messages about traditional Jewish matters. We need Jewish messages about Jewish "survival" when the Day of the Lord becomes a reality rather than a prophecy. The Middle East is in turmoil, terrorism has not only attacked Israel but has come against us right here in the United States. Terrorism is a long way off from being halted and many of us believe that the countdown to the "final prophecy" is drawing nearer, so close, in fact that we can sense the end of days upon us. Iran has continued to deceive us in their pursuit of developing nuclear weapons. Experts believe that they will have reached those goals very soon or they are hiding the fact that they already have nuclear capability. Are they not one of the major supporters of terrorism and do they not hate the western world and Israel especially? Who would they (Iran) sell nuclear weapons to if not terrorists? What of North Korea? Another threat to mankind for they too are pursing nuclear capability and are further along than we are led to believe. We don't have to guess what will occur, God has already told us all there is to know. He has provided us with the facts and it is what we do with that knowledge that counts. I would not wait too long to do something and that is to learn, to understand and to "act" upon that understanding. We need to solidify eternal insurance and our own assurance that to be "absent from the body is to be with the Lord." It is the only insurance that does not have a premium attached to it. The payment for those premiums was rendered a little over 2,000 years ago.

CHAPTER 13

Notes

1 The Jewish High Holy Holidays;

2 Prayer for the Deceased – family, relatives and friends. Standing for parents or a sister or brother and remaining seated for a friend or distant relative as was the tradition here.

3 To be justified in the simplest of explanations is to be represented by Messiah in heaven and it is shown that you have forgiveness of sin and are represented by He who sacrificed Himself for your sin. You cannot *justify* yourself before God!

4 The Jewish Primer, Himelstein, S. Dr., Pg. 71, The Jerusalem Publishing House, 1990

5 Isaiah 9:6

6 Statement printed by the Publisher in the Tanakh.

7 Exodus 19:12

8 Deuteronomy 6:4, Tanakh, Jewish Holy Scriptures, Pg. 284 The passage is from the 1917 printing of the Tanakh and was edited and changed in the 1985 printing from *"One"* to *"Alone"* Why did man choose to change what was originally written from the original manuscripts and the Dead Sea Scrolls? The reason is in the writing above.

9 There is a lack of unity among Ultra-Orthodox, Orthodox, the varied sects of Orthodox practices, Conservative and Reformed. A Doctrine is an overall understanding of the practicing of our faith that would bring us all closer and more unified.

10 Biblical term for the consummation of a marriage. In the Orthodox tradition, two "witnesses" (something shall be known) women would wait outside the door of the newly wed couple and take the marital bed-sheets to show to the Rabbi to prove that the Bride was in fact a virgin. If she was not, she had misrepresented and lied to the groom – or there had been sexual activity before the marriage. There were then options for both cases.

11 Genesis 3:15

12 Address by an Orthodox Rabbi from Miami in 1998

THE FINAL PROPHECY

13 This is a hypothetical but historic view based on extensive studies.

14 Ezekiel 39:4

15 See Daniel 9:26, Ezekiel 38:8, 11.14.

16 Mark 5:35-43 NT

17 Psalm 49:9

18 Ezekiel 26:19

19 Hebrew for Messiah

20 Previous statement from a Rabbi I referred to earlier.

21 Redemption- "the act of redeeming or the state of being redeemed, deliverance, rescue."

22 Romans 6:23 NT

Chapter Fourteen

Messiah in Prophecy and Acceptance

Denial is far easier than acceptance. As Jews we have a strong belief system and when it comes to our Judaic heritage, it is very difficult for us to change our beliefs regardless of what anyone tells us or shows us. We believe in "what we know" which has been concluded from whatever we have been taught. We have not learned beyond those "outside" acquired beliefs because we have not applied ourselves to Biblical study, seeking answers and truths, because limited time in this life seems to distract us from the pursuit of God—who should be the basis of our entire life. This may be a point for agreement however what if you were to discover that there were incredible truths that you did not know and truths that you "thought" were correct when in fact they are untrue or slanted? Not rumors or suppositions but pure, hard facts that were never taught to us so we still do not know the truths. Suppose one of those "unknowns" was that everlasting or eternal life is based solely upon the recognition of Messiah? Suppose your eternal destiny was at stake and all that the person attempting to reason with you was trying to do was present the facts, lay-out the truth, leaving the decision-making process totally up to you? It is a fair and intelligent scenario of why I am doing this so I encourage you to consider these last few Chapters very carefully. I can show you Messiah in prophecy but I cannot provide you with individual, spiritual acceptance—only He can give that to you. Man is full of picturesque, glowing and often tempting "words" that test our patience, our wills and often our belief system. In the end, the decision, the choices that affect our lives, our destinies are totally our choices. This would be especially true when the opportunity of learning truth is placed right in front of you. Then it becomes your choice and your consequence for the wrong choice. So let's continue to reason together and explore information you likely have never received from your Rabbi or your grandparents or even a Jewish relative. They, like you, did not spend a lot of time studying God's Word beyond Torah.

One of the most difficult barriers we Jews just can't seem to get past is the Deity of Messiah. Because of the total association of Yeshua with the non-Jewish or the Christian, Yeshua simply cannot (we believe) be the God of the Jews. He cannot be Deity. He cannot be "One" with God—or could He? Within the answer to that question is the insurance policy to eternal life, the policy of which the entire policy "premium" has already been paid for. The policy whose ownership was first written in blank and every name that appears on the face of the "beneficiary list" subsequently is written with indelible ink—it is written in the Jewish blood of Yeshua. If your own name is on that list, it was not included because you attended services last Yom Kippur. It is not included because you are a "good person." You have not received the insurance and the gift of eternal life by any other means than by the blood of Yeshua, the Messiah. Herein lies the single mystery that separates Jew and Christian, the single mystery that although is answered, shown and explained in Scriptures, it is the most difficult single fact for the Jewish, human mind to accept or to even deal with in the sense of Jewish thought-process.

Isaiah 44:6 declares, "This is what the Lord says—Israel's King and Redeemer, the Lord almighty: I am the first and I am the last; apart from me there is no God." Yes, those are the words of Scripture, along with Deuteronomy 6:4-5 and other verses that indicates that the Lord God is One—but God's Word also sows the seeker of Bible wisdom that He is indeed One—in three persons.

If we simply go back to my introducing you to the thoughts of Genesis 1:26 in the previous Chapter, I touched upon the fact that the Book of Creation is very clear that He (Messiah) and the Spirit of God (that equals two) was "from the beginning." God did not reveal Himself to us in that way but for the words given to Moses in describing the Spirit

CHAPTER **14**

hovering over the waters and then creating man in "Our" image, likened to "Us" and that is plural as I well defined for you. This is not a Catholic teaching or a Christian teaching or "any" teaching on any "exclusive" basis. This is God's Word telling us that He is One, but there is also a Son and a Spirit that is a part of His Holiness and all are a "Oneness" that are Three yet One. There is another verse in Genesis that I reserved for this portion of our reasoning together and that is Genesis 3:22 where God is speaking of Adam's sin and the fact that he had eaten from the Tree of Life. I will compare both the Tanakh, citing our Jewish Bible first, and then the identical verses from the New King James. Tanakh, Genesis 3:22, "And the Lord God said, "Now that the man has become like one of **us**, knowing good and bad, what if he should stretch out his hand and take also from the tree of life and eat, and live forever!" There is no denying the words of our very own Bible. The word "us" is as clear as it was in Genesis 1:26 where "Us" was also accompanied by "Our" image as well. The New King James recites the identical words for Genesis 3:22 with the exception that the word "us" is capitalized. Remaining in the Old Testament and recalling my statement that the Bible is shrouded in mystery because we have eyes that do not see—meaning we do not study, we do not search for knowledge and understanding as we should and as God has directed us in Scripture. Some of us however, do seek the truths of God and that was the over one million Jews I spoke of previously who have found these mysteries and discovered the answers in Yeshua. Remaining in Tanakh, the Proverbs (of Solomon), 30:4 declares, "Who has ascended heaven, and come down? Who has gathered up the wind in the hollow of his hand? Who had wrapped the waters in his garment? Who has established all the extremities of the earth? What is *his* name or *his son's* name, if you know it?" Once again, the only difference between the verse in Tanakh and the verse in the New King James complete Holy Bible is that the words "His" and "Son's" are capitalized out of respect for Deity. Did the verse not state "Son?"

Now we have God and we have God's Son, the One we call Yeshua and Messiah. If I were to continue along this line of pointing out the directions of Scripture, the arrows of verses that all lead to the mystery of three-in-one would be another book within this book, so let us take but

The Final Prophecy

a few more verses and remain in the Old Testament. The prophet Isaiah relates a vision to the people of Israel. The vision is God pleading with His people to repent, to turn away from sin. This is not Isaiah's words but the Word of God being spoken *as* God through Isaiah. Isaiah 48:16, "Come near to *Me*, hear this: *I* have not spoken in secret from the *beginning*. From the time that it was (the beginning) I was there. And now the *Lord God and His Spirit, Have sent Me."* The words are from God alone for only God has existed from the "beginning." God has shown us the name "I AM" from the beginning. Have you seen the message in behalf of the other two divine persons? The LORD, God and the Spirit of God—the "Lord God has "sent Me." The Lord God sent "Me" His Son, Yeshua and the "Spirit of God." The Lord God would be *Adonai Jehovah* a title for God the Father. "Sent Me" proceeds from the Father, from "I AM." If you were to once again engage one who speaks Hebrew, go to the original text and verify the perfection and the revelation of these words. There is another verse in Isaiah that reveals the position of Yeshua within the Three and that is Isaiah 9:6. This is one of those verses that only intensive study would reveal not the surface meaning of the verse but the deeper meaning as well. In the King James Bible there are five titles given and yet "Wonderful Counselor" can correctly be treated as components of but one title. The components within this verse show us that God is "One" being in three Persons. This is why his name was called "The stumbling block to the Jews" in the New Testament. That is the sad part—Yeshua came for we Jews in the first place and "His own did not esteem Him."

The most compelling argument for Yeshua as Messiah lies within the prophecies themselves, as He alone fulfilled them. Those who believe He is "yet to come" would have Him fulfilling these prophecies all over again and that is literally impossible. The most critical and intensive studies by some of the most brilliant men in history have studied, torn apart, attempted to disprove word for word, sentence for sentence and manuscript by manuscript of the Old and the New Testaments. All who set out to disprove, in the end—some after devoting a good part of their lifetimes, became believers. You can't deny something that declares truth to your brain and your soul! Many books have been published on the prophecies of Messiah however the best source of discovering them is

CHAPTER 14

the Book that God wrote, the Bible. It provides all the prophecies in the Old Testament and the details of the fulfillment of each one in the New Testament. The problem for most people is setting aside the time to study them so I have listed "some" of the key prophecies that I feel are important to your understanding the complete picture of Messiah and the end of times. The prophecies begin with and end with Yeshua.

The Seed of the Woman—Genesis 3:15 Here God declared that Messiah will come from the seed of a woman, not the seed of a man— a supernatural conception from God alone. "But when the fullness of the time had come, God sent forth His Son, born of a woman, born under the law." Betrothed to Joseph, Mary was a virgin when she told Joseph of her blessed conception. Through his love for her and after he received visit from an angel confirming the divine nature of her condition, Joseph married her, took her away and never lay with her once through the pregnancy. The main point is the virginity and purity of a woman who can be traced in genealogy directly to the line of David. We know that Joseph suffered disgrace when the local Rabbi found out of this pregnancy as the Orthodox law called for purity until the wedding night.

God's Word always supports itself and verses affirming Yeshua as Messiah are in Psalms 22 and 89. There are verses in other Psalms that allude to Messiah however these two to provide us with undeniable, direct reference to Messiah. They speak of things that only He would be able to fulfill. I will begin with Psalm 89 and after one reads this there is no other conclusion than this Psalm points directly to Yeshua. The Psalm speaks of God reiterating His covenant with David and that David's seed would rule on the throne of Israel forever. (verse 3-4) In verses 20-24 it is said that God has established His chosen one who will never be defeated. He will be God's hand across the sea and would be anointed, "...and His seed also I will make to endure forever, And His throne as the days of heaven." It surely appears to be referencing Messiah but how do we know it is Yeshua? Because only He was of the seed of David and only His seed will go on forever. Verse 26-27, "He shall cry to Me, 'You are My Father, My God and the rock of My salvation. Also I will make Him My firstborn, The highest of the kings of the earth."

The Final Prophecy

If you are thinking that the verses of Psalm 89 sound more conquering than suffering, we will interpret Psalm 22. All the prophets agree that Psalm 22 relates His suffering and His purpose.

(1) **The Seed of Abraham**—Genesis 22:18—"In your seed all the nations of the earth shall be blessed, because you have obeyed My voice." & NT Galatians 3: 16 – "Now to Abraham and his Seed were the promises made". He does not say, "And to seeds," as of many, but as of one, "And to your Seed, who is Yeshua".

(2) **Messiah would be of the Seed of David**—Psalm 132:11. "The LORD has sworn in truth to David; He will not turn from it: "I will set upon your throne the fruit of your body." Jeremiah 23:5— "Behold, the days are coming," says the LORD, "That I will raise to David a Branch of righteousness; A King shall reign and prosper, And execute judgment and righteousness in the earth." & NT Acts 13:23— "From this man's seed, according to the promise, God raised up for Israel a Savior—Yeshua." The lineage of Yeshua through Mary is traced directly to David, generation by generation in The New Testament, Matthew Chapter One, and it is precise in every name and every generation. It is also interesting to note that Joseph, husband of Mary traced his lineage to David as well.[1]

(3) **To Come from the Tribe of Judah**—Genesis 49:10, "The scepter will not depart from Judah, nor the ruler's staff from between his feet, until he comes to whom it belongs and the obedience of the nation is his." with NT Hebrews 7:14 "For it is evident that our Lord arose from Judah….."

CHAPTER 14

(4) **Messiah must come at a** *"specified"* **time**—Daniel 9:24-25 and Matthew 21:1-11 "Seventy weeks are determined, For your people and for your holy city, To finish the transgressions, To make an end of sins, To make reconciliation for iniquity, To bring an everlasting righteousness, To seal up vision and prophecy, And to anoint the Most Holy, Know, therefore and understand, That from the going forth of the command, To restore and build Jerusalem, Until Messiah the Prince, There shall be seven weeks and sixty-two weeks; The street shall be built again, and the wall, Even in troublesome times." The timing in "weeks" are literally "years" and not "days" as is depicted in Daniel 10:2-3 where Daniel is speaking of "mourning for three full weeks." In the Book of Nehemiah, Chapter Two, we see the order given for Israelites to return to Jerusalem from captivity to rebuild the wall, the city and the Temple. This was about 445 B.C. If the prophecy is mathematically calculated, you will find that the total time prophesied for the coming of Messiah was 483 years. This was fulfilled in the New Testament in Matthew 21:1-11, 9 Nisan, A.D. 30 when Yeshua also fulfilled the prophecy of Isaiah and rode into Jerusalem on a donkey on the very day that Daniel's time line depicts. The time line by Daniel also leaves one week or one seven year period that will remain as the final part or week of that prophecy. That final week is the essence of the need to reason over these facts. That "week" could begin tomorrow.

(5) **Born of a Virgin**—Isaiah 7:14 "Therefore the Lord Himself will give you a sign; The virgin will be with child and will give birth to a son, and will call him Immanuel." with NT Matthew 1:18-23 See comments on Seed of a Woman above. Also see Chapter Fourteen "Who is Messiah"

The Final Prophecy

(6) **Born at Bethlehem of Judea**—Micah 5:2 with NT Matthew 2:1 & Luke 2:3 "But you, Bethlehem, Ephrathah, though you are little among the thousands of Judah, Yet out of you shall come forth to Me, The One to be Ruler in Israel, Whose goings forth are from old, From everlasting." Did you know that this was also the birthplace of David? (1 Samuel 16, Isaiah 9:6 -7 "For unto us a Child is born, Unto us a Son is given; And the government will be upon His shoulder. And His name will be called Wonderful Counselor, Mighty God, Everlasting Father, Prince of Peace. Of the increase of His government and peace, There will be no end, Upon the throne of David and over His kingdom. To order it and establish it with judgment and justice, From that time forward, even forever. The zeal of the Lord of hosts will perform this."

(7) **Visited and Adored**—Psalm 72:10 with NT Matthew 2:1-11 "The kings of Tarshish and of the isles Will bring presents; The kings of Sheba and Seba will offer gifts." These are the three who followed a new and brilliant star that was prophesied would appear over Bethlehem when Yeshua was born. Also see #8

(8) **The slaughter of innocents by a Roman king**—Jeremiah 31:15— "Thus says the Lord: "A voice was heard in Ramah, Lamentation and bitter weeping, Rachel weeping for her children, Refusing to be comforted for her children, Because they are no more" and NT Matthew 2:16-18—"Then Herod, when he saw that he was deceived by the wise men, was exceedingly angry; and he sent forth and put to death all the male children who were in Bethlehem and in all its districts, from two years old and under, according to the time which he had determined from the wise men." King Herod the Great upon hearing of the birth of the foretold

CHAPTER **14**

child who would be King of Israel, sent his soldiers into Bethlehem to kill the first born male of each family. Even the Roman Governor had heard of the prophecies of the coming Messiah. The Governor did what the Pharisees would also do thirty years later from that day. They did not want to lose their wealth, influence and power to a "King of the Jews." Herod sent soldiers "to" kill Him and the Pharisees conspired to "have" Him killed. The first time was not meant to be and the second was the fulfillment of both His mission and the prophecies concerning His sacrifice for us.

(9) **Preceded by John** as a forerunner to announce His coming and before entering public ministry—Isaiah 40:3, Malachi 3:1, with NT Luke 1:17 and Matthew 3:1-3. John was the son of Elizabeth and anointed by God to be the forerunner for Yeshua and announced His coming under stringent, sacrificial conditions so he would have no connections with the Pharisees or with the world.

(10) **A prophet likened to Moses**—Deuteronomy 18:18 with NT Acts 3:20-22 "For Moses truly said to the fathers, 'The LORD your God will raise up for you a Prophet like me from your brethren. Him you shall hear in all things, whatever He says to you. And it shall be that every soul who will not hear that Prophet shall be utterly destroyed from among the people." Moses was set in a basket in the Nile so as not to be slaughtered by the Egyptians. Yeshua was taken out of Jerusalem and brought to Egypt to be spared the slaughter by Herod the Great. Moses was sent by God to free us from Egypt. Yeshua was sent by God to free us from sin.

(11) **A special anointing of the Holy Spirit**—Psalm 45:7 "You love righteousness and hate wickedness; Therefore God, Your God, has anointed You With the oil of gladness more than Your companions." Isaiah 11:2— The Spirit of the LORD shall rest upon Him, The Spirit of wisdom and understanding, The Spirit of counsel and might, The Spirit of knowledge and of the fear of the LORD. Isaiah 61:1, with NT Matthew 3:16, Luke 4:15-21, 43 The day that Yeshua came to the Jordan River to begin His three year ministry to fulfill all that the prophets had foretold. At that time the Spirit of God descended upon Him as a dove and the power of heaven was within Him as a man of flesh but also a Deity sent to fulfill the mission of Salvation for mankind.

(12) **Messiah was to be a "priest" after the order of Melchizedeck**— Psalm 110:4 with NT Hebrews 5:5-6—"You are a priest forever, according to the order of Melchizedek."

(13) **Messiah was to be a Redeemer for the Jews and the Gentiles as** *well*—Isaiah 42:1-4 "Behold! My Servant whom I uphold, My Elect One in whom My soul delights! I have put My Spirit upon Him; He will bring forth justice to the Gentiles" with NT Matthew 12:18-21 This is a key prophecy for Yeshua was sent to free us from sin once and for all, but also to offer the grace of God to the non-Jews long before the advent of Christianity by all Jews from Jerusalem who believed in Yeshua. The non-Jews were referred to as Gentiles.

(14) **Messiah was to begin His ministry in Galilee**— Isaiah 9:1-2 with NT Matthew 4:12, 16-23 "And leaving Nazareth, He came and dwelt in Capernaum,

CHAPTER **14**

which is by the sea, in the regions of Zebulun and Naphtali, that it might be fulfilled which was spoken by Isaiah the prophet, saying: "The land of Zebulun and the land of Naphtali, By the way of the sea, beyond the Jordan, Galilee of the Gentiles: The people who sat in darkness have seen a great light, And upon those who sat in the region and shadow of death Light has dawned." It would not only fulfill the prophecies but was so appropriate that the One who would save all those who were Gentiles, not knowing God and without the chance of Salvation, was the Jewish Messiah. It is also ironic but the fulfillment of the prophecy for our people stated, "Can anything good come out of Galilee?" Just about all that Yeshua did was in direct opposition to the hypocritical practices of the Pharisees.

(15) **Messiah was to enter Jerusalem as Hosanna**—Zechariah 9:9 with NT Matthew 21:1-5 "But when the chief priests and scribes saw the wonderful things that He did, and the children crying out in the temple and saying, "Hosanna to the Son of David!" they were indignant and said to Him, "Do You hear what these are saying?" As Yeshua rode into Jerusalem the very day that the prophets said He would, people shouted "Hosanna" and laid palm leaves and their coats before His path. Also see Daniel 9:24-25, Matthew 21:1-11.

(16) **Messiah was to enter the Temple**—Hag. 2:7-9 & Malachi 3:1 with NT Matthew 21:12 – "Then Yeshua went into the temple of God and drove out all those who bought and sold in the temple, and overturned the tables of the money changers and the seats of those who sold doves. And He said to them, "It is written, 'My house shall be called a house of prayer, but you have made it a 'den of thieves." Yeshua opened the cages of the ani-

mals being sold for sacrifices and overturned the tables where the priests and the Pharisees were making money at the expense of the poor who had to change their currency from other lands into the currency of Rome when they came to sacrifice for their sins at the Temple in Jerusalem. The money was to buy an animal to offer as a sacrifice and depending upon how much money you could afford, one could purchase anything from a bird to an unblemished lamb. This was why Yeshua overturned the money changers tables as it was about commerce and not about God's business of repentance from sin.

(17) **Messiah would teach in Parables**—Psalm 78:2 – "I will open my mouth in a parable; I will utter dark sayings of old," with NT Matthew 13:34-35. To those who would believe His words, the parables had great meaning. But to those who would not believe the very same message was nonsense to their ears.

(18) **Messiah's ministry would be characterized by miracles**—Isaiah 35:5-6 "Then the eyes of the blind shall be opened, And the ears of the deaf shall be unstopped." with NT Matthew 11:4-6, John 11:47. "Then the chief priests and the Pharisees gathered a council and said, "What shall we do? For this Man works many signs. If we let Him alone like this, everyone will believe in Him, and the Romans will come and take away both our place and nation." There was an eye witness to every miracle that Yeshua performed, miracles that no mortal man could accomplish. The blind were cured, cripples walked, deformities that were afflictions from birth were cured and limbs made whole. He brought a child back to life and the incredible day amidst hundreds of witnesses

that Yeshua brought His friend Lazarus back from the dead! These were not mere claims but witnessed miracles that only Messiah could provide. He was sent as the Great Physician to heal the sick and the broken hearted.

(19) **Messiah would be rejected by His own people**—Psalm 69:8, Isaiah 53:3 with NT John 1:11, John 7:5 –"For even His brothers did not believe in Him." The Pharisees saw to it that He was denounced so that there was no chance of His gaining the following of the people and taking their power away from them. Let us not forget that the people were expecting the conquering Messiah and not a man who was both flesh and Divinity spreading a message of love your enemies!

(20) **Messiah was to be a "Stone of stumbling to our people and a "Rock" of offense**—Isaiah 8:14 with NT Romans 9:32 & 1 Peter 2:7-8 "Behold, I lay in Zion, A chief cornerstone, elect, precious, And he who believes on Him will by no means be put to shame. Therefore, to you who believe, He is precious; but to those who are disobedient, "The stone which the builders rejected has become the chief cornerstone, and "A stone of stumbling and a rock of offense." Yeshua was and is the cornerstone of the building of a faith that could never be put down or silenced. Make no mistake, Christians suffered and died for their faith and unlike our suffering, they chose to do so in not denying Yeshua. To this very day, the voice of Martyrs can be heard all over the world, as evil attempts to defeat the good and no one of faith will give up that which is more precious than earthly life.

(21) **Messiah would be hated without cause**—Psalm 69:4—"Those who hate me without a cause Are more

than the hairs of my head; They are mighty who would destroy me, Being my enemies wrongfully; Though I have stolen nothing, I still must restore it." Isaiah 49:7, with NT John 7:48, John 15:25 – "But *this happened* that the word might be fulfilled which is written in their law, 'They hated Me without a cause." Again, we have the suffering Messiah and not the conquering Messiah, hated for not freeing the Jews from Roman rule and then being crucified on a cross which was despicable to the Jews. It was the Roman style of execution and any Jew that was crucified "had to have been" a criminal! The Pharisees hated Him because He was a threat to their very existence and their power. I personally believe that there was so much more to the Pharisees rejection of Yeshua that we will never know until we get to the place where every question will be answered. The whole problem has always been that no one can come back and tell us the answers!

(22) **Messiah would be rejected by the rulers** (Pharisees)—Psalm 118:22—"The stone which the builders rejected Has become the chief cornerstone." with NT Matthew 21:42, John 7:48. See #21

(23) **Messiah would be betrayed by a friend**—Psalm 41:9—"Even my own familiar friend in whom I trusted, Who ate my bread, Has lifted up his heel against me." Psalm 55:12-14 with NT John 13:18, 21. This refers to Judas who for thirty pieces of silver conspired to have Yeshua arrested by the Pharisees. Why? Because Judas, in his heart of hearts believed that if the Pharisees arrested Yeshua, He would then fight back and overthrow all of them and take the throne of David. He never understood and when it became apparent to him what he had done,

CHAPTER 14

he hung himself in what would become Potters Field, the "field of blood." The branch that Judas hung himself on broke and he was split open by the jagged pieces of pottery discarded there.

(24) **Messiah would be forsaken by His disciples**—Zech. 13:7—with NT Matthew 26:31-56 Even those who followed Him and loved Him were afraid when Messiah did not conquer the Romans but rather went along to be killed by the Romans, all instigated by the Pharisees. His disciples ran and hid themselves when Yeshua was arrested and even Simon Peter, one of the disciples who dearly loved Yeshua, denied Yeshua three times before the rooster crowed—and Yeshua told him that he would do so just a day before His arrest. .

(25) **Messiah would be "sold-out" for thirty pieces of silver**—Zechariah 11:12 with NT Matthew 26:15 Judas made the deal with the Pharisees, to give Yeshua away to them for Judas knew where to find Yeshua praying. He eventually threw the 30 pieces of silver back at them when he realized what he had done. But the prophets said it would be and little did this betrayer know that he was carrying out the very prophecy that was about four hundred years before he was even born. See #24.

(26) **That price would be paid for the "Potters Field"**—Zech. 11:13—"And the LORD said to me, "Throw it to the potter"—that princely price they set on me. So I took the thirty pieces of silver and threw them into the house of the LORD for the potter" with NT Matthew 27: 7—"And they consulted together and bought with them the potter's field, to bury strangers in." See #24.

The Final Prophecy

(27) **Messiah would be smitten on the cheek**—Micah 5:1— "Now gather yourself in troops, O daughter of troops; He has laid siege against us; They will strike the judge of Israel with a rod on the cheek with NT Matthew 27:30. When the Roman soldiers struck Yeshua on the left cheek, He turned His right as He had preached to thousands to "turn the other cheek" instead of fighting back. This was even more infuriating to those who wanted Him to conquer the Roman rule.

(28) **Messiah would be spat upon**—Isaiah 50:6 with NT Matthew 27:30

During the time that Yeshua was arrested and awaited going before the Roman Governor (the death penalty had been revoked from the Jewish rule and only the Roman Governor could order a man put to death on the cross) the Roman guards who mocked Him and beat Him spat on Him but once, just as the prophets declared. He did not say a word nor even verbally or outwardly show any hatred or anger towards these men. Only supernatural power could allow the flesh to take so much physical abuse and so much pain that no mere man could have ever endured.

(29) **Messiah would be mocked**—Psalm 22:7-8 with NT Matthew 27:31 and 39-44 The Roman soldiers mocked Him and placed a robe upon Him and a crown of thorns upon His head, mocking Him and laughing at Him, calling Him the "King of the Jews." See #28 above.

(30) **Messiah would be beaten**—Psalm 22 with NT Matthew 26:67, 27:26, 30. See #29 above.

CHAPTER 14

(31) **Messiah's hands (wrists) and His feet were to be pierced**—Psalm 22:16 – "For dogs have surrounded Me; The congregation of the wicked has enclosed Me. They pierced My hands and My feet;" Zech. 12:10 with NT John 19:18 John 19:37 and John 20:25 2 Prophecies depict that Yeshua had to be sacrificed. Crucifixion in that time was the only way that one was put to death. Do you realize that any of the zealots or criminals could have been put up to killing Yeshua in the night but this was the only way that the Pharisees could shame Him for all of Jerusalem to see, hence putting down any rumor or notion of His claims of Deity. Did they not know that the prophets already declared this hundreds of years ago?

(32) **Not a bone of His was to be broken**—Exodus 12:46, Psalm 34:20 with NT John 19:33-36—"But one of the soldiers pierced His side with a spear, and immediately blood and water came out. And he who has seen has testified, and his testimony is true; and he knows that he is telling the truth, so that you may believe. For these things were done that the Scripture should be fulfilled, "Not one of His bones shall be broken." And again another Scripture says, "They shall look on Him whom they pierced." This was a prophecy that no man hanging from and nailed to a cross could contrive. The rule of crucifixion was that after some hours, a Roman guard would come along with a club and break the shin bones of each man being crucified. You see, when one is nailed to a pole or cross there is a small piece of wood beneath his feet which his ankles are also tied and nailed to. He must lift himself up using this piece of wood below his feet in order to get air to his lungs. After a while, any man of less than extraordinary strength would not be able to lift himself any more and would suffocate. If a man hung too long, the breaking of the

shin bones would obviously prevent lifting oneself up. The prophecies declared that not a bone would be broken on the body of Yeshua. There were two other men who were crucified with Yeshua, one on each side of Him. (One of the two declared that Yeshua was surely Messiah). Both their shin bones were broken but when the Guard came to Yeshua, he did not because the guard saw Yeshua was dead. To make sure however, the guard took his spear and pierced the side of Yeshua and blood and water poured out. Surely He was dead and the water and blood was from the pericardium sack that surrounds the heart. Yeshua gave up His Spirit after this sack burst open as though He had died of a broken heart for the sinfulness of man. [3]

(33) **Messiah would suffer thirst**—Psalm 22:15 with NT John 19:28 #34 and 35# are related prophecies, one preceding the other.

(34) **Messiah would be given vinegar to drink**—Psalm 69:21— "They also gave me gall for my food, And for my thirst they gave me vinegar to drink" with NT Matthew 27:34

(35) **Messiah was to be "numbered with the transgressors**—Isaiah 53:12 –"Therefore I will divide Him a portion with the great, And He shall divide the spoil with the strong, Because He poured out His soul unto death, And He was numbered with the transgressors, And He bore the sin of many, And made intercession for the transgressors." with NT Matthew 27:38 To His right and His left were two other men who were being crucified who were criminals. Yeshua was not guilty of a single sin, much less any crime. Even the Roman guard below at the end declared that "surely this man was

CHAPTER 14

Messiah.

(36) **Psalm 22 – The Suffering Messiah, the Sacrifice for our Sin.** Psalm 22, written by David, was a testimony to the visions he had of Messiah. Within this Psalm you will find details that could only have been fulfilled by the real Messiah. I urge you to read Psalm 22 for yourself.

(37) **Messiah's body was to be buried with the wealthy**—Isaiah 53:9— And they made His grave with the wicked— But with the rich at His death, Because He had done no violence, Nor was any deceit in His mouth." with NT Matthew 27:57-60. A wealthy believer gave up his own tomb and went to the Roman Governor to gain permission to have Yeshua buried there.

(38) **Messiah's body would not see corruption**—Psalm 16:10 with NT Acts 2:31 "Therefore He also says in another Psalm: 'You will not allow Your Holy One to see corruption." Not one single sin could be found in Yeshua. Not a crime, not an offense, not a bad word for even the Pharisees who had Him put to death. Even the Roman Governor sent Yeshua to the Provincial Governor because he could find "no sin in this man" and surely no reason for putting Him to death as the Pharisees had requested be done to Him.

(39) **Messiah was to be raised from the dead**—Psalm 2:7, 16:10 with NT Acts 13:33-35 [4] "God has fulfilled this for us their children, in that He has raised up Yeshua. As it is also written in the second Psalm: 'You are My Son, Today I have begotten You. And that He raised Him from the dead, no more to return to corruption, He has spoken thus: 'I will give you the sure mercies of

The Final Prophecy

David.' There is no question that without the resurrection of Yeshua after three days, there could be no belief in Him as the true Messiah. Resurrection was the key factor. If it were not true, reasoned one of the Pharisees, the whole "matter" would simply go away. If it was true and it was of God—nothing could stop such a powerful truth. His resurrection could never be put-down. So important was making sure that no one stole the body of Yeshua, a full Roman Guard (sixteen men) were ordered to be placed around His tomb day and night and for the full three days and nights, no one could approach that tomb under penalty of death. The body of Yeshua was wrapped tightly in burial cloth from head to toe. This was a gauze-like cloth that when fully wrapped, was completely covered with a paste-like mixture of spices. He was carried into the tomb and placed on a rock-like ledge by the Roman Guards. This tomb was hewn into the rock of the mountain and there was no way in or out except through the front opening. The guards rolled the huge stone (that weighed several tons) into place from its perch on the slight incline, once the wedge at the front base was removed. The stone rolled into the opening of the tomb like a "wedged" seal, slamming into place forevermore—so one would think. Then, a Roman Seal was placed across the stone's edge to the wall of the tomb. That seal was a marker that clearly stated that anyone interfering with that Seal, breaking it or removing it in any way was subject to be put to death. After three days, when the tomb was found empty, one of the findings that was seen from peering into the tomb and never stepping foot within was the burial cloth, fully in tact and simply empty of the earthly body that three days ago it had encased. Yeshua did not un-wrap the burial cloth for it was perfectly formed as it had been first wrapped around Him. Yeshua appeared to His followers, His

CHAPTER 14

disciples and to over five hundred witnesses who saw Yeshua alive after the resurrection.

(40) Messiah was to ascend to the right hand of God—Psalm 68:18—"You have ascended on high, You have led captivity captive; You have received gifts among men, Even from the rebellious, That the LORD God might dwell there" with NT Luke 24:51, Acts 1:9 and Psalm 110:1 with Hebrews 1:3—"who being the brightness of His glory and the express image of His person, and upholding all things by the word of His power, when He had by Himself purged our sins, sat down at the right hand of the Majesty on high" His ascent to heaven was literally being "taken up in the clouds" the very same way that He will return after the Great Tribulation. Yeshua did not ascend without witnesses, those who watched Him until He disappeared from view towards the heavens. The event was recorded just as any of the miracles Yeshua performed were witnessed and recorded, but it was the resurrection and then His ascent that spurred the beginnings of believers that would rather die than deny any of this happened—and they were all Jewish. At first, I considered providing an account of all the prophecies however that would have practically doubled the content of this book. I also realized that alone would not create within you the belief and acceptance of who Yeshua is. Only the Spirit of God can demonstrate to you that Yeshua was and is the Messiah of Israel.

THE FINAL PROPHECY

Notes

1 Luke 3:23

2 In Psalm 22 you may read of his death by crucifixion that is portrayed in great detail.

3 He would be the substitute for our sins, the sacrifice for all times.

Chapter Fifteen

Sin and Salvation

Four of the most misused words I have ever heard are, "I'm a good person." On several occasions, I recall asking, "What is a good person?" The replies were mixed but essentially the reply was, "I don't sin!" As I look back on the lives of my grandparents, I could sincerely say that they were two people who lived a pure and decent life, however I would never say that they never sinned—we all do. The expression, *"I'm a good person"* is without merit in the natural and spiritual order of things in this life. There is no such thing as a "good person." There are good hearted people, kind and generous people and even thoughtful and loving people. Although they have wonderful attributes they are burdened with the inheritance of sin. Adam and Eve were "good persons" until they sinned against God. Noah was a good person but he got drunk and fell asleep naked. Moses was a good person yet, because of sin, he never got to step foot on the land beyond the Jordan River because he disobeyed God. His only vision of the land God gave the Israelites was from the plains of Moab before God "took him up" and his body was never found. Jonah was a good person but he ran from God's instructions and almost died as a result of his disobedience. Abraham was a good person but he lied to Pharaoh about Sarah being his sister while passing through Egypt. Abraham lied out of fear that they would kill him and take Sarah for the Pharaoh's harem. He also disobeyed God when he was told which portion of land he should occupy. He gave his nephew Lot the first choice to keep the peace between them instead of being obedient to what God

The Final Prophecy

told him to do. David was a man after God's own heart yet the same David took another man's wife as his bride after practically ordering her husband's death by having him placed on the front lines of battle. Then there was the matter of adultery that David committed with her prior to that incident. All of this sin cost David his first born son. I believe you are beginning to get the idea. I don't know how anyone can think of themselves as a quasi-righteous or a "good person" for the prophet Isaiah declares that man's self-professed righteousness is likened to "filthy rags." We tend to forget all too soon where we have been as a people and how we have survived. We owe our survival to the grace of God. Our gratefulness has turned to arrogance and God Himself has called us a stiff-necked and stubborn people. Moses addressed our ancestors as "A perverse and crooked generation."[1] When Moses completed writing the Law in a Book, he told the Levites to place the Book of the Law beside the Ark of the Covenant. Then Moses declared, "That it may be there as a witness against you, for I know your rebellion and your stiff-neck ways."[2] Moses knew the nature of people and knew that once they entered the promised freedom of their own homeland, they would succumb to the ways of the world. Simply think of the sinfulness at the base of Mt. Sinai while Moses was receiving God's commandments. What do you think has changed in all these years? The real problem is that the majority of our people do not understand the true essence of sin. We understand transgressions, trespasses and iniquities but for some reason we do not relate to the word sin.

It was sometime ago that a prominent, American psychiatrist[3] noted that there was one word that spoke for the tragic state of contemporary life. The simple word was "sin." I do not have to account for the tragedies that have beset this world that date back as far as you wish to go. Most of those tragedies that we view as horrific events were motivated by the consequences of sin. Hatefulness, greed, pride, envy, deceit, jealousy are all the results of an innate, sinful nature that only God's Spirit can overcome. We are not "good" by our own works or our nature but by the grace of God and certainly not of ourselves. It has been a difficult task convincing others that you do not have to be a bank robber or a murderer to be a sinner. Could it be that we are stuck in the mindset

CHAPTER **15**

of "self-justification?" Justifying our actions becomes automatic, without thought or regret but also without restraint. We become so used to doing certain things in our lifetime that we do not consider them as sinful but rather ordinary. The heart speaks a language of emotions and one would not deny that whether we term it passion or emotions, most of we Jews seem to have a heart filled with both. In the New Testament, Yeshua said, "For out of the abundance of the heart the mouth speaks." (See Matthew 12: 34) If a heart is filled with love, than loving words will flow from the lips, but if a heart is filled with anger, resentment and even hatred than the words of one's lips will be far from loving. The Old Testament is filled with expressions from the Torah that support this statement. Leviticus 19: 17-18 declares, 'You shall not hate your brother in your heart. You shall surely rebuke your neighbor, and not bear sin because of him. You shall not take vengeance, nor bear any grudge against the children of your people, but you shall love your neighbor as yourself: I am the LORD." Deuteronomy 13:3 speaks of the heart being filled with love for the Lord, that which allows that love to extend to mankind, "for the LORD your God is testing you to know whether you love the LORD your God with all your heart and with all your soul" There are over 300 verses in the Old Testament that deal with the "condition of the heart." Jeremiah 29:13 tells us exactly how we should find God, "You will seek Me and find Me, when you search for Me with all your heart." Out of the heart of man comes blessing and cursing. Out of the heart of man comes love and hate. Out of the heart of man comes God's Word or the evil that evil thoughts have sown over the years. That is why the profession of faith must come from the heart and not just from the lips. In the New Testament, the Apostle Paul tells us, "That if you confess with your mouth, 'Yeshua is Lord' and believe in your heart that God raised Him from the dead, you will be saved (you will receive salvation for everlasting life). It does not get any plainer than that.

Within every one of us is the knowledge that we shall one-day pass from this world. As we grow older, time seems to pass much more rapidly and we awake each morning wondering "where the time has gone." The one thing that we have failed to recognize is that nothing we do or say in this world will assure us of immortality. You can think it and you can listen

The Final Prophecy

to the Rabbis of the world tell us "All Jews go to heaven and find eternal peace." Unfortunately we have believed them but this is simply not true. Even the ancient Sadducees and the Pharisees disagreed with each other on the resurrection of man. These were two of the most powerful, Jewish ruling parties in ancient Jerusalem. (It was the Sadducees who taught there was no resurrection). (See NT Luke 20:27)

There are many aspects to being a "good person" but that is not the requirement to enter eternal life. Are you a husband who has never in his married life, focused his eyes on another woman with even the slightest lust in his heart? Are you a husband who is the spiritual leader of his home and directs the family in every Jewish Holiday, holding Bible studies and educating his children on the history of Israel and our people? Have you (man or woman) ever held malice in your heart for another or uttered a profane word against another? Have you ever cheated anyone in business? I could go on, however you get the idea. No one can answer yes to every question or profess obedience to the over 600 laws that no human being could possibly abide by. You may be a good person according to society but according to God you are a sinner. You are surely not "righteous" in the eyes of God and "heaven" does not have an "open door policy" as many Rabbis would have you believe. The Book of Proverbs tells us that, "Whom He loves He corrects?"[4] If God did not put you through trials of learning curves and you continued to repeat the same sinfulness over and over again, God knows that He will eventually lose you to the enemy, for the wages of sin is spiritual death. There is an age-old adage that states, "We should learn from our mistakes." Satan knows this weakness within human nature all too well. If you do not believe in the fact that Satan and evil truly exist, you are one of those who have been totally deceived into thinking that "going it alone" in this world is the right thing to do. Never underestimate the power of evil in this world because you are no match for that power. You are human, finite and only God can keep you from being snatched right into the pits of Sheol. Spiritual forces that exist around us is a subject that most Rabbis do not readily teach. Good vs. Evil is the battle that has claimed the lives of countless people throughout history and most are eternally suffering for taking the wrong side of that battle. There is no middle ground, no

CHAPTER 15

retreat to regroup and go back to contemplate which side you want to be on. We know what sin is and the consequences of sin. We have been persecuted, have suffered and have fought through most of the atrocities that have been waged against our people. Yet, I ask you, are we alone? Have we forgotten our history so quickly, not just American History but history that begins with Genesis 1:1. Tomorrow's history (even within the next hour of your life) is unknown to man but the ending and the new beginning is already predestined and there is no changing it or altering the course of God's will. The final prophecy will be fulfilled and it is only a matter of when.

Most of us have not learned from history and we continue to remain in our sin and in hold on to the stubbornness of refusing to understand what needs to be done to get out of it. Why do these things happen, you wonder, those "bad things that happen to good people." They are a result of sin. Two brothers, Cain and Abel, one of them filled with hatred, jealousy and the resulting murder of his own brother. Sin comes in many forms and in many variations, some of them resulting from a lack of spiritual guidance and uncontrolled anger, while others suffer from the inability to withstand temptation. Sin comes out of unchecked jealousy, hate and contempt for others who are unlike us, especially when we belittle non-Jews or minority groups and the less fortunate then ourselves, for the same God that created you is the same God that created all of mankind. Sin is your calling someone a name that is a racist remark or an insult reflecting bigotry. It is all labeled as sin because God loves all His creations and not just His chosen people. The sin itself may be minimal in your thinking, gradually becoming familiar and seemingly not such a bad thing to have done—until the consequences become a sad reality. An example would be the casual flirtation between two married people in a workplace setting that eventually leads to an office friendship that eventually leads to "My wife (husband) doesn't understand me!" The flirtation was the lure, the lunch was the set-up and the result was sin. It was gradual, building the notion that it's "okay—no one will ever know and it's only this once" and that is how the evil deception operates. Why do you think God created women to be so attractive to men? It was for the beautiful consummation of marriage, the experience of two being one, husband and wife and the bearing of God's children. Were you aware that even talking badly about your spouse to another is a sin? You are supposed to hold each other in high esteem, in a mutual commitment from the promise you made to God when you said, "I do. You promised each other a life-long relationship of marital sanctity, until "death do us part." How do many marriages fail? Couples try to make it on their own—without God. You invited God to the wedding and then you kept Him out of the marriage.

My point has been to illustrate to you in some small way that sin, in its simplest or most perverse form is part of everyday life. The battle to keep ourselves out of the throws of sin is a battle that you can not win without the army of God behind you. Satan is stronger than you are but not against God. Satan wants every Jewish soul and that is the simple truth. There is a heaven and a hell, a place with God or a place in Sheol—the place for those who have not recognized the only way to stay out of it is to turn their sinfulness over to Messiah for forgiveness. The idea is to be free from the chains binding us in a sinful condition where eventually the weight of those chains of sin will drag us down to a less than wanted eternal destination. Only the sacrifice of Yeshua could appease God for our sins. Even if the Temple in Jerusalem had been restored and you could travel there today with your family to sacrifice an animal each year and be forgiven of your sins, how long do you think the line would be of those from all over the world who came to do the very same thing before the sun set on the day of Yom Kippur? How many unblemished lambs would be required? Where would they come from? How would one priest sacrifice millions of lambs in one day? That is why Yeshua said at the final moment of His sacrifice that "It is done"—the appeasement to God had been made for all mankind. His words indicated the "blanket forgiveness" of every man's sins for He alone could bear that burden. All a man had to do was to believe that Yeshua was there for just that purpose— the first time. Once you accept this truth within your heart, the sinful ways of your life will be changed to conform to God's will for His people. You will also receive the blessing of the Spirit of God indwelling within you forever. There is no other way except through Messiah. There is no other way except looking to Messiah for not only

CHAPTER 15

forgiveness but for the spiritual strength to remain steadfast in a fallen world. You're acknowledgement of Yeshua as the One whom God sent to rescue your soul and gave you the opportunity to spend everlasting life with Him will be the words to insure your personal eternity. That is what is referred to as "the hope within us" and is the only way that man should face the reality of death. We do not change who we are. We are Jews, but Messiah was sent to free all slaves of sin, just as He released the captives in Abraham's Bosom. The Jewish souls who were waiting for Messiah saw Him when He "ascended" to "free the captives." They knew it was Him, believed in Him and were released from the place between heaven and hell that existed before His coming. Those who were there had not had the opportunity to see Him and to know Him so they were awaiting that divine moment of deliverance, to be brought to the waiting arms of God forevermore. After Messiah came, those who believed and continued to accept Him in their hearts will see that day of glory, as those who accept Him right up to The Day of the Lord will also join our Jewish brothers and sister in the heavens for an eternal life. Those who mock, who disbelieve, who continue to be duped and lied to by the evil forces of this world, will surely spend eternity with evil forces and then there is no asking, "Why— why didn't I listen, why didn't I believe." It will be too late for if you deny Him, you deny that there truly is a heaven and that leaves only one other place to spend your eternal life.

Scholars of incredible genius have set out to disprove these very words of the Bible and after years of intense study, wound up accepting Yeshua as their Messiah and the only thing that changed in their lives was that God indwelled His Spirit within each of those who committed to Yeshua. They are still Jewish. They still go to Synagogue, they did not change their beliefs or their traditions or their Jewishness. They simply found their Savior and their substitution for their sins. I would encourage you to go on the Web and check out the Messianic Synagogues throughout the United States. Send E-mails, ask questions, get answers from Rabbis who have seen the light, awakened to the truth of Yeshua and now are standing before a Congregation of Jews who will all be together in heaven when their time has come or Yeshua comes back for us. No wondering, no maybe no "when its over-it's over" but the knowledge of everlasting life within them, a hope that no man or force can take away. Once you are one of His, you can never be snatched from His hand. This is truth, what traditional Rabbis would steer you away from because the Messianic movement is opening up the doors of truth by the thousands every day. Over a million plus Jews cannot all be wrong. Write to more than two or three and then see the answers, all of one Spirit, one heart, one Love for God and finding eternal salvation through Yeshua.

Notes

1 Deuteronomy 32:5

2 Deuteronomy 31:26

3 Karl Menninger

4 Proverbs 3:12

Chapter Sixteen

The Final Prophecy

I recall the time that I was standing in front of Radio City Music Hall in New York City (around the late 1950's) and hearing a man screaming at the top of his lungs to the people entering or exiting the theater, "Repent, repent, for the Day of the Lord is near." He told everyone who would even glance his way to "seek the kingdom of God and repent of their sins—ask for God's forgiveness— before it's too late." About forty-five years later and after hundreds of end-of-the-world books and quote a few movies of the same, we are still here. We continue to exist despite many adverse, man-made problems. For one, our ozone layer is being eaten away and "global warming" is being attributed to shifts in the weather. "Holes" in the ozone have increased skin cancer risk with skin melanomas now at an all time high. There have been rising levels of toxic mercury in our oceans from unauthorized, commercial dumping. Land fills and remote dumping sites have been the scenes of the illegal burying of toxic wastes that have been seeping into our water supplies. We keep reducing the size of our Rain Forests, literally raping them of medicinal herbs, rare woods and animals for zoos and private, wealthy collections. We have yet to stop polluting our rivers and streams, campers and hikers not adhering to rules about dumping their waste. Forest fires are burning hundreds of thousands of acres of National Parks. The same fires leave the forest area and burn suburban acres and homes as well. It is these forest fires that disturb the eco-system and the habitats of many animals of which some are now included on the endangered list. Global terrorist

The Final Prophecy

attacks, the war in Iraq, a nuclear arms race in North Korea as well as Iran. Religious and political genocide in Sudan and about a dozen other topics I could list that would make an otherwise confident adult become uneasy. Perhaps that is why most people choose not to think about or discuss these negative topics, despite their present-day reality. And yet, the end of the world has not come and we go to bed each night expecting that the sun will rise tomorrow just as it has since Creation and it will all still be there in the morning—except one morning that just won't be quite what we have been used to.

Do I sound as though I am writing another "end of the world" book? We all know it could, someday, however my approach is through an exploratory acquisition of knowledge and understanding of Biblical truths, rather than tabloid speculation. This is about God's Word and heeding those words quite literally and not hiding our heads in the sand like ostriches. Spirit-filled Messianic Jews and Christians have this incredible confidence and lack of any fear when it comes to the ending of this world the way we know it, for they have inner hope and a sense of peace. Why do we as Jews continue to deny what the Messianic Jews and the Christians of the world have long possessed—this unyielding faith that there is really more to death than just death itself? This is a soul-searching journey that climaxes with a single topic, the day that the world as we know it ends and a new, righteous world is born. This book is all about priorities and whether one lives only for today's happiness or makes the choice to live for eternal happiness. It is about embracing all who are God's people and not just those who follow our traditions. We need to care about the future of our children, our grandchildren and when it is all said and done, what occurs when we take that final breath on this earth. That final moment where the reality of these familiar surroundings begin to fade, to darken and all the memories we have stored present themselves in one rapid but vivid flash before our eyes for the very last time. That is what I care about and what this book is about—the moment after you draw that last earthly breath, for to face death without eternal hope is to say, "I will enjoy my youth but when I grow old, what else is there to look forward to but to die?"

CHAPTER 16

I have been asked many times when teaching or having discussions with friends about prophecy and the Bible if I really, in my heart of hearts believe that we are living in end times. As we discover the final prophesy together, you will see how the stage is being set for the impending Day of the Lord and we are truly at the point where God might say, "They have long passed My line of grace. Let the last week of Daniel begin."[1] The Jews of the First Century A.D. thought that the Lord would return to them any day! They believed this because Yeshua had instructed them to live each day as though He would return at any time. Many have asked a single question which I deemed both intelligent and obvious. "If Yeshua promised His disciples He would come back soon, do you really believe that 2,000 years is considered soon?" I answer that simply by reminding you that a thousand years of our time is one day to the Lord. The signs spoken of by the prophets of the Bible are a reality and all that remains is for God to begin the countdown to the reality of Armageddon. The point that God has made to us in Scripture is to live each day as though on the very next day, the events of the Final Prophecy could begin. There is an urgency that I have attempted to impart to you. When I hear someone say. "Who knows what tomorrow brings!" and I know that they do not have a clue about Biblical realities, I want to weep for them. Sometimes, when it is a friend or family member and they still deny it, I weep for them and continue to pray that God will touch their hearts and awaken the realities of how short this earthly existence is when you compare it to what could be an eternal destiny. This is the proving grounds, the eternal destination is life. After all, if the world was only filled with joy, how then would we learn courage and patience so that we can be all that we can be while we are in this temporary world? Death is not the closing sunset on this world. It is the eternal sunrise—that which follows.

William Shakespeare, when he penned Mac Beth, wrote, "If you can look into seeds of time and say which will grow and which will not; speak them to me." Do you not find it strange that a great man of words would be seeking a word concerning the future? What is strange is that it is right here before our eyes in God's own handwriting—the guided pen of the prophets of Israel. True, there is no "time line" or a specific date of expectation, however it is all there. It is why I included such detail

The Final Prophecy

about the prophets and their prophecies for fully one-fourth of the Old Testament manuscripts were prophetic when they were written. There are approximately 1,527 references to the return of Messiah in the Old Testament alone. The return of Messiah is not a theory, it is Biblical truth. Man will deny but Scripture supports. Life after death, eternal life, is not a small issue but rather a most serious issue in that the days of life here are limited and the days of life God promises to those who know Yeshua are unlimited— they are eternal. Here is a simple and forthright consideration. If we who believe in Yeshua are wrong (and the Spirit says we are not) then we have lost nothing and you have hopefully gained some knowledge about the Bible and the prophets. However, if we Messianic Jews are right, it is you who do not believe that will lose everything. With God, you can't straddle the fence forever—you are either on one side or the other. Perhaps God meant this book as your personal wake-up call to fully weigh in on the side of God's truths.

Judgment is the issue, the point where God punishes the inhabitants of this earth for their sins, the iniquities that have turned this world into a modern day "Sodom and Gomorrah." We have been on the extreme side of sinful for a very long time however, once again, God's patience is longer rather than shorter. The appeal for God to hold off judging mankind this long is not because God thinks we are all going to suddenly change and turn away from sin. That can not occur until the encrusted layers of our sin have been washed clean. The world needs a new start, a new beginning so to speak, but it will not take place under the same conditions as it did when God told Noah to build an ark and be prepared for a world-wide flood! God made a covenant never to eradicate the entirety of mankind again— but God never said anything about partially wiping out mankind such as will occur in The Great Tribulation. Those who would be judged and removed from this earth and eternally sentenced to Sheol are those who rejected God and made the free choice of following evil. If you look at the Day of the Lord, the prophesied final judgment of the entire population of the earth from this simple yet purely rational analogy, not all of mankind chose evil so why would a loving God wipe everyone from the face of the earth? He would not, however there was never anything said or promised about fire or about huge earthquakes.

CHAPTER 16

God never promised that mankind would not be subjected to death by the sword of an angel or the stingers of giant locusts that were sent from the pits of hell. However, it is not as though God did not warn us and provide us with precise information concerning these judgments. They have all been forewarned and explained in His Book of Revelation in the Bible.

Remember, if you know some of the history of the Book of Genesis in the Bible, you know that Abraham had the opportunity to appeal to God on behalf of Sodom, asking that should he find any righteous men, would God spare the destruction of that city? He and God negotiated over the number of righteous people that could possibly be in Sodom— 50, 30, 10 but when it came right down to it there were none who were righteous before God. However, God gave Abraham's nephew Lot and his family the opportunity to escape from this sinful place, walk away before God poured-out His annihilating judgment upon the entire city. They were led to safety but something happened before they reached a point where Sodom was no longer in view. Lot and his wife were strongly warned not to look back under any circumstances whatsoever—but she could not resist. She was drawn to that final glance, that over-the-shoulder, fleeting look. She was instantly turned into a pillar of hardened salt. Now why would God do such a thing? All she wanted was a last look—but at what? You see, God does not honor curiosity when it is about sin. You don't experiment with sin, you know, "I'll just try drugs for a while and whenever I want to I'll quit" or an alcoholic who after being sober wants just one more drink or "I'll just take one look at that pornographic website—what harm can that be?" When God grants His loving grace He also draws His line in the sand, so to speak and one should heed the warning well—don't cross the line. Lot's wife looked back on the world. She looked back on sin and the corruption that God was in the process of destroying, pouring out His wrath in huge fireballs that within a matter of hours burnt a city to ashes along with all its inhabitants. It is almost as though she looked back out of that small part of her that was yet tempted by the world. Regardless of her outward expressions towards God previously or your outward expressions such as those in Synagogue on Yom Kippur, sinful temptations and a "last look" at those temptations of sin can turn out to be stronger than one's love and respect for God without the Spirit of God within you to strengthen you against that temptation—that sin. She could not be totally separated from the world so she became an instant part of the world—a pile of the salt of the sea and not the salt of her faith. In 1996 while I was in Israel, I passed this pillar of salt that had a small sign that read in Hebrew and English its identity and a short statement about the story. As I walked past it, I actually could see a shape, an outline in that salt that appeared to be the form of a human being. The most striking part of that pillar of salt was that the top appeared to be like a head and it was turned—towards where Sodom once existed. God had asked us to be the "salt of the earth." This was surely not what He was referring to.

The Books of Prophecy are filled with examples of God's long suffering patience because of His unconditional love for His creation—mankind. However I also submit to you that God's warnings of punishment for sin are very much *conditional*. If you cease and desist from the sins that God sent His prophets to warn you of, He may punish you but not as severely as He would have if you simply ignored His warnings. Please, if you re-read any point in this book again, let it be this particular point about sin and punishment. The Great Tribulation which occurs during that last week of Daniel is about judgments—a purging of evil from this world.

WARNING – STAY OUT- WILLFUL SIN CLEANSING

God gave warning upon warning to our people about their less-than–devoted and ungrateful hearts that were becoming hardened by the day as they murmured and complained from the time they left Egypt to the day they arrived at the base of Mt. Sinai. Now, hold that vision at Mt. Sinai for a moment and go back with me to Exodus 7:1 where God is speaking to Moses in Egypt and God declares, "So the Lord said to Moses: "See, I have made you as God to Pharaoh and Aaron your brother shall be your prophet. Then in verse 3, God informs Moses, And I will harden Pharaoh's heart and multiply My signs and My_wonders in the

CHAPTER 16

land of Egypt. But Pharaoh will not heed you so that I may lay My hand on Egypt and bring My armies and My people, the children of Israel, out of the land of Egypt, by *great judgments."*

There were ten of those judgments and you should know them well as you dip your little finger ten times at the Passover table –ten judgments against a land that enslaved God's chosen people and refused to let them go. In the final days before God's judgments are over, there will be those whose hearts are so hardened that they will not let go of the world. Judgment after judgment will be poured out upon them. They will run to the mountains, they will attempt to hide in caves and behind rocks. The judgments will increase in scope and intensity however not by any one of these horrific events does God entirely wipe out His people. This time the resulting purge of sin will be in seven's, the number of completion in the Bible.[2] When the three seven's of the judgments are complete, those who refuse to acknowledge the God of heaven and earth will not be around to enjoy that New Heaven and earth and the Kingship of Messiah. They will go down to the pit— to Sheol so they may embrace their sin in heated passion—eternally. God will purge the earth of all sin for unless sin has been vanquished, Yeshua can not step foot upon this earth. Remember that He is Holy and cannot look upon sin. He already died for the world's sin –once. This time, those who will not turn from their sin will die.

Now go back with me to Mt. Sinai. The people had hardened their hearts. Here they were just set free from the taskmasters whip in Egypt and they are already creating idolatry by the forging of a golden calf and worshipping this idol right at the foot of where God is dwelling to be among His children. But wait, that was just one of their continued sins against God! God is patient and led them to the land He promised them. God then told our people to "go and possess the land which the Lord swore to their fathers."[3] Did they listen? Did they go and possess the land? No, they sent scouts to the land, demonstrating their total lack of faith in the Lord God. They disobeyed God and the unfortunate "nickname" that our people at this time in history were tagged with was, "a sinful and evil generation." Please stay with me now as we go to the "consequence" for their sin that should tie together this analogy between the past punishments for sin and the Great Tribulation judgments. The

The Final Prophecy

scene here is Moses addressing the Israelites, "And the LORD heard the sound of your words and was angry (they were muttering and complaining and voicing distrust in God) and took an oath saying, "Surely not one of these men of this evil generation shall see that good land of which I swore to give to your fathers, except Caleb….." Then God told Moses that even he would not enter the land and then declared, "Moreover your little ones and your children who you say will be victims who today have no knowledge of good and evil, they shall go in there….."[4]

Forty years in the wilderness was the judgment, until those of the "sinful generation" were purged. They died from old age and the difficulties of the desert and a new generation was prepared, a generation that was not filled with sin and rebellion and God permitted that group alone to enter the land. Moving forward in history, the people of ancient Israel sinned. Instead of drawing the first inhabitants of the land to God, these sinners drew the Israelites into their own idolatrous sin. There was warning upon warning that was ignored although repeatedly preached by the prophets and scoffed at by the people. God finally judged them but waited a long time to do so. God had the Israelites taken captive by the Babylonians. The Temple and most of Jerusalem was destroyed along with the wall and then our people faced seventy years of captivity in Babylon. Another sinful and arrogant generation who refused to turn away from evil we're once again purged. Will we ever learn from the past in order to preserve the future, one asks? There are some lessons that provide a pleasant short-term future and a single lesson that provides and endless future. Which one do you choose?

Each incident of our history is important in order to show you that God will purge the sin through "judgments." The Final Prophecy or the final "judgments" will be no different. God will purge the earth of all those who refuse Him and who reject faith in Messiah. These are the ones who will receive the judgments—one judgment after another, progressively getting worse each time until those who could have repented and did not are the only ones left to receive the final one. The rest of the people who gave their souls, their eternal destiny to Yeshua will be with Him and not in the midst of these judgments except God's "sealed" Jewish witnesses. That has been the historic basis of God's patience, warnings, waiting and

CHAPTER 16

finally judging. It is coming soon and there is no discrimination in the judgments between those who are outright evil people or criminals and those who reject the Messiah of Israel. They are all sinners—they will be purged, they will be judged.

The Final Prophecy Fulfilled

The prophecies of end times culminate with the seventieth week of Daniel, the final period on earth before the return of Messiah. As we have noted, the first half of this period or three and one-half years, shows us but one single sign that it has begun. The final seven years will bring cleansing of the ungodly by judgment and destruction. Finally all that will be new and sinless under the Kingship of Messiah ends the ordeal and the new heaven and earth begin. Where will you be in all of this if tomorrow morning the first sign is given?

The sign is the removal of all of God's children from this earth who have recognized Yeshua and have professed Him as the true Messiah. Not the Messiah of the Jews or the Messiah of the Christians but the Messiah of mankind. It is part of the entire plan, the prophetic declaration of what God planned since the beginning—the free will to profess one's faith in what God has told us in His Word. If you recall I asked you who do you believe, God or man. We have all had that choice and not having made the right choice would become obvious when that day arrives. Each and every "believer" will be removed from this world. Remember Enoch who never tasted death but was "taken up" to be with the Lord? [5] As Enoch was here one moment and gone the next, so will every person of faith be "taken up" to be with the Lord. The world will see its share of the false teachers and prophets but the most dreaded will be he who falsely professes to be the Messiah. We can't say that they weren't warned!

"And Yeshua said to them, "Take heed that no one deceives you, for many will come in My name, saying, 'I am the

The Final Prophecy

Messiah,' and will deceive many." [6]

He will proclaim himself and exalt himself and everything will be peaceful for the first three and one-half years. On the very last day of that time frame the world will discover who this self-professed Messiah really is in the Temple in Jerusalem. This will be the "abomination" that will mark the beginning of the Great Tribulation.' "Therefore, when you see the 'abomination of desolation,' spoken of by Daniel the prophet, standing in the holy place (whoever reads let him understand) then let those who are in Judea flee to the mountains" (Matthew 24:15-16). This is not speculation, nor is the Great Tribulation exclusively for the Christians and not for the Jews. It is for every human being who dwells upon the face of this earth. What puzzles me is that the very substance of all we are as Jews began in the wilderness. Admonitions that God Himself gave to our people at Mt. Sinai, warning us that the Lord GOD will not allow anything to come before Him or in place of Him, especially the things of the world. God calls it idolatry and in those times it was about worshipping carved images of wood or stone idols. God will not take a back seat to anything, especially inanimate objects that won't even be here in years to come, rusting or breaking or become something you have grown tired of and simply discard or give-away. Someone once told me that "their Rolex watch would run for a hundred years because it was so well made." I paused, looked at the watch, looked back at the person who made the remark and replied, "How will you know?" The point is simply our time limitation—we have limitations and God does not. God can wait for several thousand years for His creation to go full circle, from holiness to sin to punishment and back to holiness. The Book of Deuteronomy Chapter Four is all about what God did not want His people to do. These instructions and admonition dealt mainly with the prophets warning against worshipping anything except God and continued through a review of the Ten Commandments and other laws that God set down for His people Israel, "then beware lest you forget the Lord who brought you out of the land of Egypt, from the house of bondage. You shall fear the LORD your God and serve Him, and shall take oaths in His name. You shall not go after other gods, the gods of the peoples who are all around you

CHAPTER 16

(for the Lord your God is a jealous God among you lest the anger of the[7] Lord your God be aroused against you *and destroy you from the face of this earth.* God has expressed His love for His people Israel but His people Israel continue to sin against Him. Remember that God is Holy, loving and just and being "just" means He must punish sin. Within the same verses, Moses talks about loyalty to God and remembering that without Him they would still be slaves in Egypt (See Deuteronomy 4:20-25). More than anything else, God's chosen people were to be the expression of His love, the light of His Spirit, bringing praise and worship to Him from all whom our Jewish presence touched. Our people were to be all of this by simply keeping the statutes.

Let's just say for example sake that you were moving and the night before you head for your new home in a totally strange city that you have never been to before, an angel comes to you in a dream and gives you some instructions to live by when you get there. It seems that this new city you are moving to has mostly atheists living there. "WHAT," you exclaim, "I, a faithful Jewish person chose to move to a city of Gentiles!" However there is a reason for all things and the angel informs you that God is going to use you as His witness in a powerful way. You move to the new city and meet people who have some exciting ways of living, tempting and pleasurable things that you have never experienced before. You are new to this town and of course, you want to fit in. However you observe sexual immorality, idolatry, parties every weekend, gambling, adults using profanity in their conversations and if that's not bad enough—there isn't a Synagogue in the entire town! At first you are sorry you moved but after a few weeks, you begin to get used to these ways. You begin to reason with yourself, "Let's face it, I live here now so I might as well follow the old adage of when in Rome do as the Romans do and simply enjoy myself!" All that God had taught you and raised you up to live by and uphold suddenly becomes a blank—as though it never happened. You do not follow God's instructions and move right into the condition of flagrant sin. God can not look upon sin and the more you sin the more you become separated from God. You continue to sin until it seems absolutely normal and the distance between you and God grows further and further apart until it is no more. You are now lost, a victim of temptation, separated from God. Your only hope is to turn away from your sinfulness and go back to the arms of God.

For those of you who do not believe that God judges and will ultimately destroy those who sin against Him, it is critical that you understand that there exists a "line of grace" or a period where God will be patient and send all kinds of warnings in different ways, attempting to turn His people away from the sins against Him. When the warnings have been many and the sins continue, God will then judge the sinfulness and punish the sinners. Did God not instruct our ancestors "Only take heed to yourself diligently keep yourself, less you forget the things your eyes have seen and lest they depart from your heart all the days of your life. And teach them to your children and your grand children, especially concerning the day you stood before the Lord your God in Horeb, when the Lord said to me, (Moses) 'Gather the people to Me and I will let them hear My words, that they may learn to fear Me all the days they live on the earth, and that they may teach their children (to fear me as well."[8] In the following verses of Deuteronomy 4, Moses speaks specifically of carved images that people worship instead of the Lord God, and if they do evil in the sight of God and provoke Him to anger, "I call heaven and earth to witness against you this day, that you will soon utterly perish from the land which you cross over the Jordan to possess; you will not prolong your days in it but be utterly destroyed." When the last days come upon us, judgment will come upon every human being whose heart has been hardened like the example of the man who moved to another town and adapted the sinfulness of his surroundings. These would be the ones who literally refuse to acknowledge God and they will surely perish in their sins. Have you taught your children and your grandchildren the ways of God so that they may follow His Word from generation to generation and to fear Him? [9] There is no difference in the carved images of ancient times to the idolatry that is prevalent today in modern times. The world has become more sinful than God's patience will endure much longer. Just because it has not occurred in several thousand years, we tend to disbelieve that it will ever come and we go about our lives instinctively and surely not in accordance with what God has said He wants from His people. Don't be fooled, we have all crossed God's line of grace. We are

CHAPTER 16

all sinful and all are ripe for the judgment. It's not too late to change your heart. Even rough, dry and cracked skin can be softened with creams. The salve for a hardened heart is the daily washing of the heart in God's Word and turning away from the things of the world that bind us and prevent us from having that closeness with Him. Do not be fooled and do not rest in the false confidence that "I am Jewish and a blessed people. We are the chosen, 'The 'apple of God's eye' and God would never wipe us all off the face of the earth." The Bible shows two very convincing arguments that suggest you are sadly mistaken. One was the 40 years in the wilderness and the other was 70 years in Babylon. The forthcoming one has been called The Great Tribulation. The prophets called it The Day of The Lord.

PERSECUTORS BECOME HIS FOLLOWERS

THE RESURRECTION – THE FINAL PROOF

The night before the Pharisees arrested Yeshua to put Him to death, those who followed him were very much upset. He told them He was about to leave them. "WHAT? You, the Messiah, having been with us for three years, showing us all these miracles, teaching us all these things and now you're leaving us alone to face the Pharisees and the unbelievers?"[10] I can only imagine that His disciples were in utter shock. It must have been a frightening experience for them for one simple reason. They believed in Him, they knew who He was. There was not a doubt in their minds that Yeshua was the Messiah and now He told them He was leaving, "to be killed for them!" They were both confused and disappointed for in all that He had taught them about love, I believe that they were still waiting for Yeshua to wipe out the Romans. There existed some doubt among His disciples, however they had never known or had seen anyone like Yeshua. One who claimed Deity, who healed the blind, caused cripples to walk and those with leprosy to be instantly cleansed. Who else could He be? They asked Him point blank where He was going

The Final Prophecy

and Yeshua told them, "Where I am going you can not follow Me now, but you shall follow Me afterward."[11] Yeshua knew that His ultimate destination was from death to resurrection, down to rescue the captives in Abraham's Bosom and then ascending to heaven. He would be in the eternal realm awaiting those who believed in Him. If you think it is difficult for you as a Jew to believe in Yeshua, let me tell you this. Every single man, woman and child who followed and believed in Him from the time He came until after His earthly death, were all Jewish. One of His biggest adversaries was a respected, Roman-born Jew (considered as a citizen of Rome although he was Jewish as he was born there) who had been personally raised up and tutored by the most prominent Rabbi of those times since he was a child, Rabbi Gamaliel. This man I speak of was Saul, one who came from a long line of respected Jewish leaders in the Temple. He too did not believe in Yeshua at first, and made his quest in life to persecute and imprison anyone who spoke the name Yeshua. Saul, this respected man of God, with high status in the Temple of Jerusalem from a long line of Jewish leaders, learned in every aspect of Torah and a godly man who was a hater of those who professed their faith in Yeshua. This Saul became the most widely known and revered "follower" of Yeshua and was renamed Paul, the man who wrote most of the New Testament Bible. How and why is another story— but it is so very important for you to understand that a man such as this did not devote the rest of his life to follow Yeshua and profess Him as Messiah because of some whim or claim of deity. In fact, the self-claim of His Deity would never have been enough to spur a world-wide movement that could never be put down to this very day. You see, after He was crucified and after three days had passed and the tomb was empty, over 500 people saw Yeshua, spoke with Him, broke bread with Him and interacted with Him. The hole in His side and the spike-holes in His wrists (some say hands but were actually the wrists)[12] were the proof that He was crucified and was dead. Now He was alive—resurrected, absent from an entombment with the burial wrappings still in place on the concrete slab within that tomb. His resurrection was the seal of faith that was immovable. Saul was on his way to persecute more believers in Messiah when he had his own spiritual encounter with Yeshua and never looked back. Saul

CHAPTER 16

(Paul) became the man who spread the truths of Yeshua throughout the world until his own martyrdom occurred in defending the very faith he once persecuted. He never stopped being Jewish because he believed in Messiah. He never renounced or stopped practicing His Judaism. Saul who became the Apostle Paul was a Jew who had come full circle, a "completed" Jew for the Spirit of God was now in him as a believer in the Messiah of Israel. I and so many Messianic Jews have never stopped being Jewish. We have never given up our customs, our Passover Seders, our celebration of "Rosh Hashanna" (Jewish New Year) or dancing like David danced and singing like David sang in worshipping the Lord our God. The difference is in our spirits and in the Spirit that binds us with unyielding faith in the kingdom to come.

The twelve disciples of Yeshua also saw Him during the forty-days He allowed Himself to be seen by those he knew and had walked with for those three years. Even "doubting" Thomas fell to his knees when he saw Yeshua walk into an upper room the disciples used for meeting in and for prayer. Yeshua instructed Thomas to go ahead and touch the hole in his side or the holes in his wrists from where the spikes had been driven. Thomas fell to his knees and knew with his entire being that this was Messiah, renouncing his disbelief and pledging his life to Yeshua.

As for truth in one's beliefs, it has been said that self-preservation is the strongest instinct a human being possesses. It is against man's nature to give-up his life for another. Perhaps we might do it for our children, our wife or a beloved family member, but would all twelve of the disciples who followed Yeshua chose to die for a lie? Would twelve men who could have saved themselves from a horrible, torturous death actually choose to die because they could not renounce that which they knew to be the absolute truth? "Renounce Yeshua publicly and live" was the deal they were each given, but they could not do so. They knew then what Yeshua meant when He said that they could not be with Him then but would soon "follow Him." He told them that He had gone to "prepare a place for them and in His Father's house were many mansions." (NT John 14:1-3) They knew that the moment they too drew their last breath that they would be with Him forever. Would you die to promote a lie? Would you give up your life to be nailed to a wooden cross in order to

The Final Prophecy

facilitate some lie? No fame, no fortune left to your wife or your children, just a horrible death. You knew that if you rejected the truth it would be the same thing as rejecting God and you would be damned for eternity. I believe under those circumstances you would surely die for the truth because in order to have the courage to allow it to happen, your soul had to belong to Yeshua.

Twelve men died for the truth, not for a lie.

> "Let not your heart be troubled; You believe in God, believe also in Me. In My Father's house are many mansions; if it were not so I would have told you. I go to prepare a place for you. *And I will come again* and receive you to Myself; that where I am, there you may be also."[13]

This was the first time Yeshua had mentioned coming back for them. It was the first time that Yeshua told them directly that when He came back, "He would receive them to Himself". This is known in prophecy as the "Rapture" or the "taking-up" of all those who believe in Yeshua from this earth for a very compassionate and well defined reason. They would have a view to the events of the Final Prophecy from heaven.

THE FIRST SIGN

This is the sign that tells us it has begun, the sign you would rather be a part of than a witness to. There is no warning, no evening news broadcast the night before or an afternoon "news flash" the day of, it just happens. In the twinkling of an eye every single person in the world who had ever professed their belief in Yeshua, Jew and Christian alike are gone! If they called upon the name of the Lord even one second before this event occurs, they will be taken-up— millions of "Enoch's" raised from

CHAPTER 16

the earth to the heavens. If it was a pilot flying a plane he would be gone. If it were a conductor on a railroad car, he would be gone. If it was your waitress about to place something on your table in a restaurant, the plate would likely smash to the floor for she would be gone. If it was a famous chef in a restaurant, the food would be burning on the grill but he would not be there. Is this difficult for you to fathom? From every city, every country, every business and every home—they would be gone. I know that this is something unprecedented, almost an unbelievable event, but nevertheless, an event that we have been long informed of. We claim it is impossible for millions of people to simply disappear in the twinkling of an eye—there would have to be some trace of someone! Are you then saying that God can take one but not one million or millions if He wanted to? I think that if God could create the heavens and the earth in six days, God can assuredly remove all believers from the earth when and how He chooses. He's God! Take Enoch as an example.

> "So all the days of Enoch were three hundred and sixty-five years. And Enoch walked with God; *and he was not.*"
> Genesis 5:23

It might appear to you that Enoch simply "died" however in this Chapter of Genesis, all others who were mentioned such as all the descendants of Adam, the Bible states that Adam "dies" and not that he was "no more." Then there was Seth and Seth "dies" after he begets Enosh who begets Cainan and then Enosh "dies" and God's Word goes on to name those who were begotten, their days on the earth, stating plainly for each one except Enoch—he "was not." Enoch was a man of God, who walked with God which translates to Enoch pleasing God by practicing all of God's ways and loving God more than life and surely more than the world. Enoch was raptured, taken up and never tasted death. The believers who walked with Yeshua and loved Yeshua and believed in Yeshua

The Final Prophecy

were "taken up." They never tasted death but rather were *"received to Myself"* which was what Yeshua told us that all who believed in Him would be—received unto Him, their spirits now in heaven. They were now in their heavenly bodies and not their earthly bodies. The body that God will give to us for our eternal life is not perishable like the flesh of our earthly body. What happens to our earthly bodies is that they are totally gone—disappeared and not to be found for they were transformed and that is why there is not a trace of one human being who is gone. Many will say that there was a loud sound in the clouds like a "trumpet" and that the next moment it was over—in the twinkle of an eye. It was the end of their days on earth but the beginning of the *Final Prophecy.*

It would not take any major news station (whoever was left at these stations who were not believers) but moments after it occurred to declare this incredible phenomenon. Suddenly, people were gone, houses deserted, cars at the curb side or perhaps crashed with the keys still in them but no one in the driver's seat! Planes that fell out of the sky that left full and crashed with only a few passengers on board—the rest missing! The word that would be out will be that believers in Messiah have been "removed from the earth." Oh, there would be some newscasters who realized what had happened, some officials in Government who would be left and others who would realize intelligently that the prophecies of end times were really happening. Then, while the world is still in a state of utter confusion, a voice will be heard on all the television and radio stations that will declare the "truth" of what has occurred. He will be authoritative and wise. He will sit before the television cameras of the world and proclaim that those who were removed were basically "evil" and they worshipped a false Messiah—that's why they were removed from the earth. He will reveal all the reasons for these events, all the explanations that the non-believing world was waiting for— that God removed them so that the earth could be cleansed. Who is this to proclaim such lies, and what of all the Jewish believers who loved and believed and trusted Yeshua? Oh, we are with Him—all who believed are with Him, however this new "leader" is lumping us all into the simple category of being "evil" and now we were gone. Those remaining on earth will be led to believe that the world is finally a "better place"— a world of peace and of brotherhood!

CHAPTER 16

> "Then if anyone says to you, 'Look, here is the Messiah' or 'There' do not believe it. For false Messiahs and false prophets will rise and show great signs and wonders to deceive."[14]

This famed leader rises up and proclaims his divine power and his ability to now bring peace to the world. This man will even promise to bring absolute peace to the Middle East. He will cease all wars and will unite the world in brotherhood. This all sounds and appears so wonderful could it be that this is the "true" Messiah? Was Yeshua really not the "true" Messiah and those "believers" have actually been duped all these years? All will be confused except those in the world who knew in their hearts that the true Messiah just brought all His children to be with Him and here they are, those who would not believe are now standing and wondering what will become of them. However, peace surely comes and quickly. This false "Messiah" will make a pact with Israel and he will stop all the fighting and the unrest not only in that region but throughout the entire world. He will help Israel rebuild the Temple and even help them to begin sacrifices once again. He has united all of mankind, appearing to have unlimited power in negotiating and stabilizing the world. He will be endorsed by the United Nations and surely the Confederacy of Nations and all their Eurodollars will be right behind him. He has shown more power in his leadership than any man in history and why not. He is the Antichrist, the one who was prophesied in the Bible, but who in the world is powerful enough to renounce him or go against him? Most of the world will not denounce him for most of the world is suddenly very well-off. There are suddenly several million Christian and Jewish believer's homes that are vacant all over the world. First to arrive and claim their house is first to have it! Cars, clothing, jewelry, works of art, bank accounts, cash in homes, and everything else that was left behind is all up for grabs. Can you imagine a homeless guy finding a four-bedroom three-bath home stocked with food and every convenience he needs? All the bank accounts and investments left behind by these believers will now be the property of the new Government—the One World Government and the one ruler.

The Final Prophecy

Everything is wonderful and everyone is at peace. Does this not sound like the promises that were made by Messiah? World peace, everyone happy and content, having all the things they need and life is so good—but only for three and one-half years. Israel is at peace and has not known one single enemy or threat since this "leader" helped them to rebuild the Temple in Jerusalem. Adorned with all of the finery and splendor that was likely compared to the Temple that Solomon once built, sacrifices were now taking place, priests appointed from among the noted Rabbis of Jerusalem and some from other parts of the world [15] and every day, in every way, all are counting their blessings.

According to the events of this time period, shortly after the pact with Israel is made and before the events of the Great Tribulation begin, the Prophet Ezekiel tells foretells of a country that is North of Israel (the conclusion of who this country might be is not perfectly clear. Some Biblical scholars feel that it could be Russia or some part of the Soviet Union) They will not be alone and will be joined by some other nations in this great attack on Israel detailed in Ezekiel 38:5-6. The timing of this event also is a matter of scholarly speculation however I will give you an overview of these events. These are the events that fulfill the 333rd prophecy that heralds in the new age, the new heaven and earth and the rule of the true Messiah. The armies that invade Israel will be literally wiped-out because the Protector of Israel, our God will intervene supernaturally (Ezekiel 38:19-39:5) including God creating a huge earthquake amidst the invading armies (Ezekiel 38:19-20) and if you know Old Testament history and the sound of the trumpet that confused an entire army to fight among themselves, this is the mirrored event that God creates and they do so, confused and literally killing each other. (Ezekiel 38:21-23) "I will call for a sword against Gog throughout all My mountains, 'says the Lord God.' Every man's sword will be against his brother. And I will bring him to judgment with pestilence and bloodshed. I will rain down on him, on his troops, and on the many people who are with him, flooding rain, great hailstones, fire and brimstone."

This defeat will only serve to strengthen the Middle East and the evil one who is ruling it. Having lorded power and defeat over the European Confederacy by now, this is even a greater defeat that may now claim was

CHAPTER 16

his and he will use this to elevate his incredible power and raise the level of fear among all the remaining people of the world. Revelation speaks of his power over all tribes, nations and tongues all sanctioned, for God has His ultimate plan and we who have read the prophecies know the ending already! You must imagine that the people of Israel are feeling very good about all of this for they are in the wake of this new power and supposedly under the protection of this great ruler. They never read the New Testament Book of Revelation or if they did, had no faith in it—now they will be living it! As for those who disappeared, it is amazing how fast we can forget people when our fickle selves are safe, at peace and with every luxury one could ask for. However, their blessings are but for three and one-half years, for on the last day of that precise time period, something happens that brings a shocking reality to the Israelites who have been blinded once again— this time by a false Messiah.

The Final Time Frame

The final period of the Great Tribulation begins on the day following the first three and one-half years, the halfway mark of the Seventieth Week of Daniel. "Then he shall confirm a covenant" (that which the false Messiah did in the beginning of this time period with Israel) "with many for one week" (that was supposed to be seven years) "But in the middle of the week" (three and one-half years into the covenant) "he shall bring an end to sacrifice and offering" (this is at the Temple he helped Israel to build at the beginning of this covenant). "And on the wing of abominations shall be one who makes desolate, Even until the consummation which is determined, is poured out on the desolate."[16] This is the day and the moment that he who claimed to be the friend of Israel and the mighty new leader of the world, reveals himself. On the day that marks the second half or the last period of the prophecy, the Antichrist walks into the Temple with a pig being dragged behind him. He goes directly to the sacrificial altar of God (I am sure that many of the Temple priests try to stop him however the Bible is not clear if he comes with an army of men or simply a few with great physical power.) He places the pig on the altar

The Final Prophecy

and cuts the throat of the pig, allowing the blood of the pig to pour out all over God's sacrificial altar. The "abomination" that has been prophesied occurs and the entire world now knows who this man really is. You see Satan had been cast down from heaven once and for all and instills all his power into this man who is now a powerful world leader. Now perhaps this is something that has repulsed you and has awakened some anger because of a pig being sacrificed on the altar of God— the very altar where sacrifices of unblemished lambs and red-heifers are being offered-up to the Lord. This was even more than an "abomination" to our people of Israel, this was an offense in the face of God Himself—but then again, God knew it would happen since He was the One who began the countdown to the prophecy in the first place.

The Mark of the Beast

"666"

> "He also forced everyone, small and great, rich and poor, free and slave, to receive a mark on his right hand or on his forehead, so that no one could buy or sell unless he had the mark, which is the name of the beast or the number of his name."
> (Revelation 13:16)

> "Here is wisdom. Let him who has understanding calculate the number of the beast, for it is the number of a man: His number is 666." (Revelation 13:18)

CHAPTER 16

Can you imagine a one-world Government with a single monetary system? One man has all the say that affects the finances of every human being in the entire world and has the control of all world currency? Surely you know about the Euro Dollars and the joining of the European nations for it occurred long before the fulfillment of this prophecy. This "confederation" was a sign for those of us who have watched for these signs, not the false signs or the predictions of the soothsayers or false prophets but what Yeshua said would mark the coming of "the end of the age." What was once independent, becoming united, those who were many now acting as one, joining economical powers to become a greater world financial power. Who in the fifties or sixties or even the seventies would have ever thought it possible?

Imagine waking up one morning after three and one-half years in your peaceful and secure lifestyle and you need to go you shopping. You turn on the morning news and there is an announcement by this false Messiah of the world that goes something like this. "Good Morning my brethren and it is the dawn of another wonderful day as a united world, filled with peace, tranquility, brotherhood, all that we could ever need. To make things even easier, this will be the dawning of a new age of financial convenience. No more worrying about ATM's or running short on cash-on-hand, nasty credit card bills and so on. You see, all of this no longer will exist beginning today. The World United Government announces the new "Living Chip," a simple microscopic chip that will contain all of the necessary information for you to shop, bank and have total financial freedom. No more mail boxes full of monthly statements and bills. Now with a sweep of your hand or the scan of your forehead, you can conduct all financial transactions and only one simple statement each quarter right on your own computer screen. Paperwork gone, bulky wallets filled with cash and credit cards gone, no more theft—just financial freedom. You may obtain your application and your chip at any one of many convenient locations that are now established throughout the cities of the world—most of which will be in your local food store. Turn in all your cash on-hand at these locations today in exchange for your very own microchip since as of now, cash has ceased to exist. Your personal chip will take but moments to inject and it is so small it passes through a tiny needle like the one you would have had your flu shot with."[17]

This portrayal is not a spoof or some fantasy. It is a portrayal of this prophesied event that will take place almost immediately after the Antichrist is exposed. After the first half of the seven year period, after the abomination on the Temple altar in Jerusalem, the world finds out that the monetary system is about to be replaced. No more cash, no more savings accounts, no more checking accounts and no more credit cards. The world "leader" knows that to control mankind and have total power you must control the needs of the masses, their staple, everyday needs. The best way to do that is to make them all go through your system! How could this be possible? Is it possible? The answer is "yes," and this system has been available for some time. If you look back in time and consider all the changes that have happened in this world in the past few decades, they did not happen overnight. They occurred gradually, one step at a time so that not too many people notice and those who did were quick to forget. People are truly fickle and that goes for you and I as well. We soon forget that which annoys or concerns us, thinking that we have no control over these matters so "why should we worry about them?" The First Amendment to the Constitution of the United Stares, for one example. Did you think twice about freedom of speech and self expression turning into the actual act of explicit sex on the screens of the movie theatres of the world? The main argument of the sleazy lawyers who represented the porno-kings was that it did not violate Judeo-Christian rights because if we did not want to see it—just don't go to the theater! Would that be likened to ancient times when if you did not like what was going on in Sodom, you would be told don't live there? Did you ever think you would hear profanity in its most profound form spoken in these movies as though they were punctuation marks instead of words? Did you ever think you would see the day that the word "God" or the Ten Commandments were not permitted in public institutions? How about gun laws where assault weapons could be sold at gun shows, reduction of prison sentences for violent crimes, partial-birth abortions and I believe I have made my point. These changes occurred through the courts, one motion at a time, one trial at a time and one case at a time. All the things that point to the Final Prophecy are being set-up one at a time,

CHAPTER 16

gradually and over the past years during times that we were not even paying attention to them until some judge signed his name and it was too late. The "Chip" is no exception, having been developed and quietly spoken of but surely not as loudly as abortion or stem cell experiments.

Back in 1995 there was talk of a Scientist who had been working on and who developed a micro-computer chip so tiny that it could pass through the opening of a hypodermic needle. He mentioned that it would be used, as one example, to keep track of pets who were reported as missing at the rate of thousands per year in all major cities. The problem at that time however was in energizing this chip as it was so tiny that the battery could not supply enough power but for a short period. The breakthrough in this "chip" came when the Scientists working on the project announced that instead of a battery, they had developed the chip so that its power source came from a "heat exchange" within the body itself—humans or animals alike. Want to know where it all went from there?

THE EXPERIMENT

Guelph, Ontario (Canada) was selected as the base for the first pilot project and the chips were made into what was called the "Smart Card." The launching was successful because the records showed that 93% of the merchants in that city responded and participated by accepting these "Smart Cards" that were designed to make us a "cashless" society. This "Smart Card" is a replacement for the credit cards that have had a magnetic strip across the back of them as the "chip" is a micro-chip and therefore necessitates no magnetic strip to be on the card that could be scratched, de-magnetized or inadvertently destroyed. Look at the technology and the implications of the technology rather than the application and the fact that God's Word has warned us about the chip, (biblically referred to as "the mark of the beast") for several thousand years. The very same microchip that is implanted in the card is the very same microchip that can be injected under the skin and the natural question

THE FINAL PROPHECY

should be "where?" Remember the "heat transfer" from the human body to power the chip? Scientists have found that the two places that produce the best heat transfer while applying a simplified scanning application of the chip is the forehead or the right hand— just under the skin at the top of the hand or the center of the forehead. Should you accept this chip, everything about you, everything that speaks for who you are is now a matter of controlled record. This occurs on a global scale and there are no exceptions. Everyone will receive this chip or mark or they can not buy or sell—anything!

To those who will say that "it will never happen," my answer is, "It already has happened." The company processing this technology is a company whose controlling interest is owned by Master Card or was at the time this information became available— in the depth that I was able to research it. If 90% of the banks in Canada are utilizing this system, how long will it be before the banks of the United States and Europe follow the move? In fact, this "Smart Card" which you can readily research yourself on the Internet, has the following excerpt stated on one of its Web Sites.

---

*"Introducing the Monex ®Electronic Cash, a key, value added smart card application available now as part of the **global OneSMART™ MasterCard ®program.***

Note the word "global?" The advertisement goes on to say,

* Our strategy is simple: We're focused on providing you with the technology, expertise and flexibility you need to give your customers anytime, anywhere, any-device access to their payment accounts—now and in the future. Whether payment is made at the point of sale, or with a mobile phone, set-top box, PDA, or PC, we are committed to ensuring the same fast, reliable, secure payment experience that account holders have come to expect from the MasterCard brand.

*The above was copied word for word from the advertisement that appeared on their website.

The words of Revelation describing the mark of the beast could have been science fiction until this technology began to be used in 1996. Additionally, the company who manufactures the "Smart Card" when

CHAPTER 16

they first began production[18] titled this the **M**ulti-tech **A**utomated **R**eader **C**ard. The bold on the first letters of each word are mine so that you can obviously determine what it spells! Who said that the "Mark" of the Beast could not be spelled "marc" instead of "mark?" The root word of the name of the company that owns this technology is "dexter" which means "right hand." That is where I suggest that you check the Internet and conduct your own research to confirm all that I have stated. Simply search under "Smart Card" and apply the information you read to end times prophecy.

In the meantime, what plan could be devised to get us gullible American-consumers comfortable with all of this? Simple, let's start with animals as I previously mentioned. Today you can hardly walk into any Vet's office and not find a stack of brochures on the ultimate protection for your pet. After all, collars fall off, dog tags can be lost and how would you be able to get your beloved pet back? "Now you can with the simple, under-the-skin injection of a microchip that contains all your personal information so that the dog that is found may be reunited with its owner." (Excerpt from an actual advertisement at my Vet's office!) Sounds smart, doesn't it? What is our level of comfort in it being applied to human beings? What of promoting it under the actual record of mix-ups at Hospital Nurseries as well as black market baby kidnapping and a few other reasons like the kids on the milk cartons of this country who are lost? A tiny microchip, under the skin of your baby's hand and no-one will know it is even there except it will be traceable by any Police or any authority with the technology.

But the new microchip, the one that you will have to have implanted to buy and to sell will be a "required" form of obtaining even the most basic things of life. You simply pass your hand across the scanner when you finish shopping and your account at the "World Bank" will be debited for the amount of the purchase. The actual implantation of this "chip" is known as the "Mark of the Beast" and everyone and anyone who takes this mark, who allows the implantation of this chip is making the statement that they are standing on the side of Satan and not placing their trust in Messiah. I can equate this lack of faith to our own people thousands of years ago at the base of Mt. Sinai, not trusting in God and not having enough faith that God would send Moses back down with their Commandments. Accepting the things of the world, needing the things of the world and worshipping the things of the world by giving in and accepting this Mark—after all, our ancestors accepted a golden calf, did they not? Those who will accept the Mark will do so out of fear—the fear of being put to death. Take the mark or lose your head at the old-fashioned guillotine. For the purpose of simplicity and understanding, I have purposely not included every verse of the Book of Revelation or the precise timing to the events but have kept these events in a semblance of order in context with what the Book of Revelation describes and as a type of "commentary." If you have never picked up a Bible or never read a single verse from the prophets then it is my prayer that God speaks to your heart and you make the effort to do so. There is no exaggeration in all of this and no Hollywood special effects. There are no actors or actresses and no script. God wrote the script and it is His Word that is available for you today. This is all that God told His prophets and all that they wrote. This is your chance to visualize and to fully understand all the facts with your mind and your heart—in that order. This is the chance to not be one of those who will face these terrible times wondering what is next should you wake up tomorrow and we who believe in Messiah are gone! The Day of the Lord is technologically and politically closer than further away, more so then it has ever been.

Notes

1 Paraphrased from a Biblical understanding God's admonitions to our people.

2 See the explanation and examples of *seven* in Appendix "A' – Questions and Answers

3 Deuteronomy Chapter One

4 See Deuteronomy form our people's refusal to follow God's instructions

CHAPTER 16

of entering the land in 1:19 to God's admonishment through Moses in 1: 34-39 and then their being turned away back into the desert for forty years in verse 41. It was all a matter of faith, of belief and of honoring God before those who lived in the land of Canaan.

5 Genesis 5:21

6 NT-Matthew 24:4

7 Deuteronomy 6:12-15

8 Deuteronomy 4:9 emphasis mine

9 This word *fear* is used as in *uncompromising respect, awesome respect.*

10 Authors phrasing of Biblical text but in total context.

11 John 13:36

12 There remains controversial teaching between His being nailed to the cross by His hands whereas Medical Doctors and studied Theologians know that it would not be feasible to drive a spike through one's hand that would hold the weight of that person to the cross bars. There is a soft spot in the wrist that is between two bones that are like a "Y" or a wishbone in shape and that is where the nails would be driven to hold a man upon a cross. This is a small controversy and is not the issue or the point. He was crucified for us—that is the point.

14 John 14:1-3

15 Matthew 24.23 NT

16 Note that this is an important part that is in The Final Prophecy II which reveals everything taking place through the eyes of a Rabbi and his family who are called to come back to Jerusalem and become one of the priests of the Temple.

17 Daniel 9:27 Parenthesis/emphasis mine.

18 Authors adaptation

19 It is not known if they still use that name but did so in Canadian advertisements when they introduced the Smart Card.

THE FINAL PROPHECY

Chapter Seventeen

The Great Tribulation

The Great Tribulation is not a matter of "if" it will actually happen but rather "when" it will happen. It is the final week of Daniel's prophecy (seven year period) and is also foretold by the Old Testament prophets as "The Day of the Lord." When it occurs there will be many who will actually accept the truth and understand that they were wrong, wrong in believing what they were told by Rabbis and by those who did not believe in the prophecy of end times and wrong in not believing the prophets and God's warnings. These are the ones who will become the "faithful" in this time and will ultimately stand with God. There are also those who will continue to disbelieve and not budge from their sinful natures. Despite all the devastation that will be going on, they will continue to challenge all goodness and righteousness and even God Himself. The face of this earth will also be changed as devastating events, mostly catastrophic in proportion will destroy the "lay of the land" by fire and pestilence. This will be "judgment time" and will begin directly following the "abomination" that will occur on the altar of the Temple in Jerusalem. Israel will quickly recognize that the man claiming to be their Messiah is actually one who has obtained his power from Satan. It is my opinion that those of our people, the Messianic Jews will have been long gone with the Christians on the day that it all begins. Many of those who were not part of the "rapture" (those taken-up before the events begin) will immediately come to know and understand that the Messianic Jews and

The Final Prophecy

the Christians were actually with God and not removed from the earth because they were evil. (This is the explanation that will be given for their disappearance) If there are any Bibles left on earth, many will scramble to obtain a copy and read the New Testament and the Book of Revelation to see what will next occur. What will be going on in the heavens at this time has been told to us by the Jewish prophets of Israel. Remember that God gives us ample warning before He punishes us for sin. His patience and His grace are extended for us to recognize our sin and that is more than generous when you consider the over 2,000 years of fulfilled Biblical prophecy that God has provided us with to learn from!

The prophet Zechariah portrays one of the strongest expressions of the return of Yeshua and His eventual ruling over the nation Israel in Zecharia 9:10. Remember that there must be repentance, forgiveness and restoration in Israel and the forgiveness of the sins of the people. It is through Israel that God will bless all the nations of the world but that will be in the future after God judges the nations who have dealt badly with His Israel (See Joel 3:9-17) When it is all over and the cleansing of the world's sin is complete, Messiah will reign and all the world will worship Him in Jerusalem. (Joel 3:17)

It is now time for the judgments or the time that God declares that "enough is enough" and begins the final countdown towards The Day of the Lord, the Great tribulation, the purging of the world's sinners who will not repent, who will not recognize the true Messiah. These are the people whose hearts will have become so hardened that they will never recognize truth. They have been living a lie for so long that they can not distinguish between what is right and what is wrong. They are lost in their sin and doomed to the consequences of that choice. All of the talk, all of the books and movies and all of the chiding and rebuking by those who did not believe that this day would come is now a moot point, for it has arrived. I can not even imagine being on earth and knowing in my heart that someone once told me, warned me about these times and that I walked away disbelieving and thinking that the one who told me was a fool.

In the heavens there is a scroll that contains Seven Judgments. They are sealed, having been sealed for several thousands of years (in our under-

CHAPTER 17

standing of time) and are about to be opened. Only He who is worthy may open these seals and all eyes in heaven turn to Yeshua. He alone shall begin the judgments, for He is the "Lamb of God" who removed the sins from those who believed in Him. Now, those who refused to believe in His truths will pay the price.

> "You are worthy to take the scroll, And to open its seals; For You were slain, And have redeemed us to God by Your blood. Out of every tribe and tongue and people and nation, And have made us kings and priests to our God, And we shall reign on the earth. Worthy is the Lamb who was slain, To receive power and riches and wisdom, And strength and honor and glory and blessing." [1]

There are seven judgments in this scroll and by no means assume that they are the "only" judgments. These are only the beginning of all that was foretold that the Great Tribulation would be. These seven scroll judgments are but the prelude to the seven "Trumpet Judgments" which begin in Revelation 9:7 and then the final "Bowl Judgments" in Revelation Chapter 16. (There are seven of each set of judgments, seven being the number of "completion" in the Bible) The earth and all who remain on it will go through more chaos and horrible destruction than was ever seen in history. God gave us every warning by sending seventeen prophets who recorded it all for us to foresee. All of this should not be a surprise to most—except those who refused to look into the biblical truths of Messiah.

The First Seal

When the "first seal" is opened, one on a white horse who is called "Conqueror" and having a bow in hand will be sent out to "conquer" which literally translated means to "kill." In this verse he is given a crown which makes him a type of ruler. The interpretation I have found leans towards this being the Antichrist. Although we have spoken of the power he has had up until the Great Tribulation begins, the timing from his revealing himself by the abomination on the altar of the Temple and this point of riding out with heavenly permission to kill leaves an important observation unexplained. From the description in the Bible that is depicted, take note that the bow he is given has no arrow nor is there any mention of any other weapon being carried in his hand. This could then be the Antichrist who conquers through his present control of the world government and more so politically than with warfare.

The Second Seal

When the "second seal" is opened by Yeshua it will denote great conflict on the earth. The rider who will be sent out will be on a horse which is fiery red, and he will be given a sword. He is instructed to take all the "peace" from the earth so that people will have great conflict, with anger and outright rage that will ultimately result in their killing one another.

The Third Seal

The "third seal" when opened declares that this rider is on a black horse with scales in-hand and is ordered to create a great scarcity of food and staple goods so that there will be very little left on the earth to sustain those who are still left. Starvation is a horrible weapon.

CHAPTER 17

THE FOURTH SEAL

The "fourth seal" when released will send out a "pale horse" and the rider will be named "Death." The power will be given to this rider to have dominion over a fourth of the earth and to kill "with sword, with hunger, with death and by the beasts of the earth."[2]

THE FIFTH SEAL

When the "fifth seal" is opened it will be some good news for those who did not take the Mark of the Beast. Those who did not take the Mark and found themselves beheaded will also find themselves instantly in possession of a new spiritual body. They will also find themselves instantly in heaven with all those who had been taken-up before this all began. They will be clothed in white robes and told to wait a little while longer until all the trials taking place now and to come on earth are completed. Those who would be martyred for Yeshua would be so and it was all concluded—who would be in the pit and who would join them in the heavenly realm.

THE SIXTH SEAL

In the opening of the "sixth seal" there will be a huge earthquake and the sun will grow black while the moon becomes red like blood. Then the stars from the heavens will fall upon the earth and both mountains and islands will be totally moved from their original positions on the earth. When this occurs, all who thought they were brave will run and hide themselves as the Prophet Isaiah told us would happen, long before this day ever came. Another testimony of the Word of God, the foretelling of the things of this world— if only we would heed their warnings before rather than after.

The Final Prophecy

> "They shall go into the holes of the rocks, And into the caves of the earth, From the terror of the LORD And the glory of His majesty, When He arises to shake the earth mightily. In that day a man will cast away his idols of silver And his idols of gold, Which they made, each for himself to worship, To the moles and bats, To go into the clefts of the rocks, And into the crags of the rugged rocks, From the terror of the LORD And the glory of His majesty, When He arises to shake the earth mightily."[3]

And

> "Fall on us and hide us from the face of Him who sits on the throne and from the wrath of the Lamb! For the great day of His wrath has come, and who is able to stand?"[4]

Who is able to stand indeed for no man can hide from God's wrath nor will he find shelter when God has finally declared judgment on all of the sinfulness of mankind.

> "Then I saw another angel ascending from the east having the seal of the living God. And he cried with a loud voice to the four angels by whom it was granted to harm the earth and the sea, saying, "Do not harm the earth, the sea or the trees till we have sealed the servants of our God on their foreheads. And I heard the number of those who were sealed. One hundred and forty-four thousand of all the tribes of the children of Israel were sealed."[5]

The number 144,000 is not, in the opinion and interpretation of many scholars a literal number but rather a "symbolic" representation. When I began to study the Book of Revelation some years ago, I too wondered

CHAPTER **17**

at first reading, That's it? Only 144,000 of our people will be left in Israel when this is all over? Of course I did not take into account the number of those Messianic believers who were already in heaven with the Lord. There are several choices to select from in the interpretation of this number. Could this be the "redeemed" of God at the end of the age prophetically foretold or are these people literally martyrs who God will preserve through the Great Tribulation? We see that the "seal" is a mark of God rather than the mark of the Beast. Going back to the very night that the Angel of Death "passed-over" Egypt, our ancestors, under the instructions of Moses, made a protective-type seal on the doorposts of their houses. This seal would save them from the death that was taking the first born of the households of Egypt. This was a reversal of the curse that Pharaoh declared against the children of Israel. The prophet Ezekiel also spoke of a "seal" in Chapter Nine which was also placed on the foreheads of those who rejected sinful abominations.

> "Now the glory of the God of Israel had gone up from the cherub, where it had been to the threshold of the Temple, And He called to the man clothed with linen, who had the writers inkhorn at his side and the Lord said to him, "Go through the midst of the city, through the midst of Jerusalem, and put a mark on the foreheads of the men who sigh and cry over all the abominations that are done within it. [6]

God then told others that after this "seal" had been placed on the foreheads of the ones who turned away from the sinful abominations, destroy "all" who were left— young or old, man or woman, adult or child. If they did not have the seal on their foreheads they died. What happened in Egypt on the doorposts of the houses of God's chosen is so close to the "seal" on the foreheads of those who chose to follow the Lord that one can only surmise that God, even then was providing us with a correlation that would be familiar to those who followed the Lord.

The Final Prophecy

In the Great Tribulation, we see that there were abominations committed at the Temple which is described in Ezekiel Chapter Eight. When one defiles God's holy Temple, the Glory of God departs from that house of worship. In this case, Ezekiel was being shown the abominable sins of idolatry and animal worship and perverted practices—right in God's holy house. So, God's glory is no longer in the city and the warnings have been long given. God's Spirit is no longer among the people and those who defied sin and remained faithful to the Lord were marked on their foreheads—they were saved from those who looked for the seal before slaughtering all those who remained without it.

In the Book of Revelation and in the specific time frame we are now referring to these people as "virgins" which is symbolic of their not being taken-in by the sinfulness of the world but rather remaining faithful to God. The 144,00, are the "redeemed" ones who I believe were indeed not martyrs as some suggest, but rather "servant's of God" who are true to the Lord in their beliefs and their faith. This faith was naturally reaffirmed once they realized who the true Messiah of Israel was. Some Commentaries on this subject will present other views or interpretations such as they were not all Jews, however if they were not Jewish, how were they chosen from the twelve tribes of Israel? They are likely to be completed Jews[7] who gave their hearts to Yeshua and now instead of martyrs are witnesses to the revelation of the true Messiah of Israel. The problem has always been that Jewish witnesses should have been conducting this kind of witnessing several thousand years ago. It was those who crossed over the Jordan into the "Promised Land" and became just like the heathens rather than bringing the heathens to God. This is the opportunity to get it right, to go out during the Great Tribulation and speak of the forgiveness and the everlasting life that could be afforded those who are still resisting the salvation of Yeshua. Those who defy the beast and refuse taking the mark and were killed for that stand, are taken up to heaven and wait until the moment that their garments (now white robes) will be literally dipped in blood from their sacrifice. That is symbolic of the blood of the Lamb Yeshua and His sacrifice for us. There is a time where God welcomes them all and they join those who first came in the rapture just before the Great Tribulation began.

Chapter 17

The Seventh Seal

The "seventh seal" when it is opened will bring no immediate action. In fact, there will be absolute silence in heaven for about a half an hour. Seven angels will stand before God and each of these angels will be given seven trumpets.

The Trumpet Judgments: The First Trumpet

The first trumpet that is sounded will produce hail and fire and that hail will be mingled with blood. One third of all the trees on earth will be burned away and the grass of the earth will be scorched, burned as black as coal. The angel who will throw down this fire will use a "censer." This is a golden pan that in the days of the Temple was suspended from a rope or a chain and was used to carry the burning coals. These coals were used to ignite the fire where incense was being offered up to the Lord. Now, in the days of judgment, this "censer" will not be used to heap burning coals upon a fire to honor God. It will be used to heap burning coals upon the heads of those who will still be upon the earth and who have not honored God.

The Second Trumpet

The second trumpet that will be sounded will send a huge object that will appear as a mountain, totally ablaze with fire that will come crashing down into the sea. A third of the sea will become blood and a third of the living creatures, all the fish and all the marine life will die. Do you remember Moses standing before Pharaoh telling him to let God's people go? Moses dipped the tip of his staff into the Nile right before the eyes of the hard-hearted Pharaoh. As the rod touched the water, a small, red ring that appeared as blood began to widen and as it did it spread across the

THE FINAL PROPHECY

Nile until all its waters were of blood. Every living creature that dwelled within or upon the Nile died that day and the stench covered the land.

THE THIRD TRUMPET

At the sounding of the third trumpet, a star is released from heaven. It falls to the earth burning like a huge torch, falling into a third of the rivers and springs of the water on earth. The star shall be called Wormwood and will contaminate the water supply so that many people will die from the lack of drinking water.

By this time it would seem that no human who was left on earth would doubt that they were witnessing the judgments of God, The Day of the Lord. One would think that everyone on earth would be falling on their knees in repentance, begging God's forgiveness and asking God to have mercy on them. Biblical prophecy however, foretells us that they will not. The fact is they will do quite the opposite. The remaining unbelievers will be standing and shaking their fists at God as all of these judgments are being cast-down upon the earth. They will not submit, they will not give-in and they will not profess God as their Savior. They resist the truth before them, many running to hide in caves thinking that they can escape God's judgments. In essence, they are attempting to hide from God.

When the fourth trumpet is sounded, this time it will be the heavens themselves that are affected. One third of the moon and the stars will all be darkened, so that one third of both the day and the night will be without light.

The sounding of the fifth trumpet is where the word "torture" becomes a "kind" word. A star will fall to earth (this star is believed to be an angel or angelic being) who will have the key to the pit of hell. Once opened, a great billow of black smoke will emerge from the pit and will darken everything— but that will not be the worst of it. Out of the smoke from the pit will come locusts, not ordinary locusts but enormous one's, each equipped with a stinger that make this locusts look like giant scorpions. These stingers will come against everyone left on the face of the earth,

CHAPTER 17

stinging them over and over again until people actually beg to die—but they will be unable to.

The sixth trumpet when blown will signal the angel who will be at the river Euphrates. The angel will release four other angels who have been waiting for this day to carry out the judgments of the Lord. They will be released to allow the killing of one-third of mankind who are left upon the earth. An army of over 200 million horsemen will attack to kill that one-third of mankind. Their breastplates will be red like fire, with blue and yellow colors. The heads of their horses will be like lions but their mouths will spew fire like dragons but they will indeed be horses. Fire, smoke and brimstone will be their weapons. Those who will be left, according to biblical, prophetic accounts, will still be hard-hearted, enough so that they will not repent of their sins, even after all that they witness. What does it take to bring men who have been hardened in sin all their lives to fall to their knees and ask God for mercy and forgiveness? Some will simply never bend their knees to anyone, even God and that is the result of a life of sin. They will have an eternity in Sheol to think about it!

The Bible tells us that a "pause" will take place between the sixth and the seventh trumpet, almost as though God in His infinite mercy will provide a brief respite— a time to reassure all of His children that He is sovereign and all that is happening will soon be over and all believers in Him will herald in the "new" Jerusalem.

As such, let us also pause here for a moment and reflect on the events that have occurred thus far. No man can "pause" the Great Tribulation when it comes upon us but I can pause in this writing, to ask if at this very time in your life, are you someone who is hiding from God in the caves of your disappointment or you're unbelief? Although the Great Tribulation is not yet upon us and there are no balls of fire being thrown from the sky, are the "signs of the times" and all that is available to you in the Word of God not enough to convince you that you are really a sinner in need of a Savior? Can you seriously be aware of all that has happened and continues to happen in this world since 9-11 and not believe that the signs of this day are beginning to become vivid? If God were to say tomorrow that "enough is enough" and by His will He begins the countdown on the Final Prophecy, are you one of the people who will be

The Final Prophecy

watching from a balcony seat in the heavens or will you be one of those who will be looking up at it all coming down!

The opening words of Chapter Ten of the Book of Revelation declare, "I saw still another mighty angel coming down from heaven, clothed with a cloud," Some Bible scholars say that this is Yeshua, however when you look up the word "another" in the original Greek text, you will find that this means "one of the same kind" or a "created being." It is also not one of the seven angels who have been assigned to blow the trumpets of the seven trumpet judgments. It appears that this angel is of "great rank" in heaven and filled with strength and splendor. This angel shall declare the Messiah and states that there should no longer be any delay in the sounding of that seventh trumpet. The mystery of God was about to be completed, announcing Yeshua as the true Messiah and declaring the words of the prophets to be true and correct. This angel had what appeared to be a "rainbow," a reminder of God's covenant with Noah and a sign that His people are protected while the guilty are punished. God has also been mercifully patient in waiting over 2,000 years for the earth to purge sinful generations and to teach future generations, just as God told us to do in the desert out of Egypt and in the captivity of Babylon. "And these things you shall teach diligently unto your children."[8]

Then, John, the one who received this revelation from the Lord was told to "eat this book" in the hands of this angel and John did so, noting "it was sweet to the taste and sour to the stomach." The sweetness is likened to God's Word, sure and revealing when read and "digested" or learned, but the sourness within John's stomach was to remind him of God's awful judgments that were now being poured out upon the earth. I personally believe that Yeshua weeps when each of these judgments are poured out. These are souls He was unable to save, the ones who "got away" for any number of sinful reasons. Arrogance, pride and traditions never brought anyone to salvation. These who never made the first calling to heaven before the Rapture could also be the hardened ones, the non-believers who loved the world, cared only about the things of the world and never believed there was even a God much less a Savior, a Messiah who was sent to free them from the chains of the pit.

CHAPTER 17

Keeping with the sequence of events, there are now two men, witnesses on earth who go about preaching the goodness and forgiveness of God. Naturally Satan will not stand for this display of God's power because he (Satan) wants every single soul who had not been "taken-up" down in Sheol with him. Out of the pit he comes, in person, killing the two witnesses who have been preaching Yeshua to every person looking on. Satan kills the two so that all may see them die—by his own hand. This will be Satan's way of mocking God and swaying those who are left on the earth to remain faithful to him. To illustrate his power and flaunt this killing of God's own witnesses even further, he leaves the dead bodies lying in the street for all to see! I can almost see Satan pointing to the two dead witnesses of God, saying, "Look at them now—dead, lifeless, just like all those who are on the side of God will be."[9] Mock God, will you? After three and one-half days of these two "witnesses" lying dead on the street, the breath of God enters them, even as their bodies were beginning to have the stench of death. The people who had walked by them prior to this, surely mocked them and mocked God. Then, a thunderous voice from heaven declared, "Come up here" and in front of all these hundreds of witness, the two men physically ascend towards heaven. Can you imagine being there and seeing this happen? Two dead men standing to their feet, God calling down for them to come and join Him in heaven and they begin to levitate and rise towards the clouds!

This should be a familiar scene to those who recall the miracles of Yeshua and His calling Lazarus to "come out" from his grave after having been dead for several days. The ascent to heaven should also be familiar for it was before all those witnesses that Yeshua ascended to heaven, exactly forty days after His resurrection. If that was not enough to convince all who were left on earth of the power of God, within the very same hour there will be an enormous earthquake where seven thousand people will be killed and a tenth of the entire city will fall into complete ruins. The initial laugh belonged to Satan but the final one will always belong to the Lord. Those previously hard-hearted and shaking their fists at God, after witnessing all of this and the fact that they, the worst of the heathens were still alive, gave glory to God in heaven. At this point would you not realize God's sovereignty, His power and the truth of His covenants, those

The Final Prophecy

which the world should have heeded a long time ago— especially before the Great Tribulation? Now you the reader have that same chance. It is still not too late but He is coming soon. Is your heart right with Him ?

The seventh trumpet sounds its formidable blast and this time, voices from heaven could be heard everywhere. I picture it as an outdoor event where millions of people are attending and there are speakers in heaven directing the sound which now announces, after this trumpet sounds,

> "And there were loud voices in heaven saying, 'The kingdoms of this world have become the kingdoms of our Lord and His Yeshua and He shall reign forever and ever."[10]

At this point, if you were there in heaven with those who were now with the Lord in their eternal bodies, watching all of this occur, you would have seen twenty-four elders who sat before God on their thrones, fall down on their faces, prostrate before the Lord in worship and adoration. These twenty-four were twelve of the disciples that followed Yeshua who promised them that He would be with them one day in His Father's house and the other twelve were the leaders of the twelve tribes of Israel. In unity they all cried out, "We give thanks, O Lord God Almighty, The One who is and who was and who is to come, Because you have taken your great power and reigned, The nations were angry and your wrath has come, And the time of the dead that they should be judged , And that You should reward Your servants the prophets and the saints, And those who fear your name small and great, And should destroy those who destroy the earth."

Let's not forget in all this revelry that the people who are left upon the earth are those who have taken the Mark of the Beast, have defied the Lord, have cursed heaven and shook their fists every time that another judgment was poured out. It is nearing the end but the end will be the beginning. In fact, it will be a beginning that is inconceivable in vision because words could not describe what God has planned for those who

CHAPTER 17

love Him and are faithful to Him.

After the twenty four Elders declared their words, one could hear and see in the heavens, lightening, noises, thundering and there was an earthquake and great hail that fell as the temple of God was opened in heaven and the Ark of God's covenant could be seen.[11] Now there were great goings on in heaven and I had said that I would not recount every single detail but rather save that for your own reading of the Book of Revelation.

There were varied signs that occurred in heaven, from a woman, child and dragon to another dragon, fiery red and having seven heads. His tail drew a third of the stars in heaven and threw them to the earth. Much of these symbolic occurrences come from the Book of Daniel, Chapter Seven. In Chapter Thirteen of Daniel we are told of a beast from the sea. This was the one to wage the war against all who were not in the Lambs Book of Life, those left upon the face of the earth who defied every chance and reason to get right with God. This is where heaven speaks of the Beast and the number of his Mark which is 666. This is the final gathering of all those left to take the Mark or die, to worship Satan or be killed. The Bible tells us that in these end times there is no exception. Rich man or poor, servant or master, king or his subjects, no one escapes the demand of the evil one to take the Mark or die. The 144,000 that were sealed before much of this occurred? They were standing on Mount Zion with Yeshua by this moment in the course of events. A voice spoke to them, a voice likened to running waters and loud thunder. Then there were harpists playing their harps and a new song was being sung before the throne and that song could only be sung by the 144,000 "who were redeemed from the earth."[12]

If this were a Broadway play I would tell you that the final act is about to begin. The curtain is going down on the old and is coming up on the new when the three angels are seen flying in the midst of heaven who cried out, "Fear God and give glory to Him, for the hour of His judgment has come." Judgment—the Day of the Lord has come and the heavens have spilled-forth God's wrath, yet there will always be someone who will ask, "Is there more?" It would appear that much of the earth has been cleansed but not entirely, for sinners still remain on the very earth that a holy Messiah is soon to step foot upon once again. The earth must be fully cleansed of all sin, so to answer the question, yes—there is more to come. The "final" judgments known as the "seven bowls of God's wrath" are still ahead, yet amidst all of this tribulation, God is still merciful for He could have simply wiped the planet clean with one fiery scoop—but He did not, giving time for those who would finally repent to do so. God does not want another person to perish eternally because of their sin. The angels call for those who are left to repent and to give up their ways and come and worship God. They were warned by the other angel to not take the "Mark of the Beast" or surely they would die in the eternal lakes of fire. Those who would not heed God's warnings from His servants are predestined to perish.

The Bowls of God's Wrath

The first bowl is poured out and horrific sores comes upon every single person who has the Mark of the Beast and worships the image of the Beast.

The second bowl is poured out on the sea. This time, not a third or a portion of the sea is turned to blood as it was in the last judgments but the "entire" sea is turned to blood, killing every remaining living creature that is in the sea.

The third bowl is poured out upon the remaining streams and rivers. Now all the drinking water of the world is turned to blood so that there is no more drinking water.

Another angel pours out the fourth bowl upon the sun. As a result, the sun intensifies and becomes so hot that anyone who walks outside will be scorched.

The fifth bowl is poured out on the throne of the beast and total darkness comes over the "kingdom" of the beast, the evil one and all his evil followers. There are cries of unimaginable pain and torment.

CHAPTER 17

The sixth bowl is poured out and it dries-up the river Euphrates. This allows a direct path for the enemy to attack Israel.

> "Then I looked and behold a white cloud, [13] and on the cloud sat one like the Son of Man, having on His head a golden crown and in His hand a sharp sickle."[14]

Another angel who came out from the Temple and crying out to Him in a loud voice telling Him that the time had come to reap, for the harvest of the earth was ripe.

> "Thrust in your sharp sickle and gather the clusters of the vine of the earth, for her grapes are fully ripe. So the angel thrust his sickle into the earth and gathered the vine of the earth and threw it into the great winepress of the wrath of God. And the winepress was trampled outside the city and blood came out of the winepress, up to the horses bridles, for one thousand six hundred furlongs."[15]

The "winepress" is the "wrath" of God on those of the earth who have truly allowed their hearts to remain wicked and unyielding to God. The sharp sickle will reap them quickly while the winepress denotes a literal "bloodbath" of a battle that will not take place in Jerusalem but rather outside the city. After all, Jerusalem will be the home of the Lord for the future Kingdom and even in times long passed, God promised to spare His beloved city. Those who are faithful do not have to witness the final bloodbath. The prophet Zechariah prophesied of the attack that will come against Jerusalem in the "last days."[16] We know this for Zechariah uses the term "in the end" so we know that this is the final battle of Armageddon. When God speaks of a big battle, think about one

The Final Prophecy

thousand six-hundred furlongs! In modern measurement, that would equate to about 200 miles! This battle is more fully described in the New Testament Book of Revelation 19:11-21, however verses 11-12a to me are the verses that all Messianic Jews and Christians alike have awaited since Yeshua promised to return, this time in triumph.

> "Now I saw heaven opened, and behold, a white horse. And He who sat on him was called Faithful and True, and in righteousness He judges and makes war. His eyes were like a flame of fire, and on His head were many crowns."

An angel just before this all occurs, goes about insuring that all the prayers of all God's people for judgment had been answered— before this battle was unleashed. The slaughter was very severe, to say the least, a battle if fought in the central valley of Israel could well see blood that would run about four feet deep in troughs in some places. In Ezekiel Chapter thirty-nine it is all foretold. One did not need an armchair view to know what the results of this battle would be. God's prophet had already told us some several thousand years before the first drop of blood is ever spilt in this valley.

> "And I will send fire on Magog and on those who live in security in the coastlands. Then they shall know that I am the LORD. So I will make my holy name known in the midst of My people Israel and I will not let them profane My holy name anymore. Then the nations shall know that I am the Lord. The Holy One in Israel. Surely it is coming and it shall be done, says the Lord God. This is the day of which I have spoken."[17]

CHAPTER 17

The valley, according to the Word of God will be called "Hamon Gog." In order to cleanse the land after Armageddon, it will take Israel about seven months to remove the corpses of men and horses from this battle. God declares that the name of the city where these remains are buried shall be called "Hamon Gog" as well. There will be no mistake as to this battle and its outcome for God will be glorified. God speaks of this in His Word as the final sacrificial meal, symbolically saying that all of Israel will feast at His table of defeat--feast on the horses, riders and with all men of war. (Symbolic of the defeat in this great battle) God's tolerance for men of war has been exhausted and no one will come against His Israel and survive, ever again.

Now it was time for the seventh and final bowl to be poured out. When that occurs, there will be a voice that comes from heaven that will fill the air with the words, "It is done!" There will be noises like thunder, there will be lightening and a great earthquake larger in scale and intensity then man has ever before known or will ever know again. The results will be that the cities of the nations will fall. The islands will be gone and the mountains will not be found. Then hailstones so huge that they will be the weight of a talent will come upon the earth. The few left, those who chose to remain will still be cursing God and shaking their fists at the heavens. A "talent" weight is about 75 pounds so you have an idea of the size of the hailstones that will be hurled upon the earth. The devastation will appear to be total in scope, while above in the heavens, those who were believers and had given their hearts to Yeshua were at a huge banquet table that was the "Wedding Supper of the Lamb of God" the feast and celebration in heaven that awaited all of God's faithful children. Those who were beheaded and died for the sake of Yeshua were in their own heavenly bodies and were joined to this table for they had proven their loyalty to the Lord and were now celebrating and worshipping with Him.

In the final Chapters of the Book of Revelation we see the symbolic fall of Babylon which has always represented evil in the Bible. This portion of Revelation is filled with symbolism and vivid descriptions of the glory that is given to God and the glory that is bestowed and given to Yeshua. This is depicted in Chapters 18 -19 of the Book of Revelation and I would

THE FINAL PROPHECY

encourage you to obtain a commentary or better yet, a Study Bible that contains the Old and the New Testaments. Read these Chapters and the entirety of the Book of Revelation for yourself. Read God's Word and be blessed for God tells us that "whoever reads the Book of Revelation from the Bible will be blessed." Likewise, in Revelation 22:20 God warns us that anyone who adds or takes away from His Book of Revelation will receive the curses of what has been portrayed.

In the ending of Revelation, Satan is bound up and thrown into the pit for a term of one thousand years. The description of the incredible, awe-inspiring beauty of the new heaven is beyond my own words. Oh, I could recite the verses here but how can I describe a "River of Life" running down from the throne of God. Can you picture the scene of a lion and a lamb resting side by side together? How can I explain to you that there will be no more curses or judgments, no more suffering, pain or sorrow? How, beyond that which the prophets have written can one give you the vision of what you will endure if you continue to follow the ways of the world? Yeshua tells us toward the end of the final Chapter, "I am the Root and the Offspring of David, the Bright and Morning Star." It is He alone that will claim His rightful throne in Jerusalem, ushering in the New Heaven and Earth and one thousand years of peace and righteousness in Yeshua.

When I think of this coming time I am filled with a sense of joy for I imagine the "completion" of all our brethren on the earth. I think of their justification before God, their sanctification in being cleansed of all sins so that we all sit together at the banquet table watching the finale of the events below on earth. Perhaps your child or wife or grandchildren will be sitting beside you or across from you! In some instances, there are those who will see a departed parent or even a departed child. They will be in spirit and in their heavenly new bodies, for God's Word leads believers to the conclusion that we will indeed know each other in the heavenly realm but not as we were but as God transforms us spiritually. But what of the tragedy if you were there and one of your children, a parent or a loved one was below in the midst of the Great Tribulation? You watched them and cried out to them but they could not hear you and if they did, would they listen?

CHAPTER 17

It reminds me so much of the Bible story of the man who did not even give a crumb from his table to the poor beggar who sat outside his marvelous house and starved while this man gloated in his cruelty. When they both died, the beggar was taken to Abraham's Bosom and the rich man wound up in Hades. As it were, the rich man looked up and saw the beggar whose name was Lazarus, (not to be confused with the friend of Yeshua who was raised from the dead) just across a chasm where he could not reach him. The rich man's tongue burned from the heat of Hades, and he cried out to the beggar that he might dip his finger in water and cool his tongue. But Abraham answered for him and explained in so many words that the beggar was now awaiting his reward and the rich man was where he should be for his cruelty to the poor beggar. Then the rich man cried out and asked that someone from the dead please warn his brothers at home of this reality—that they might be saved from this torment and would surely believe someone who returned from the dead to inform them! Father Abraham's answer was swift and direct, "Why would your sinful brothers listen now when they would not listen to Moses and the prophets?"[18]

In a word, God has sent all His prophets to warn His people in every way He could, giving us plenty of time to understand, to learn the wisdom and the knowledge of His Word. We seem to wait, procrastinate until the many opportunities have already passed us by and then we cry out for mercy or for help. If you listen to teachers or those who claim that Messiah is in Brooklyn or Messiah hasn't come yet you have been listening to men who usually have an agenda for stating direct contradictions of God's Word. They will have to answer for that before the "Judgment Seat" of God or possibly the Great Tribulation if it should come before their appointed time is over. They may be blind to the truths of God but why should you not remove the veil from your own eyes? Can the blind lead the blind? Can you learn or advance in wisdom or understand the things of God when you are listening to men who are blind to God's truths? Yeshua addressed this when He said, "And He spoke a parable to them: "Can the blind lead the blind? Will they not fall into the ditch?"[19] That is the point, the place where man who does not see truth will lead you right into the ditch—or is it the pit? There are those that have eyes

The Final Prophecy

but never see truth for they are followers of the influential, the rich or the powerful. Men's agendas are built on the weaknesses of the followers.

You have just read and I pray, reasoned through the events of the Final Prophecy, accompanied by actual verses from the Book of Revelation and from the prophets of Israel. You have had a verbal vision of what "suffering vs. eternal joy" looks like. If it did not capture some serious thoughts about your eternal destiny, there are no further, human words that I could end this book with that would convince you that God wants you to receive His eternal salvation. If you have indeed seen the wisdom and the truths that have been portrayed in this journey through the Bible, as well as the prophecy of the Old Testament than perhaps you are one of the fortunate fellow Jews who will not be on the face of this earth when the Final Prophecy is fulfilled. There is no middle ground here, no hedging and no sitting on the fence. Don't you think it is time that you got right with God? All you have to do after all the years you have denied Yeshua is to go to Him in prayer, ask Him for forgiveness and for the "key" to the door of eternal life.

You either purchased this book or it was given to you by a friend, someone who loves you and knows that your eternal destiny lies in your next move. I pray that this book has been a "journey of truth" for you. If you want to get right with God and recognize the saving grace of Yeshua, than all it takes is belief— a belief within the depths of your heart that should be crying out to you right about now that Yeshua is the Messiah. The prayer that you can say in the privacy of wherever you are comfortable, is your profession of faith. God is only interested in your heart, for that is all He sees within every human being. Where is your heart? Who has it and who or what takes up space within it? Yeshua said,

> "Also I say to you, whoever confesses Me before men, him the Son of Man also will confess before the angels of God. But he who denies Me before men will be denied before the angels of God."[20]

CHAPTER 17

On the last page is a simple prayer that is offered only as a "guide" should you not be used to praying. Your own, heartfelt words is all that God wants to hear—the sincerity and the devotion to Him as Lord and Messiah of your life. Perhaps it is the right time and you know it in your heart of hearts. Don't allow the enemy to claim your soul for you are far too precious to God. He will not open the door to eternal life through any other means or way because you think you are a "good person!" There is only one way to heaven and His name is Yeshua. One of the most frequently asked questions I hear from my Jewish brothers and sisters who have intellectually arrived at the conclusion that Yeshua is the Messiah is, "What will happen to me if I believe, if I say this prayer, am I still Jewish? Where do I worship Him?" Do I still go to the same Synagogue? What do I tell my friends? What do I say to my family?

These are very real questions that I have been asked and questions that you should never be embarrassed to consider. If you are Jewish, having been born Jewish and never went to Synagogue a day in your life—you are Jewish. If you are a devout Jew who is in Synagogue every Sabbath, keeps the Sabbath and all the Holidays, you are Jewish now and you will be a "completed Jew" just as the one who has never even entered a Synagogue—we who have been born Jews will always remain Jews. Upon professing your faith in Yeshua, you do not leave your faith or change your faith. What will happen is that all you have been doing in observance of your faith will be that much more enriching and meaningful. You do nothing that God does not lead you to do. The prayer said from a searching heart with truth is the final connection, the indwelling Spirit of God that will live within you— for you will then be His "completed" child. You will be a Jew who sees, acknowledges and acts on the truths of Yeshua. I encourage you to look-up the Messianic Synagogue sites on the Web and find a few listings in the area in which you live. Call and speak to the Rabbi and ask him all the questions you have within your heart. Let him know you have read this book and you want to speak to him personally—should you desire to do so. There is nothing wrong in seeking Messianic support, in fact it is encouraged. If you have not said this prayer or feel that you really did not mean it when you did, go to that Messianic Synagogue on the very next Sabbath, attend the Services and allow the Spirit of God to minister to you. Ask the Rabbi to pray with you in person and possibly answer any remaining questions. I too welcome your questions and comments and I implore you not to allow that "small voice" within you to be silenced by doubt, fear, lies of the past or human opinion. This is a decision that is between you and God and no one else. As I personally reflect on the day that I made that decision, I can only give thanks for the many blessings that I and my family have been recipients of and the incredible peace I have enjoyed within me. I know that I am a child of God, adopted into His family and His Kingdom "forever." I once wished that someone had handed me a book with these truths when I was a young man seeking the answers to life. I soon learned however that "God will restore all the years that the locusts have eaten away." The Old Testament is filled with verses such as these that all lead to one's individual belief and personal faith in Messiah.

The End –or is it your beginning?

Notes

1 Revelation 5:9-12

2 Revelation 6:7-8

3 Isaiah 2:19-21

4 Revelation 6:16

5 Revelation Chapter Seven

6 Ezekiel 9:3-4

7 Referred to earlier as those who profess their faith in Yeshua as Messiah.

CHAPTER 17

8 See Deuteronomy 11:18-21

9 Author's illustration

10 Revelation 11:15-16 2nd part 17-19

12 Author commentary on verse Nineteen of Chapter Eleven using the words of the passage.

13 Revelation 14 – The Lamb of God and His 144,000 saints who were sealed.

15 Also prophesied by Daniel- See Chapter 7 of Daniel, Old Testament

16 Revelation 14:14

17 Zechariah 14:1-5

18 Ezekiel 39: 6-8

19 NT Luke 16:19 Parable of the Rich Man and Lazarus

20 NT Luke 6:39

21 Luke 12:8

22 In crucifixion, the only way a person on the cross could gain air into their lungs was to push their body up, utilizing the small wooden block that was below their feet. Breaking the shinbones would naturally prevent a person from having this ability and they would die more quickly. Prophecy dictates that they would *not break one of His bones.*

If you have questions or comments, please do not hesitate to e-mail me personally at **jayministry@msn.com**

For additional copies of this book for friends who have yet to fully understand the glory of Yeshua, go to **www.master-press.com**

The Final Prophecy

> *"And it shall come to pass afterward,*
> *That I will pour out My Spirit on all flesh;*
> *Your sons and your daughters shall prophesy,*
> *Your old man shall dream dreams,*
> *Your young men shall see visions.*
> *And also on My menservants and on My maidservants*
> *I will pour out My Spirit in those days.*
> *And I will show wonders in the heavens and in the earth;*
> *Blood and fire and pillars of smoke.*
> *The sun shall be turned into darkness,*
> *And the moon into blood.*
> *Before the coming of the great and awesome day of the Lord.*
> *And it shall come to pass, That whoever calls on the name of the Lord*
> *Shall be saved.*
> *For in Mount Zion and in Jerusalem there shall be a deliverance,*
> *As the Lord has said*
> *Among the remnant whom the Lord calls.*

The Prophet Joel, 2:28-32

The day of the Lord is declared nineteen times in the Old Testament by the Jewish prophets of Israel. He is coming soon.

May the Lord richly bless you and cause His countenance to shine upon you and bring you peace, contentment and the joy of His salvation for an everlasting life, Amen

Prayer:

Dear Yeshua, I exalt You and praise You for Your goodness, Your mercies and Your blessings— Please forgive my sins Lord and wash me clean so that I may stand before You this day forgiven and cleansed of the sins that have separated me from You. May Your Spirit live within my heart, guide me and preserve me as I profess my faith in You, my Lord, My Savior and my Salvation for now and for evermore. Amen.

Upon saying this prayer, "welcome," into the family of God. Shalom, my brethren. This year in Jerusalem and if not, surely next year! God bless you and keep you, now and forever. Amen

THE FINAL PROPHECY

Yeshua in the Bible

A Partial Listing of the Prophecies Fulfilled in Yeshua

DO YOU BELIEVE IN PROPHETIC FULFILLMENT?

Since these ancient prophecies, Isaiah 11:11-12 declared the independence of Israel—it was fulfilled. Jeremiah 31:10 in 599 B.C. declared the "re-gathering" of our people and in 1948 the fulfillment of this prophecy was seen in the Israeli Declaration of Independence which stated that, "The State of Israel is now open to Jewish immigration and to the ingathering of our exiles." The prophet Ezekiel in B.C. 600 prophesied of the "high ground war" and that Israel would prevail. In 1967 Israel indeed prevailed in the Sinai War. Ezekiel also declared what Israel would do with the desert soil and we surely know the transformation of Israel from sand dunes and barren land to land that is *"tilled and sown"* as Ezekiel 36:9 so declared. Ask yourself if you can really look deeply into the fulfillment of all that history has shown us and still not believe.

SEED OF THE WOMAN

The prophecy that came from the lips of God Himself. Not the "seed of a man" denoting that there had to be a man and a woman involved but the "seed of a woman" –no man, a virgin, a Divine seed.

Genesis 3:15   Galatians 4:4

Through Abraham

Genesis 22:18   Hebrews 2:16

Through Isaac

Genesis 21:12   Hebrews 11:17-19

Through Jacob and Judah

Genesis 28:14   Matthew 1:2
                                  Hebrews 7:14

Time on Earth Foretold

Daniel 9:26   Mark 15:37

He Would Come Through the Line of David

See "Birth" below.
2 Samuel 7:12-13   Acts 13:23

Born of a Virgin

Can a man arrange who his own mother would be, especially one who came through the line of David?

Isaiah 7:14   Matthew 1:18,21

Born in Bethlehem of Judah

Can a man arrange for the place of his own birth?

Micah 5:2   Matthew 2:1

The Final Prophecy

A Prophet like Moses

Deuteronomy 18:15　　　　　　　　　Acts 3:20-22

He shall come from Galilee

Isaiah 9:1-2　　　　　　　　　Matthew 4:12, 16, 23

Shall enter publicly through Jerusalem

It was prophesied that Yeshua would enter Jerusalem on the back of a donkey in "His humility" and yet the path into town was lined with people who laid palm branches and coats in His path.

Zechariah 9:9　　　　　　　　　Matthew 21:5

His Tenderness and Compassion

Not a word of frustration or anger to anyone.

Isaiah 40:11　　　　　　　　　Matthew 12:15,20

His Performing Miracles

Giving sight back to the blind, curing cripples and cleansing the lepers was witnessed by hundreds of people. It was no secret as to what He did although Yeshua in His humility and knowing that the Pharisees were sure to question these miracles, told most of those He cured to tell no one. At one point a man who was blind from birth as the New Testament declares was questioned as well as his parents. His answer was simplistic and true, "I was blind and now I see!"

Isaiah 35:5-6　　　　　　　　　Matthew 11:4-6

HE SHALL BE REJECTED BY HIS OWN PEOPLE

Psalm 69:8   John 1:11 and John 7:3,5

REJECTED BY THE JEWISH RULERS

They stood to lose their power, their positions and their financial compensation if they acknowledged that Yeshua was truly the Messiah. The more I study the more I am convinced that they knew *exactly* who He was. However they had to save themselves and Yeshua came to save us!

Psalm 118:22   Matthew 21:42

SOLD-OUT FOR THIRTY PIECES OF SILVER

Judas accepted thirty pieces of silver from the Pharisees to betray Yeshua by leading them to where He prayed every evening.

Zechariah 11:12   Matthew 26:15

HIS PRICE GIVEN FOR THE POTTERS FIELD

The thirty pieces of silver that Judas received from the Pharisees for betraying Yeshua were used to buy this field. It is also the place that Judas hung himself in his remorse for what he had done. The field was used to discard broken pieces of pottery.

Zechariah 11:13   Matthew 27:3,7

SUFFERING BEYOND HUMAN CAPACITY

Psalm 22:14   Luke 22:42,44

See "His Silence"

The Final Prophecy

His Suffering for Us

Yeshua did not have to die as He did. At any time He could have avoided all of this suffering and His crucifixion. He was not killed but rather gave up His life as the final Atonement for our sins.

Isaiah 53:4-6   Matthew 20:28

His Silence during all Suffering

Only One with Divine power could have withstood the beatings and the suffering and not cry out, scream, complain or say a word to his accusers or during His beatings. The Roman whip that Yeshua received 39 lashes with was designed to wrap around the body and tear the flesh in pieces for they were embedded with glass and pieces of metal. Not a sound? Could a mere human being withstand such physical cruelty?

Isaiah 53:7   Matthew 26:63
Matthew 27:12,14

Nailed to a Cross

Psalm 22:16   John 19:18
John 20:25

Lots would be cast for His Garments

It was prophesied that the robe they placed on Him, mocking Him as "King of the Jews" would be gambled for and it happened precisely as the prophets predicted as several Roman soldiers cast lots for his garments.

Psalm 22:18   Matthew 27:35

Numbered with the Transgressors

Isaiah 53:12   Mark 15:27-28

Yeshua in the Bible

He Interceded for His Own Murderers

If someone were murdering you, would you ask that they be forgiven?

    Isaiah 53:12   Luke 23:24

Not a Bone of His Shall be Broken

See "Pierced" below.

    Exodus 12:46 – Psalm 34:20   John 19:33

He Would be Pierced on the Cross

To insure that Yeshua was dead and they did not have to break his shin bones,[21] a Roman soldier took his lance and drove it into the side of Yeshua. Out gushed blood and water, the fluids of the pericardium sack that protects the heart. It is said that Yeshua died of a broken heart and not from the crucifixion.

    Zechariah 12:10   John 19:34,37

Would be Buried with the Rich

A man went to the Roman Governor and asked that Yeshua be place in a tomb where only the wealthy were buried—prophecy fulfilled.

    Isaiah 53:9   Matthew 27:57-60

His Resurrection

Without the resurrection of Yeshua, none of this would matter. It is the key to the fulfillment of all prophecy and that which the faith and belief that He was and is the Messiah is based. Many theories have been launched against the resurrection but like those who did not believe the Bible, the more they investigated the more convinced the experts became that this was truly the Messiah.

The Final Prophecy

Psalm 16:10   Luke 24:6, 31, 34

His Ascension to Heaven

There were witnesses to His ascension who saw Him "taken up into the clouds" and disappear. Remember Enoch?

Psalm 68:18   Luke 24:

He Shall Sit at the Right Hand of God

Psalm 110:1   Hebrews 1:3

His Priestly Reign in Heaven

Zechariah 6:13   Romans 8:34

Rejected by the Jews and Accepted by the Gentiles

Isaiah 11:10   Acts 10:45